DOGSCAPING

Creating the Perfect Backyard and Garden for You and Your Dog

BY TOM BARTHEL

Andrew DePrisco, Editor in Chief

Jarelle S. Stein, Editor

Jennifer Calvert, Associate Editor

Elizabeth L. Spurbeck, Assistant Editor

Camille C. Garcia, Assistant Editor

Brian Bengelsdorf, Senior Art Designer

Karen Julian, Publishing Coordinator

Additional photographs courtesy of/reproduced with permission of: **Jeannie Harrison/Close Encounters of the Furry Kind (www.cefkphotos.com)**—cover (central image); **Karen Taylor**—pages 1, 5 (top), 9, 11, 14, 16 (top), 18, 23, 25, 27 (top), 32 (top), 41, 54, 58, 60–61, 79, 81, 91, 103, 113, 123, 125; **Shutterstock® Images**—pages 3, 4, 5 (bottom), 6 (far left), 48, 51, 52, 53 (bottom), 62, 63 (bottom, right), 70, 84, 85, 92 (bottom), 94 (bottom), 115, 135; **Jean Fogle**—pages 5 (second from bottom), 105 (bottom); **Isabelle Francais/BowTie Inc., and Gina Cioli and Pamela Hunnicutt/BowTie Inc.**—pages 17, 82; **USDA Agricultural Research Service**—45, 105 (top, photo by Ken Hammond); **American Horticultural Society (www.ahs.org)**—page 136; **U.S. National Arboretum, USDA-ARA**—page 137.

Library of Congress Cataloging-in-Publication Data

Barthel, Tom.
  Dogscaping : creating the perfect backyard and garden for you and your dog / by Tom Barthel.
    p. cm.
  Includes index.
  ISBN 978-1-933958-33-0
  1. Organic gardening. 2. Landscape gardening. 3. Dogs—Health. 4. Dogs—Housing. I. Title.
  SB453.5.B38 2010
  636.7'083—dc22
                    2009023292

BowTie Press®
A Division of BowTie, Inc.
3 Burroughs
Irvine, California 92618

Printed and bound in the USA
15 14 13 12 11 10 09 1 2 3 4 5 6 7 8 9 10

Dedication

Dedicated to my wife, Rachel, whose support and encouragement breathe life into so many of my dreams; also to my dog, Dakota, who enthusiastically tested the theories and methods found here—along with my patience.

CONTENTS

Acknowledgments

The author would like to extend a special thank you to all of those who have shared their gardens, dogs, and green lifestyles with him. Without their generosity, this book would not have been possible.

A big thank you to: Laura Klein and her dogs, Bamboo and Truffle; Leslie May and her dogs, Gracie and Johann; Sandy Pfister, Jerry Perrone, and their dog, Teddy Bear; Laura McKenna and her dog, Roger; the Smith family (Amanda, David, Evangeline, and Gabriel) and their dogs, Scooby, Violet, and Belle; Andee Whiters and her dogs, Mallory and Moose; Cheryl Colburn and her dog, Copper; Tamma Rae Stewart and her dog, Chloe; Claudia Konieczny and her dog, Isabella; Marie and Tim Konieczny and their dog, Clancy; Lillie Kopke, Dan Rapelje, and their dog, Chloe; Bob and Kyle Kirkby and their dogs, Dewey and Dixie; and Steve Kopke and his dog, Star.

Introduction

Dogs and the outdoors go together as naturally as peas and carrots. But if these two are meant to coexist harmoniously, why do so many of our yards and gardens bear the scars of conflict? Muddy, rutted lawns, overturned flowerpots, uprooted vegetables, and minefields of dog waste plague our would-be idyllic landscapes. Worse yet, those landscapes sometimes wreak havoc on our all-too-curious pets, who can become gravely ill after ingesting toxic plants and chemicals commonly found in the very yards they delight in exploring. So why does this conflict between dog and yard exist? Because we are not designing our yards and gardens with our pets in mind, not thinking how to make the yards an organic whole, and not thinking how to live greener.

The various topics in this book, *Dogscaping*, promote harmonious, healthy, and sustainable yard and garden spaces designed with your pet in mind. With a few back-to-basics principles put in place, every outdoor space has the potential to be canine compatible, environmentally friendly, and beautiful. Learn the rules of engagement found here, and you can create the backyard of your dreams. It is possible to do so without yelling until you're blue in the face, without chasing your dog from one corner of the yard to the other, and without spending weekend after weekend patching bare spots in the lawn.

Consider this book the start of a journey to a more peaceful outdoor coexistence with your pet. That begins, in chapter 1, with gaining greater insight into who your dog is (including the purpose for which his breed was developed) and why he uses your outdoor space the way he does. By understanding who your dog is, why he acts the way that he does, and how he moves about outdoors, you can learn to balance his needs with your own needs and, by doing so, turn your yard from a war zone into a lush and beautiful oasis.

The following chapters show you how to accomplish just that. Topics covered include information on how to choose plants that possess both beauty and dog-tested durability, a task that presents the greatest challenge for most beginning gardeners. *Dogscaping* is full of solutions for this problem—telling you about winning plants that can be found at most nurseries in the United States—and for many other problems you may face. Be aware, however, that some of the plants recommended in this book have the potential to cause adverse health effects; plant poisoning may or may not be a concern with your dog. Much of the risk lies in your dog's personality and how he uses your outdoor environment. If in doubt about a plant, consider the personality of your dog, and consult your veterinarian.

Maintaining a planted environment that is not hazardous for your dog makes for a steep challenge in several ways. In the pages of this book, you'll also find out how to keep your pet safe and your environment clean through organic weed and pest control. You'll discover as well how to give your plants a boost with organic fertilizers so they will have a fighting chance against canine chaos.

Don't let yourself be intimidated by the notion of organic gardening, which often conjures images of hard, intense labor in an age in which chemical weed control and fertilization hold the appeal of instant gratification and ease of use.

Natural alternatives can be far easier to use in gardening and lawn care than you may imagine—and often can be made inexpensively from ingredients that you may already own.

In *Dogscaping*, you'll learn the basics of how to take yard waste and turn it into your own supergrowth fertilizer. You will get tips on how to keep your flowers and shrubs looking their best, and you'll discover how to give your lawn a boost and grow an abundance of organic fruits

and vegetables. The book also covers landscaping with decks, gazebos, and other structures.

In addition, in various vignettes throughout the book, real organic gardeners will share their secrets about outdoor life with their organic dogs. From the concrete jungles of Los Angeles to the north shore of Lake Michigan, dog lovers are finding battle-tested ways of integrating their dogs into their outdoor environments.

Dogscaping gives homeowners— from beginning gardeners to experienced ones—all of the tools that they will need to create an outdoor lifestyle that welcomes their pets, while also providing a beautiful environment in which they themselves can relax and enjoy nature. This book shows you how to respect your dog and your earth while appreciating what both of them have to offer. You and your pooch can go greener with spectacular results.

CHAPTER 1

Balanced Living

Living in harmony with your dog begins with acquiring a better understanding of his outdoor needs and desires, as well as your own. A good place to begin is by learning more about your dog's breed—specifically, the characteristics and the purpose for which it was developed. Is your dog a terrier, with a deep-seated need to dig out hidden prey (involving a lot of yard excavating)? Or is he a sporting breed, with the need for speed, racing from

one end of your yard to the other (ripping up grass along the way)?

Because every dog is an individual, not just a member of a breed, you also need to observe how your dog spends time in your yard. What does he do, and where does he do it? Does he regularly patrol the fence line, looking for suspicious characters? Does he have a favorite lounging spot, or two? Where does he usually eliminate?

While you are learning about your dog and watching him scamper about your yard, you should also be considering what it is you want to gain from your yard or garden. By taking a look at the big

picture of your dog's natural outdoor habits and your own expectations for outdoor living, you'll discover how to begin to make beneficial changes to your outdoor environment. A holistic approach that takes into account your needs and those of your dog represents the best chance you have for creating a harmonious outdoor space.

Decode Your Dog: Breed Characteristics

The purebred dog arose out of the need for greater specialization of man's best friend. Whether hunters, herders, or

companions, each canine breed was developed for specific purposes, to carry out particular jobs. Even though the majority of dog owners no longer hunt with their Afghan Hounds or herd with their Shetland Sheepdogs, each dog's sense of purpose is deeply ingrained in his genetic code.

That same sense of purpose defines how your dog will use your outdoor space. Discovering your dog's purpose and how you can accommodate it in the best possible way will form the basis of how you tailor your outdoor space to meet his needs as well as your own. The American Kennel Club (AKC) has divided its recognized dog breeds into seven official groups. Consider which of the following groups your dog fits into and the general characteristics of his group.

MOVERS/PURSUERS: HERDING BREEDS

The Herding Group—which includes the Australian Shepherd (*right*), the Border Collie, the Old English Sheepdog, the Shetland Sheepdog, and the two Welsh Corgis—consists of active dogs originally bred to round up and

Understanding the characteristics of individual breeds is key to yard and canine concordance.

move a variety of farm animals. In the absence of livestock, herding breeds often attempt to gently herd their owners, especially small children. Today, people choose these dogs for their intelligence and trainability.

When designing your outdoor spaces with a herding dog in mind, take into account his desire to actively pursue and herd nearly anything that moves. Fencing or other structures that define and contain your property serve the needs of these breeds best.

Expect these dogs to wear ruts in the grass along fence lines bordering sidewalks, and other areas where they can see people and animals. Their tendency to herd and protect make this habit nearly impossible to break. In chapters 2, 7, and 8, we'll discuss ways

you can accommodate these habits and disguise their muddy side effects with landscape materials and plant choices.

Because many herding breeds also respond well to training and need lots of exercise, owners often teach them a wide range of skills, from catching Frisbees to retrieving balls or decoys. You need to make accommodations for such activities in your yard. Plan to include a long runway for fetching and agility obstacles or a launch pad for aerial Frisbee catching.

HUNTERS/CHASERS: HOUND BREEDS

The Hound Group, which includes such diverse breeds as the Foxhound, Basset Hound (*right*), Beagle, Bloodhound, Dachshund, and Greyhound,

were developed for hunting purposes. By scent, sight, or both, these tenacious hunters will eagerly sniff out and pursue rabbits, foxes, and vermin. As household pets—not used for hunting—these breeds are sought after for their energy, stamina, and friendly personality.

When creating an outdoor space with the needs of a hound in mind, consider adding ways for your dog to indulge his natural hunting and tracking instincts safely and appropriately. For safety's sake, a fence is an absolute must for a yard with a hound. It prevents wandering: when hounds catch a scent on the breeze or see a squirrel across the street, they are likely to bolt with little regard for boundaries or busy avenues. In addition, the Dachshund, the smallest member of the

A hound's enthusiastic howl alerts owners to interesting scents on the wind and possible quarries for the hunt!

Hound Group, was bred to hunt and dig for vermin, especially badgers. Pet Dachshunds may like to dig in backyard gardens and lawns or under fences.

Because wandering and digging habits are the result of generations of selective breeding within the Hound Group, you must have realistic expectations about what your dog can and cannot do. With some extra planning, you can meet your dog's needs and your own, creating an appealing landscape that also safely contains him.

PATROLLERS/ PROTECTORS: NON-SPORTING BREEDS

The Non-Sporting Group encompasses a wide variety of dog breeds, ranging from protectors and vermin exterminators to exquisitely groomed status symbols and devoted companions. Each breed is the result of the unique human need for traits like safety and companionship. Breeds such as the Bichon Frise (*below*), Boston Terrier, Bulldog, Chow Chow, Dalmatian, Lhasa Apso, Poodle, and Shiba Inu serve this need with the best of them.

Non-sporting breeds continue their traditions in the backyard. They are likely to investigate unusual situations and strangers with great interest. In general, they are loyal, gregarious, and full of courage.

An outdoor space that respects the needs of non-sporting breeds reflects the diverse purposes for which these dogs were developed. Fencing that allows them to see their surroundings and investigate neighborhood activity indulges their curious nature while holding back

While You're Watching

With notebook and pen at the ready, you can do more than observe your pet's behavior patterns; you can do some advance planning for plant selection.

Plants thrive when placed in areas that match their sun and shade requirements. Each plant you choose for your garden space has an hourly or intensity requirement. Full sun equates to six or more hours of sun exposure. Part sun/part shade indicates four to six hours of sun. Full-shade plants require four or less hours of indirect or dim light.

Note where the shadows fall across your lawn, as well as the time of day you made the observation. Record the amount of sunlight potential flower beds or vegetable gardens usually receive at various times.

Before long, you'll have a complete sun/shade map of your outdoor space to further help you narrow down plant choices.

he strangers and wildlife of which these breeds have no fear.

Expect a non-sporting dog to trample plants close to property lines and fenced boundaries. Avoid conflicts in the yard and garden by giving him the opportunity to patrol his territory, looking for intruders. Disguising a chain-link fence may take more ingenuity if you share your yard with a non-sporting breed that craves an unobstructed line of sight, but there are ways to honor your desires and those of your dog. (See Screening, Running, and Patrolling Paths in chapter 2.)

SPEEDSTERS/ RETRIEVERS: SPORTING BREEDS

As a group, sporting dogs were developed for hunting waterfowl and other birds. These breeds, including most spaniels, retrievers (*such as the Golden above*), and pointers, have active and vigorous personalities. Such attributes make them popular additions to busy households.

Developed to spring into action at a moment's notice to retrieve fallen ducks or flush a flock of grouse from a stand of prairie grass, sporting breeds exhibit higher energy and activity levels than do most other breeds. In the backyard, their greatest need is vigorous daily exercise.

Crisscrossing lawn and garden spaces at warp speed, these breeds can reduce even the most manicured outdoor environment to a muddy mess in a few short days. Yards designed with these breeds in mind survive and thrive when open spaces are planted with tough turf grasses or replaced altogether with stone pathways. Sturdy woody shrubs and protective barriers around more delicate perennials and annuals guard against the dogs' active habits without sacrificing the beauty of nature.

Sporting breeds present the most difficult challenges when homeowners are creating a harmonious landscape. However, as the following chapters will discuss, you can accommodate their

Secret to Success:
Understanding the Individual

Not every dog fits so nicely into the seven AKC categories. Mixed breeds (such as this Husky/Mastiff mix) often reflect one or more of the official breed groups, and purebreds themselves may behave contrary to their genetics, depending on their level of socialization and training. From time to time, dogs just have quirks. A Labrador Retriever may behave more like a terrier—tenacious and fearless—or a Scottie may live under the assumption that he was born a hound—howling at fresh scents on the breeze.

The important point to remember in the beginning stages of planning a harmonious yard and garden is you need to learn your dog's particular characteristics and behaviors and keep them in mind. If you ignore those needs and plan for a beautiful landscape for beauty's sake, you'll end up in constant conflict with your dog.

POUNCERS/DIGGERS: TERRIER BREEDS

...ctive habits while maintaining the ...eauty and functionality of your yard.

...he Terrier Group was first developed ...o control vermin and provide food. ...s hunters and killers of rats, mice, ...nd other woodland creatures, terrier ...reeds possess special personality traits: ...ourage, determination, and spunk. ...hese often feisty, energetic breeds ...ange from the diminutive Scottish, ...orfolk, and Cairn to the spirited Soft-...oated Wheaten (*left*), the majestic ...iredale, and the powerful American ...taffordshire.

In the home and yard, these dogs ...ypically will not tolerate the presence ...f other dogs and are always ready for ...boisterous confrontation. As a conse-...uence, backyards require fencing that ...ivide the terrier's space from the space ...f nearby dogs. Solid fencing and dense ...lantings in areas with exposure to ...ther neighborhood pets keep tempera-...nents in check.

Most important, the dogs likeli-...st to dig can be found in the Terrier ...Group, bred to unearth quarry. Bored ...erriers can wreak havoc on your yard ...nd garden, as well as pose a danger to ...hemselves by digging under fencing.

LOUNGERS/ SIDEKICKS: TOY BREEDS

...*oy Group* is a general term used to ...escribe small breeds whose main pur-...ose in life boils down to companion-...hip. Lap dogs and constant sidekicks, ...hese breeds vary widely in tempera-...nent and appearance. The ever-more-

popular Chihuahua, Pug, Shih Tzu, and Yorkshire Terrier (*above*) round out the most popular toy breeds, with the Maltese, Pekingese, Pomeranian, and many others not far behind. As living spaces shrink and the demand for portability grows, so too does the demand for these low-impact dogs.

A variety of yard and garden environments stand up well to life with toy breeds. They make less waste, dig smaller holes, and create fewer ruts and wear patterns in the grass. Damage they create can be easily patched or hidden by a well-placed potted plant.

Their curious nature and petite stature, however, put toy breeds at greater risk for exposure to toxic plants and chemicals used to control pests and weeds. Organic gardening practices serve an important role with toy breeds (see chapters 2 and 8). Their small bodies often react quickly to even minimal exposure to toxic chemicals. Because they are short and low to the ground, their mouths and other mucus membranes are particularly vulnerable to poisoning.

Their quick, active movements also lead to special risks. Without careful

supervision, they may chew and swallow harmful plants in the blink of an eye, before you have the chance to intervene.

RESCUERS/BRUISERS: WORKING BREEDS

Many of the working breeds, including the Alaskan Malamute, Boxer, Bullmastiff, Doberman Pinscher, Great Dane, Newfoundland, Rottweiler (*left*), and St. Bernard, were bred to haul sleds, rescue stranded boaters, and guard expansive estates. They were initially developed out of humankind's need for a strong companion to help with life's heavy lifting.

The dogs' size and strength require several basic accommodations when owners design their outdoor environments. When sufficiently motivated, a large muscular dog from this group may crash through even the sturdiest garden gate or mow down a freshly installed picket fence as though it never existed.

In addition, the size and volume of dog waste generated by dogs of this stature can quickly overwhelm even a large yard. Yellowed grass and harmful bacteria from feces make for a very unpleasant and potentially unhealthy outdoor environment.

Observe Outdoor Behavior: Field Notes

Any holistic approach to creating an outdoor space begins with observing how your dog behaves in his outdoor environment. This can take several days, even weeks, of careful study. Note where your pet eliminates, where he patrols, the paths he frequently takes, the way he uses your property, among other activities.

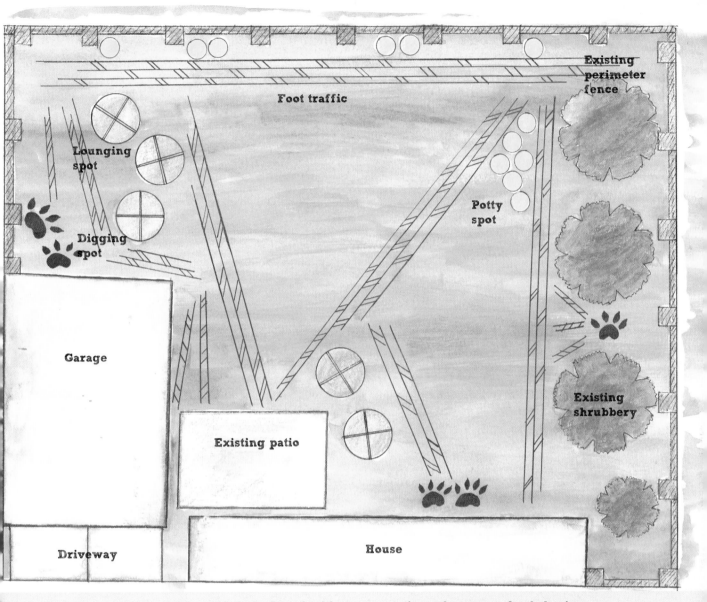

This diagram shows the layout of a sample backyard with representations of common dog behaviors.

Dogs have daily routines just like we do. Without even thinking where we're going, we get in the car each morning and drive to our workplaces. If along the way a traffic jam or construction detour sends us in another direction, we end up confused, frustrated, and late for work—angry at the change in our daily routine.

Like humans, dogs thrive on habitual activities and get upset when those are interfered with. They prefer to run in the same spot in the garden. They mark the same trees with their scents each time they venture outdoors. They take the same paths on their sentinel patrols. They deposit their waste in the same area nearly every time they eliminate. (Sometimes, of course, dogs will spread their activities all over the yard and garden, but generally patterns develop, with the animals choosing the same spots over and over again.)

Several days of careful watching will reveal your dog's routines. Recording your findings in a notebook provides a quick and easy way to translate what you see into data you can use when you begin choosing the locations of plants, pathways, and other landscape features.

The information you gather should include locations your pet uses for his routine activities, the paths he takes to and from the house, and any patterns he creates with running and patrolling behaviors. Using a basic line drawing of your house and yard, you can label these locations and patterns, as in the example illustration shown on this page. In chapter 2, you'll see how this information can be converted into a more detailed diagram that will help you make decisions that balance your dog's needs with your own.

If during the observation phase of design you find that your dog's activity is widespread and difficult to pin down, you may have to consider whether it is

An artist enjoys the peace and solitude of a secret garden, an area walled off to keep out curious dogs.

practical to plant your yard and garden with much of anything. Dogs love the outdoors for vastly different reasons than we do, and they have a hard time understanding the need for grass and brightly colored, fragrant flowers. Their desire for running and digging may supersede your plans for anything else.

A Dog-Free Zone: Exclusion vs. Inclusion

A dog who has access to your entire yard and garden, and uses this privilege to its fullest, may run roughshod over anything you plant. If this has been the case with your dog, you'll need to decide whether a little exclusion would better meet your needs.

Most dog owners want to share everything with their beloved pets, but if petunias are your passion and your dog likes to dig, creating a small dog-free zone could allow you to grow the fragile flowers you love without depriving your dog of his fun. Novel options abound for creating areas where Fido simply can't follow.

One approach is to construct a "secret garden"—a simple walled or fenced-off corner of the yard with a sturdy garden gate—as an area free from trampling and digging, where the most delicate plants can be grown in peace. A secret garden can also serve as an intimate retreat for you, a place to relax away the stress of the day without having to worry about stepping in dog waste while stopping to smell your beautiful roses.

There are many other approaches you can take for protecting parts of you

Purple verbena (*Verbena* sp.) grows safely in a hanging basket out of the reach of Clancy, a Shetland Sheepdog.

...arden. Following is a sampling of ways ...o have your cilantro and eat it, too. ...ther methods will be explored in more ...etail in later chapters.

CONTAINER GARDENS, HANGING BASKETS, AND WINDOW BOXES

...afely elevated out of a dog's reach by an ...legant pot, container gardens take lush ...lantings, by the potful, to any corner of ...he yard. If a curious pooch still inves- ...gates a little too closely, simply move ...he container to a different location or

Tabletop Transformation

The practice of tabletop gardening consists of creating a simple tray atop an elevated surface. With adequate drainage and soil, this container of sorts makes the perfect spot for growing nearly anything. Once you have your piece of furniture, here is how to go about making it into a garden.

1 Create a frame using wood, flexible landscape edging, or other appropriate material for the surface you are working with. Make sure it borders the perimeter of the flat surface where you want to do your planting. Flip the table upside down and attach the frame from underneath the table's edge.

2 Drill holes in the tabletop or surface where your garden will sit to allow for drainage.

3 If the surface already allows for drainage, as in the case of a metal bistro table, add window-screen or weed-barrier fabric to the surface to prevent dirt from falling through larger spaces.

4 Fill the tray you've created with a thin layer of gravel to promote drainage. Then, fill the tray the rest of the way with soil, plant with your favorites, and enjoy.

elevate it further by placing it atop a deck rail or stack of flagstones.

Hanging baskets also raise plants out of canine reach. When people think of these baskets, they automatically envision preplanted pots filled to the brim with one of four or five common trailing flowers and vines. But these dog-free little gardens don't have to be limited to flowers and vines. Hanging baskets are perfect for planting a wide variety of foods, such as tomatoes, peppers, and even root vegetables. You can have the garden you always wanted—high in the sky.

Another elevated gardening platform is the window box. These charming additions to the home enhance curb appeal while keeping colorful favorites safely out of the reach of curious paws. Easy to make and install, they also instantly transform a home's façade.

CLOCHES AND COLD FRAMES

Cloches have been used by gardeners for centuries to extend the growing season and protect plants from damage. A *cloche* (French for "bell") can be made from glass soldered into a boxlike shape or translucent plastic film stretched over a tomato cage or decorative frame. Popular since Victorian times, these small "bells" can be placed over delicate plants when dogs are out and removed when they go back in. Instructions for making a cloche can be found at www.gardenersworld.com/how-to/projects/cloche-seeds/.

A cold frame is basically a small enclosure with a transparent roof, built low to the ground, that can function as a mini greenhouse, extending the growing season up to a month on either side of summer. Cold frames can also be used

Identifying conflict areas will help owners to minimize them, keeping pets as happy as this Belgian Sheepdog.

to keep out nosy dogs who would otherwise damage tender young vegetables and budding flowers. Cold-frame boxes and tunnels made from inexpensive PVC pipes and covered with transparent plastic film have long been tools of the trade in the professional grower's arsenal. You can easily make them yourself (check out www.extension.umn.edu/yardandgarden/ygbriefs/h137season extenders.html) or buy a kit. You can also easily disassemble cold frames and store them in small spaces when not in use.

TABLETOP GARDENS

Your favorite annual flowers can have a place of honor (and safety) in your outdoor space. Tabletop gardening makes your dream of lush landscapes possible with less maintenance and worry about doggy destruction. This creative and newly popular hobby offers a unique alternative to the ground-level gardening experience.

Start by hitting tag sales and flea markets to find a small table or other piece of furniture you like. Bargains are best when shopping for a piece of reusable furniture that will be exposed to the outdoors. Any piece of furniture with a flat surface can be made into an elevated garden with a few simple modifications. Once you have the perfect piece of furniture, follow the instructions in Tabletop Transformation on the opposite page to build a great elevated garden.

Minimizing Conflicts with Planning

With these methods and many more, the most energetic dogs and beautiful gardens can coexist peacefully. You don't have to sacrifice beauty and personal taste for your dog's needs. Stressful conflicts between dog and human can be minimized with the right blend of realism and creative planning.

CHAPTER 2

Site Planning and Plant Selection

With copious notes on your dog's backyard habits, you can begin planning the intended layout of your dog-friendly landscape. How you orient the site and how you choose your plants make all the difference in creating a harmonious environment for both you and your pet. A three-pronged approach to site planning and plant selection presents the most comprehensive way to achieve blissful coexistence.

First, make a diagram that includes information from your observations of your dog's use of your outdoor space. Second, take the time to select plants that will stand up to your dog's level of activity. Third, make sure the plants you choose are not toxic, which can harm your dog.

With these points in mind, you'll reap the benefits of a design that's both practical and beautiful. Integrating your desires with your dog's needs stands out as the core philosophy of creating a dog-friendly outdoor space. Good site planning and proper plant selection provide the blueprint for building your green utopia.

Plan for Paradise

Drawing a detailed diagram of your backyard space provides a logical plan of action before you dig the first shovelful of dirt. Laying it all out in this way prevents mistakes and wasted resources during the execution phase of your plan. Your diagram can be as simple as a rough sketch or as elaborate as the professional design produced by many landscape architect firms. The important point about creating your site plan is that you include all the information you need to make the appropriate plant choices later. The illustration on the following page shows one example of a comprehensive map that reflects all of the factors discussed here.

Get creative. Make it fun. Getting excited about drawing a plan that embraces your love of the outdoors and

Flowers surround a Soft Coated Wheaten Terrier. Site planning includes selecting the right plants for you and your dog.

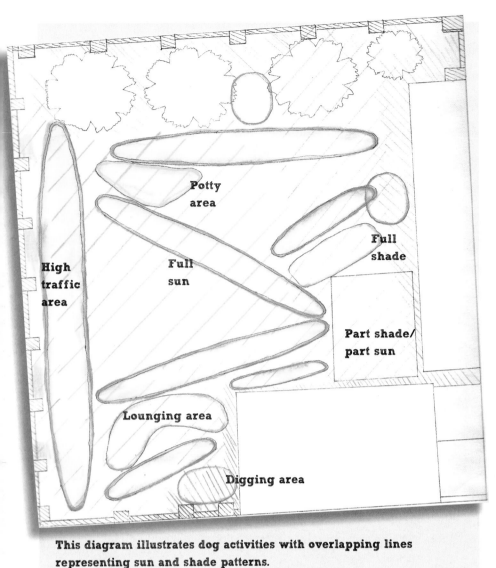

High traffic area

Potty area

Full sun

Full shade

Part shade/ part sun

Lounging area

Digging area

This diagram illustrates dog activities with overlapping lines representing sun and shade patterns.

At this time, it also helps to document the sun, soil, and moisture conditions of your property. You need to consider these factors, which influence the success or failure of whatever you plant, when making your final plan selections. Overlaying the diagram with transparent sun and shade patterns, as seen in the illustration at the left, takes into account different plant species that thrive in bright and dim light. It helps to draw directional arrows representing north, south, east, and west. Areas with southern exposure generally receive full sun, whereas eastern and western exposures receive partial shade and northern exposures receive full shade. Wet areas often characterized by clay soils, and drier areas, which typically contain added sand, can be indicated by similar transparent zones.

Although it may seem like a jumble of lines and colors at first, the resulting diagram will provide you with a very useful, personalized guide to plant selection.

Be in the Zone

The overlapping zones, now evident in your landscape plan, illustrate where conflicts between your dog's needs and your own desires may arise. The plan will help you to pinpoint the perfect locations for beautiful landscape plants and features or indicate where you should locate a special dog garden (as discussed in chapter 10).

For example, an area where your dog likes to patrol daily, which is also in full shade with sandy soil, may seem like an impossible area to beautify. In fact— indicated by your careful observation— it's the perfect spot to create a doggy digging pit. The low walls of the pit will

your love for your dog will make the experience that much more rewarding. You don't have to be a Frederick Olmstead (designer of New York's Central Park) to create a solid landscape plan, but you do have to put some energy into the experience.

Start by drawing in your property lines, including any existing fencing. Then insert all structures, including sheds, fire pits, garages, and other outbuildings. If drawing your plan on paper, go big; you'll be grateful when you don't have to squint to identify your labels and planting zones.

Next, transfer the information you've gathered on your dog's patrolling,

digging, eliminating, and other daily habits to the diagram. It helps to assign a color to each behavior and transfer that color to the diagram as a band or an oval. You'll need to see where these behaviors overlap with other factors to determine the best plant choices and features for your space.

Then add to the diagram any existing plants or garden structures in the space. Use simple color guides (such as green circles to represent shrubs or, irregular shapes with colorful dots for perennials or annuals) to allow you to see how they relate to the activity and overall look of the outdoor environment you are attempting to create.

A creative gardener has designed a mulch pathway lined with white stones and flanked by two hound statues to draw people to the back of the garden.

d structure to an otherwise unattract-
corner of your yard. You can also
ighten this dark area of your yard by
inting the sides of the structure. Best
all, the space indulges a dog's natural
sire to dig—in a safe environment that
far from the flower beds.

By contrast, a zone rarely used by
ur dog that gets a fair amount of sun
uld be the perfect area for a cut flower
rden, which will beautify your home
d yard all summer.

Interpreting the zones and finding
e perfect plants suited for each area of
ur outdoor space can be somewhat of
hallenge. With thousands of plants to
oose from, making the final decision
which ones to add to your space can
em overwhelming. To help narrow

This English Springer Spaniel, Dewey, likes to meander through the garden near the pink and white peonies.

A white Labradoodle, Dakota, pauses beside a honeysuckle vine, a good choice to mask digging.

down the possibilities, consider focusing first on plants that are more likely to survive interactions between canine and Mother Nature.

Sun and water requirements for plants are widely available; what you can't find on a plant tag, your local nursery is information on which plants stand up best to your dog's daily rigors. Surprisingly, there are plants that thrive in spite of the most dogged behaviors.

TOP VINES FOR CANINE EXCAVATORS

COMMON NAME	SCIENTIFIC NAME	LIGHT	ZONE*	BLOOMS
Carolina jasmine	*Gelsemium sempervirens*	Full to partial sun	5–9	May–June
Clematis vine (*above*)	*Clematis viticella*	Full to partial sun	4–9	Late June
Honeysuckle vine	*Lonicera heckrotti*	Sun to shade	4–9	Late June
Kentucky wisteria	*Wisteria macrostachya*	Full to partial sun	3–9	April–June
Trumpet vine	*Campsis radicans*	Sun to shade	5–9	July

* For more information on your local AHA Heat Zone and USDA Plant Hardiness Zone, see the appendix.

Deal with Digging

Dogs dig. It's a fact of life. Whether it's an attempt to circumnavigate a fence, find the source of an intriguing smell, or an activity indulged in for the sheer thrill of it all, this behavior represents one of the most significant challenges to creating a beautiful lawn and garden. As root zones and foliage are repeatedly disturbed by digging, most plants suffer the same fate—a slow and untimely death.

At first glance, it may seem as though no plant among the thousands commonly found in the landscape could possibly withstand an aggressive digger. But the plant kingdom has amazing diversity, offering great options, such as vines. If you plant fast-growing vines in zones near your dog's digging spot, you can train long tendrils to attach themselves to trellises or outbuildings near this area. As they bloom, vines offer a colorful backdrop to places pitted by frequent digging.

Drawing the eye upward and away from inevitable dog damage is a great diversionary tactic to help you cope with the occasional crater. Safely out of the way of busy paws, vines easily flourish. Choose one of your favorites or use several types for multiple colors or longer blooming periods. See the table Top Vines for Canine Excavators (opposite page) for suggestions about what to plant.

Screening, Running, and Patrolling Paths

In their daily wanderings in search of intruders and of other suspicious

Secrets to Success: Respect Your Dog

Creating a focal point in your outdoor space—an area where your family will spend the majority of their time—allows your dog to be a part of the family action. This center of activity indulges your dog's deeply ingrained social instincts.

If you want to create a harmonious outdoor space, respect the traffic patterns and territorial habits of your dog as shown on your landscape diagram. Successful dog-oriented yards allow dogs to be—first and foremost—dogs. Make sure your final plan provides opportunity for similar patterns identified by observing your pet. Don't obstruct worn paths and bathroom areas. Plan to place durable plants in these locations—plants that tolerate heavy paw traffic and urine exposure. These are just a few of the important factors you need to keep in mind during the planning stages.

This diagram shows representations of a planned patio and pergola (*bottom*), tiki bar (*top, left*), and fire pit (*top*); the placement of the structures takes into account the usage patterns of the family dog.

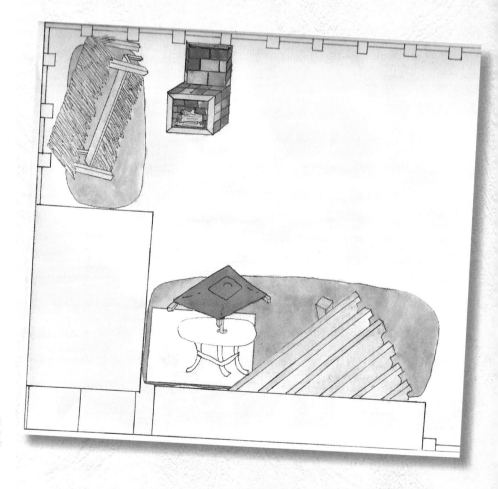

It won't take Dewey long to wear a dirt path along this wooden fence. Sturdy bushes will help hide the path.

neighborhood critters, dogs easily wear paths in the dirt along fence lines. For many breeds, the tendency to patrol and to sprint back and forth over the same course day in and day out is in their blood. Trying to stop these behaviors only leads to an anxious, frustrated dog, yet muddy ruts caused by repeated patrolling beside chain-link fencing look plain ugly.

Careful selection of woody shrubs will serve your need for a beautiful yard and your dog's need to patrol. You can hide perimeter wear and tear—and a chain-link fence—with their colorful leaves or flowering branches with a variety of sturdy shrubs. Their dense foliage hides a variety of landscape blemishes, and when set back 2 or 3 feet from the fence, these shrubs still allow your pet engage in one of their favorite activities.

TOP SHRUBS FOR ATHLETES

COMMON NAME	SCIENTIFIC NAME	LIGHT	ZONE*	BLOOMS
Red-twig dogwood	*Cornus alba sibirca*	Full to partial sun	5–9	May–June
Smoke tree	*Cotinus coggyria*	Full to partial sun	4–9	Late June
Forsythia	*Forsythia intermedia*	Sun to shade	4–9	Late June
Burning bush	*Euonymus alata*	Full to partial sun	3–9	April–June
Lilac (*right*)	*Syringa vulgaris*	Sun to shade	5–9	July

* For more information on your local AHA Heat Zone and USDA Plant Hardiness Zone, see the appendix.

Signs and Symptoms of **Poisoning**

Even with the best risk-management and prevention strategies, accidents happen. Early symptom identification makes all the difference; treatments work best when administered early, before the toxins have a chance to cause permanent damage.

The following symptoms may occur immediately or with delayed onset (up to fifteen to twenty-four hours).

- Confusion, heightened excitability
- Digestive upset—increased salivation, diarrhea, vomiting, lack of appetite
- Excessive tear production
- Neuromuscular impairment—lethargy, labored breathing, seizure, paralysis
- Rash, excessive scratching

If you suspect your dog may have been poisoned, contact the American Society for the Prevention of Cruelty to Animals Poison Control Center (888-426-4435, there is a consultation fee for this service) and your veterinarian for immediate assistance.

Many woody shrubs tolerate aggressive pruning and stand up to most canine activities. So, as the shrubs grow, you can if you wish, trim them up from the ground to allow enough space for your dog to travel and lounge beneath a shaded canopy. This creates an attractive, shady getaway that is great for hot summer days. The majority of these species don't mind the soil compaction created by heavy paw traffic and generally coexist well with dogs. See the table on the opposite page, Top Shrubs for Athletes, for suggestions about what types of shrubs to plant in your yard and garden.

A yellow Labrador Retriever rests in a favorite spot. If parts of your lawn suffer from a lounging canine, plant a durable ground cover.

Accommodate Loungers

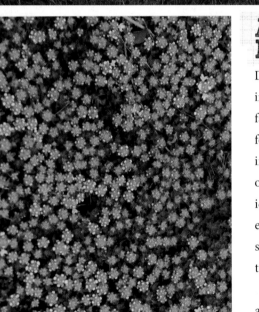

Dogs enjoy few things more than a nap in the sun. Of course, where the sun falls is also likely to be the best place for growing ornamental plants, making these overlapping zones common outdoor spots of conflict between your ideal garden and your pet. On hot days, even plants in the shade get their fair share of abuse as dogs seek a cool spot to escape the dog days of summer.

Often planted in rock gardens, as accents to flower beds, or between stepping stones, ground covers also have a stunning effect when planted in large mats over areas dogs frequent. Tough ground covers offer the perfect solution for lounging areas. They tolerate stepping, rolling, tossing, and turning while providing color and texture to a garden setting. Choosing ground cove does your dog and you a favor, becaus they make the ground softer and more enjoyable to sleep on and softer to step on with bare feet. See the table below Top Ground Covers for Dozers for sug gestions on what to plant.

TOP GROUND COVERS FOR DOZERS

COMMON NAME	SCIENTIFIC NAME	LIGHT	ZONE*	BLOOMS
Elfin thyme	*Thymus serpyllum*	Full to partial sun	4–8	June
Irish moss (*above*)	*Sagina subulata*	Partial sun to shade	4–9	May
Miniature stonecrop	*Sedum requieni*	Full to partial sun	4–8	June
Labrador violet	*Viola labradorica*	Partial sun to shade	2–10	April
Snow in summer	*Cerastium tomentosum*	Full to partial sun	3–9	May

* For more information on your local AHA Heat Zone and USDA Plant Hardiness Zone, see the appendix.

Eliminate Elimination Problems

When nature calls, dogs deposit their waste without concern for the possible damage they may cause. Even the most patient gardener gets frustrated when constantly dealing with scorched, dead landscape and bare patches of earth. By choosing plants for the outdoors that tolerate the chemical properties of dog waste, you'll minimize lost plants and tension between you and your dog.

Contrary to popular belief, the damage to plants is caused not by the acidity (or pH) of dog urine and feces but by the high concentration of nitrogen in the waste. This overfertilizes the plants, causing them to burn. Nitrogen burning is characterized by dry, brittle, and yellow to brown foliage and leaves on either the entire plant or one side. (Strategies for minimizing nitrogen burn will be discussed in further detail in chapter 8.)

Although most tender annuals and nonwoody perennials are most affected by repeated exposure to dog waste, some popular plants for the garden not only

Chloe, a Husky/Mastiff mix, and this Weigela coexist peacefully in the yard. Weigela stands up well to the high concentrations of nitrogen from dog waste.

tolerate high nitrogen levels in the soil but also thrive in spite of it. In fact, the majority of flowering, woody shrubs have high nitrogen requirements and can better utilize frequent, concentrated doses of dog urine than other plants. Consider adding these plants to areas where your dog does his business. See the table below on Top Potty-Spot Plants for suggestions about what to plant.

Don't be limited by the suggestions offered here; answers to problematic clashes with dog behaviors come from the most unlikely places. Your nearest wilderness park may hold the best advice for selecting the right options for your outdoor environment. Filled with native plants, public spaces can offer much inspiration.

If sweet-smelling honey-suckle is native to your area, add it to the garden for beauty and durability.

TOP POTTY-SPOT PLANTS

COMMON NAME	SCIENTIFIC NAME	LIGHT	ZONE*	BLOOMS
Rose of Sharon	*Hibiscus syriacus*	Sun to shade	4–9	August
Weigela	*Weigela florida*	Full to partial sun	4–9	June
Viburnum (*above*)	*Viburnum* sp.	Sun to shade	3–9	May
Spirea	*Spirea vanhouttei*	Sun to shade	3–8	April
Shrub rose	*Rosa rugosa*	Sun to shade	2–7	June

* For more information on your local AHA Heat Zone and USDA Plant Hardiness Zone, see the appendix.

Acquire Native Wisdom

When you choose plants best suited to your local climate and conditions—the ones that have evolved over thousands of years to thrive in your neighborhood—you may discover some of the most vigorous, and surprisingly beautiful, plants you've ever seen. Natives have evolved to withstand even the harshest conditions in your local environment. In spite of bitter cold, searing heat, drought, and floods, they bloom year after year. Natural durability and sturdy growth habits make natives a perfect fit for yards with dogs. These plants are simply better able to handle what life throws at them.

Find the best natives in your area by taking your dog on a hike. Spend some time outdoors, where you can observe the blooming and growing habits of the plants in your local climate. Note a few plants you like, and contact a local conservation group or your bureau of fish and wildlife to find out how to get them for your garden. You may be surprised to discover that natives for your area are already widely available at your local nursery.

Forget what you think you know about natives. Native landscapes feature more than sparse wildflowers and drab, scrubby plants. Some of the most stunning plants make their ancestral homes right here in the United States. Columbine, phlox, black-eyed Susan, honeysuckle, sunflower, and many other colorful plants can be found throughout much of the country, growing happily and vigorously in the wild. Consider adding a few to areas you and your dog want to enjoy. Another benefit of landscaping with natives is that they tend to attract local wildlife, particularly beneficial insects such as bees and butterflies, which pollinate garden fruit and vegetable crops.

Ornamental grasses, such as this miscanthus are fast-growing, easy-to-maintain additions to gardens.

Other native plants make great additions to any garden where dogs frequent, simply because they're just plain tough. Hardy and durable, these plants make sense for active households.

Appreciating Ornamental Grasses

In the plant kingdom, many of the toughest of the tough fall into the broad category known as ornamental grasses. In recent years, the skyrocketing popularity of ornamental grasses has resulted in greater variety and availability of these appealing plants.

A trip to any nursery yields at least a few choices for gardeners who want to add these to their landscapes. Available in all shapes, sizes, and colors, grasses add texture and movement to any outdoor space.

Although most grasses require full sun and bloom near the end of summer (which makes them ideal for the most gardeners who are extremely patient), they seem as if they are tailor-made for life with dogs. Their winning attributes are numerous:

■ Grasses exhibit extensive and diffuse underground root systems, perfect for soil compacted by heavy paw traffic.

■ Grasses require scant amounts of nutrients, making them well suited for even the poorest soil types.

■ Their wide, fast-growing blades stand up better than turf grasses d to the rough-and-tumble habits of active canines.

■ Grasses seldom require soil amendments, limiting or eliminating the need for fertilizers in areas where dogs may accidentally inges chemicals.

■ Grasses continue to offer visual interest during otherwise desolate times of the year, drying to a golden hue in areas with even the harshest winters.

Prevent Poisoning

Before you finalize your list of plants for your backyard makeover, you need to address the issue of potential plant poisoning of your pooch. In fact, although your dog has never shown any sign of poisoning, your yard may already contain toxic plants. Assessing your dog's risk for ingesting plants is more important than avoiding all toxic plants. (*Note:* As touched upon in the introduction, some of the plants recommended in this book have the potential to cause adverse health effects. Much of the risk lies in your dog's personality and how he uses your outdoor environment. Consult your veterinarian with concerns.)

It goes without saying that dogs tend to explore the world with their mouths and are at a greater risk of ingesting toxic plants. If you frequently catch your pooch putting his chompers on leaves and other frilly textured plant parts—just for the sake of investigation—you need to give more consideration to your final list of plants. You'll want to avoid plants with even mildly toxic potential.

However, if the only plant your pet seems interested in is the occasional blade of grass, the risk is comparatively much lower. Certain potentially toxic but sturdy plants may be appropriate for your landscape when your animal interacts with the outdoors by galloping rather than grazing.

Moderate- to high-risk dogs need to avoid a short list of particularly volatile and potentially deadly plants with the capability to damage or severely impair digestive structures and organs. Here are ten common toxic landscape plants (for a complete list visit the American Society for the Prevention of Cruelty to Animals at www.aspca.org):

- Azalea/rhododendron (*Rhododendron* spp.)
- Caladium (*Caladium* spp.)
- English ivy (*Hedera helix*)
- Foxglove (*Digitalis purpurea*)
- Holly (*Ilex* spp.)
- Hydrangea (*Hydrangea macrophylla*)
- Jimsonweed (*Datura* spp.)
- Lady's slipper (*Cypripedium* spp.)
- Larkspur (*Delphinium* spp.)
- Lily-of-the-valley (*Convallaria majalois*)

If your yard contains any of these or other toxic plants, you don't necessarily have to tear them out or avoid using them. Be aware of the potential for harmful exposure and take appropriate measures to lower your dog's risks.

Minimizing risks is the key to preventing plant-poisonings. Of course, your dog should not be left to roam unsupervised for long periods of time with free access plants. In addition, you can use barriers to prevent dogs from accessing poisonous plants—or at least to discourage him from coming in close contact with them. Barriers don't have to be ugly. Creative options, including other plants, have been used with high success rates. (Read more about creative barrier techniques in chapter 9.)

Keep It Simple

Risks, benefits, durability, colors—the list of factors to consider goes on. It's enough to make even a seasoned gardener's head spin. Outdoor life with dogs offers many challenges, but choosing the right plants doesn't have to be one. Keep it simple. Choose a handful of your favorite plants that match your dog's lifestyle, and spread them throughout the landscape. This philosophy makes trips to the nursery less overwhelming and creates a cohesive yard and garden environment rather than the hodge-podge look of a botanical museum with one of everything.

Caladium, below, is a common toxic plant. For your dog's safety, remove it from your outdoor environment.

Organic Gardeners, Organic Dogs

Life with Truffle and Bamboo

Bamboo and Truffle, a terrier mix, roam the grounds.

Laura and John Klein
Los Angeles, California

A day in the life of Truffle, a terrier mix, and Bamboo, a Lab mix, begins with a brisk lap around the block, pulling owner John Klein behind on Rollerblades. The dogs' boundless energy and shining coats are the results of an organic lifestyle, courtesy of their health-conscious owners, who tend expansive chemical-free gardens that keep these two active dogs full on a diet of organic fruits and vegetables.

Laura Klein, publisher of Organic Authority.com—a Web site and blog dedicated to organic living—first became interested in organic gardening when she attended culinary school. She found, through trial and error, that organic fruits and vegetables simply tasted better than their counterparts and that using them produced a far superior end product.

Then Laura started researching organic foods and getting into the science behind conventional farming practices. She learned how food cultivation contributes to human, animal, and planet health. What she found changed how she thought about nutrition and formed the basis for big changes in her lifestyle. With her veterinarian's stamp

Bamboo, a Lab mix, high-fives owner Laura Klein.

approval, she extended those changes to her dogs' lifestyles.

"When I got my first dog, Bamboo, my vet recommended that I start feeding her raw vegetables, a little bit of fruit, and raw meat," Laura says. "I thought that made perfect sense, so we started doing that. She eats any fruit and vegetable you put in front of her."

Not surprisingly, the cornerstone of Laura and John's life and pet-care philosophy is a diet rich in organic fruits and vegetables. Organic produce from their all-natural front- and backyard gardens fill the Kleins' pantry.

Truffle and Bamboo, both rescued from a local pound, have thrived as a result of their owners' organic outdoor lifestyle. Hooked on raw fruits and vegetables introduced at an early age, these two dynamos help themselves to fresh tomatoes and strawberries, eagerly plucked straight from the vine as they ripen in the California sun.

"Introducing them to raw vegetables and some fruits at such a young age has been great," Laura says, "because now they are two and three, and they pretty much take any vegetable I give them. People are shocked when they see it."

With some inventive ways for keeping her gardens pest free, Laura has enjoyed the benefits of organic produce with less effort than you might think.

Snails: "You can use a shallow dish and pour a little beer in it. Dig a little hole; put the dish in there. They just crawl in and die."

Bugs: "Orange oil is a contact toxin for flies and things that eat your plants. When you spray it directly on them, they can't fly."

Weeds: "You can put down a cover crop or wood chips, but it's also just going to take some good ol' elbow grease. It's not as time consuming as people think. It's actually fairly simple."

For the benefit of her family—four-legged members included—Laura has dedicated her gardening practice and life to achieving better health and longevity.

"Reducing [dog] exposure to environmental toxins is important," she says, "because they're showing up with the same diseases we are, and we're wondering why."

CHAPTER 3

Organic Pest and Weed Control

The phrase "organic gardening practices" evokes images of barefoot communes and so-called flower children for many people. True, a getting-back-to-nature approach comes, in principle, from more free-spirited thinking. But today, people everywhere are discovering what organic gardening really represents is a desire to avoid putting potentially toxic synthetic ingredients into their soils and over fruit and vegetable crops.

Dog owners, in particular, find themselves drawn to this approach to outdoor living, which minimizes the potential for their dogs to come in contact with irritating, harmful chemicals. Although debate continues as to whether or not organic fruits and vegetables taste better than their conventionally grown counterparts, most people will agree that this all-natural approach produces equally beautiful and productive plants when gardeners follow its core principles.

So what exactly does it mean to garden organically? At its foundation, organic gardening simply means working with nature, rather than against it.

It doesn't mean surrendering an entire season's crops to chewing insects, diseas and weeds. Instead, it focuses on using nonsynthetic fertilizers, pest deterrents, and weed-control methods to replenish what is used up by your plants. It represents a balanced approach to working with the environment to grow flowers, fruits, and vegetables by using plant- an animal-based products instead of artificial ones. Organic gardeners replace wh they take in a cyclical way—by recycling reusing, and reinventing what it means honor and respect the earth and the gift it gives us.

This chapter, and following chapter will explore in more detail the tenets of organic gardening and how you can eas ily implement these techniques in your outdoor environment in order to achiev beauty, bounty, and a safe environment for you and your dog.

Puppies, such as this Golden Retriever, are particularly vulnerable to toxic outdoor chemicals; organic alternatives are safer.

Golden Retriever Copper, lies beside a basket of wilted flowers, which should be watered promptly as to not attract insects.

Proper Plant Selection for Pest Control

Organic pest control starts with plant selection. When choosing plants for your landscape, make sure you select varieties well suited to your local climate and soil type. A mismatched plant may struggle to survive in your yard and garden. At the first sign of illness, plants give off chemicals that can be detected by passing insects and other pests. Because their natural defenses are weakened, sickly plants act as magnets for pests that then spread to nearby plants that would otherwise grow well.

Before you purchase plants at the local nursery, examine them carefully. Plants exhibit several signs of illness or weakness that would predispose them to pest infestation. You may not notice these signs at first glance, so take a moment to look at the following aspects for telltale signs of problems.

Foliage color and condition: These speak volumes about a plant's health and innate pest-resistant defenses. Stay away from plants with yellowed leaves. Recent research suggests destructive garden pests are attracted to light green and yellow leaves, which indicate that a plant's natural ability to defend itself has been compromised. Avoid plants with wilted leaves; even with a healthy dose of water they may not recover.

Root appearance and number: The roots that feed your plants need to perform well. If they are damaged, the plant's ability to deliver nutrients—necessary for flower and fruit production—will be impaired. Before you buy a plant, turn the pot on its side, and look for roots protruding from the drainage holes. If present, these roots should be lean, white, and tender. Mushy, dark, rotting, or tough roots indicate that the plant has not been cared for properly in the greenhouse setting. If an excessive number of roots are emerging from the bottom of the pot, circling around the base of the plant, look for a plant that isn't so crowded. If a plant has already outgrown its pot, it may not adjust well to transplantation.

Stem appearance: Floppy or brittle stems, stems with dark spots, or stems with a yellowish color are signs of poor plant health. Stems that look strong and sturdy indicate a healthy plant, one that is likely to thrive in your garden. Look also for multiple stems in the same pot; these will multiply and spread faster, giving you more bang for your buck.

Soil color and odor: The surface soil in the pot should appear free from green or whitish growth, which suggests mold and fungal infestation that can spread to other plants in the garden. A quick sniff should indicate a clean, freshly turned soil scent. Avoid plants that smell sour or rotten. Use this opportunity to look for tiny crawling or flying insects that often take up residence during a plant's stay in the store. Leaving these pests at the store is one of the best ways to start with a clean slate.

Nonchemical Approach to Pest Control

No garden is perfect. Some pests will invade, eat their fill, and damage your garden and landscape plants no matter what you do. Even plants regularly sprayed with toxic chemicals exhibit some signs of pest damage. However, how you care for your plants will help keep the bugs at bay and eliminate the need for toxic pesticides that can make your dog sick. These practices have been designed to prevent large-scale damage and crop failures, and when executed correctly, they will do just that. So, once you have added the plants to your outdoor environment, take the following three-pronged approach to nonchemical pest control to dramatically reduce the number of pests in your garden.

PRACTICE BASIC GARDEN HYGIENE

Basic yard and garden hygiene leaves destructive pests nowhere to hide, and appropriate day-to-day care ensures optimum plant health. Make sure to follow these key organic gardening cultural practices.

Dig or till thoroughly. Dig or till the soil thoroughly before planting anything. Working the soil in this way exposes hidden larvae and other critters that can be easily picked off by birds or baked in the sun. It also forces pest eggs deep into the soil, preventing them from emerging at all.

Don't water too often. Excessive watering causes soggy soil, which can result in root rot, weakening the plant. As the plant weakens, it becomes a susceptible host for pests.

Fertilize appropriately. Adding too much compost at once makes the surrounding dirt rich in nutrients that plants aren't able to use. Those nutrients end up feeding parasites and grubs, which can also attack your plants.

Pick up dead or dying material. Dead or dying plant material must be removed promptly. Excessive amounts of rotting leaves and stems create perfect places for harmful insects and parasites to thrive.

Inoculating with Pathogens

This black hollyhock (*Alcea* sp.) has been damaged by insects.

For nontoxic insect control, fungi and other pathogens deadly to pest insects or their larvae can be added to the soil of affected plants. Just as pathogens affect people and other organisms, they also affect insects and parasites. Inoculating your soil with these pathogens and fungi, harmless to people and animals, provides an even greater security blanket against crop loss and the need to use toxic chemicals. For example, gardeners frequently use a naturally occurring bacteria available at most nursery supply stores—milky spore (*Bacillus popillae-Dutky*)—to control the larval stage of the incredibly destructive Japanese beetle (*Popillia japonica*) with high success rates.

This wildflower garden has been invaded by weeds. Some basic garden hygiene could help to keep the weeds at bay.

A katydid nymph perches on a dayliliy petal. If you remove such insects by hand, you avoid the dangers of toxic insecticides.

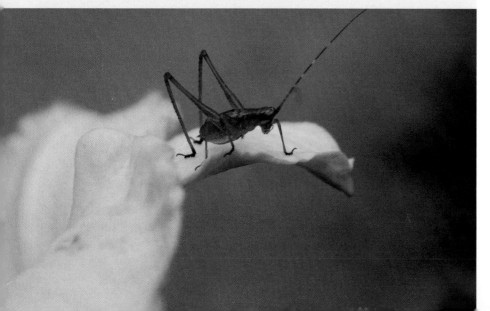

Weed frequently. Frequent weeding is necessary to remove shady hiding places where opportunistic pests can take shelter.

CATCH PESTS IN THE ACT

Other nonchemical methods for controlling pests include simply catching them in the act of destruction and disposing of them before they have the chance to multiply. Although, not for the faint of heart, these mechanical, rather than chemical, methods of pest control provide a highly effective way to keep the pests as well as the harmful chemicals out of your yard and garden and away from your pet.

A beneficial spined soldier bug kills a Mexican bean beetle, a foe to snap beans and soybeans.

Pick insects off plants. Plucking caterpillars and other large chewing insects, such as grasshoppers, off your plants quickly reduces the damage they cause. Drop them in a jar of soapy water as you collect them. The large soap molecules clog their respiratory structures, quickly euthanizing them.

Put up barriers. To prevent crawling pests from scaling trunks and stems, use barriers such as spreadable pastes made from saps and resins. Spread them directly on the bases of your plants. Cutting pests off at the ground forces them to look elsewhere for a meal.

Wash plant leaves. Washing plant leaves with a strong jet of water works well in removing insects with sucking mouthparts. These often tiny insects, such as aphids, stick tightly to plants by embedding their long, tubelike mouths into plant tissues. A forceful stream of water is all it takes to tear them away and prevent them from returning.

Utilize traps. To capture pests, hang traps in the garden for flying bugs, or lay traps on the ground for crawling creatures. Traps use natural pheromones that mimic hormones given off during insect breeding periods. Curious creatures enter and get stuck to sticky substances inside the trap or are prevented from exiting by specially shaped funnels. Then, simply dispose of the traps in the trash bin.

LET MOTHER NATURE HELP

Biological control of pest species involves letting Mother Nature take care of, well, Mother Nature. By encouraging beneficial organisms that eat harmful ones, you can solve your pest problem —courtesy of the food chain. Several techniques help lure hungry bugs to your yard that will eat the bugs that eat your plants.

Put in plants that beneficial bugs like. The nonpredatory adult phases of insects are frequently drawn to sweet-smelling, nectar-rich flowering plants. Include these plants in your garden, and these beneficial insects will come

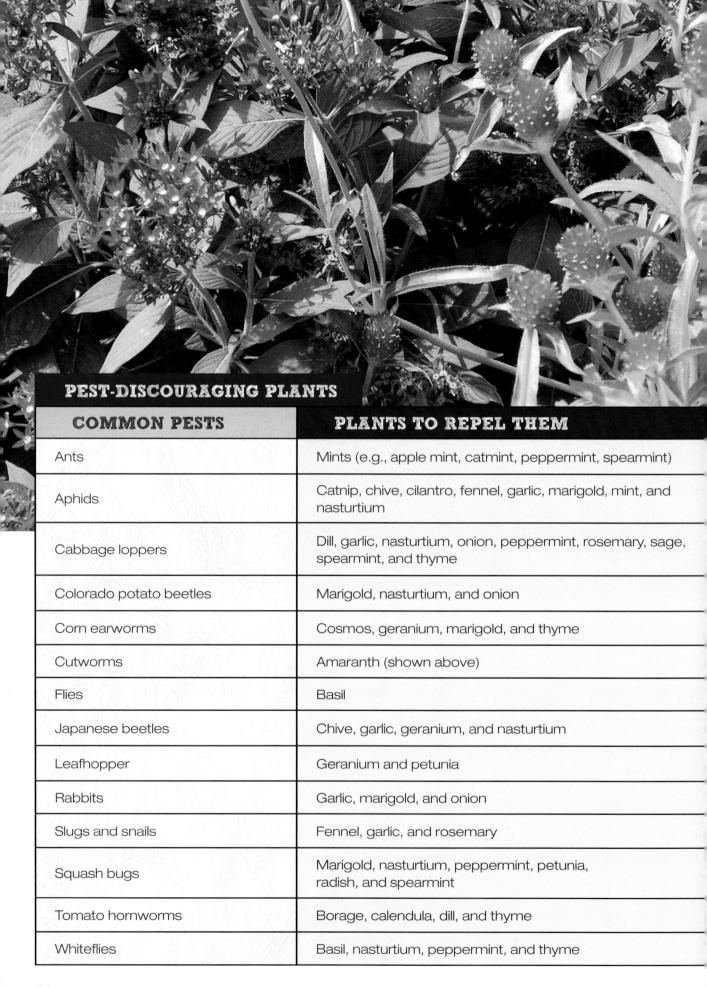

PEST-DISCOURAGING PLANTS

COMMON PESTS	PLANTS TO REPEL THEM
Ants	Mints (e.g., apple mint, catmint, peppermint, spearmint)
Aphids	Catnip, chive, cilantro, fennel, garlic, marigold, mint, and nasturtium
Cabbage loppers	Dill, garlic, nasturtium, onion, peppermint, rosemary, sage, spearmint, and thyme
Colorado potato beetles	Marigold, nasturtium, and onion
Corn earworms	Cosmos, geranium, marigold, and thyme
Cutworms	Amaranth (shown above)
Flies	Basil
Japanese beetles	Chive, garlic, geranium, and nasturtium
Leafhopper	Geranium and petunia
Rabbits	Garlic, marigold, and onion
Slugs and snails	Fennel, garlic, and rosemary
Squash bugs	Marigold, nasturtium, peppermint, petunia, radish, and spearmint
Tomato hornworms	Borage, calendula, dill, and thyme
Whiteflies	Basil, nasturtium, peppermint, and thyme

Luring **Ladybugs**

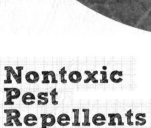

Gardening organically requires a little active participation from Mother Nature. She supplies the beneficial insects that protect your plants from the destructive ones, but there are a few things you can do to give her a helping hand. Plant a few flowers relished by ladybugs, and you'll encourage them to stop by to drink some nectar, lay some eggs, and control common aphids—all without the use of pesticides.

Favorite ladybug plants include cilantro, cosmos, dill, fennel, geranium, red clover, sweet alyssum, and yarrow.

The purple flowers of this ornamental garlic not only provide color to a garden but also discourage pests.

to drink the sugary syrup, mate, and lay eggs. Those eggs will hatch and grow into hungry larvae, which will seek out and devour pests. The cycle repeats, naturally controlling your bug problems.

Get beneficial bug eggs. Lacewing, ladybug, praying mantis, and other beneficial bug eggs can be purchased at nursery-supply stores, online, or through mail-order businesses. By putting them in your garden to hatch, you'll ensure a good supply of beneficials in your garden environment. Even if they eventually fly away, they're likely to deposit a few eggs first—perpetuating the next generation.

Conserve some pests. Although it seems counterintuitive, leaving some pests in the garden really is a good idea. Without any food, beneficial insects won't be there when you really need them. It's worth sacrificing a plant or two to ensure a ready supply of nature's helpers.

Avoid pesticides. Pesticides not only remove entire populations of food for beneficial insects but also kill the beneficial insects themselves. Use of pesticides removes nature's biological control measures from the equation— and puts your dog at risk for accidental poisoning.

Nontoxic Pest Repellents

Thousands of years of anecdotal evidence support the use of companion planting for managing garden pests. The philosophy that some plants growing nearby repel the pests often found on other plants has not thoroughly been studied by science, but it has been proven in organic backyards over the course of many generations of family gardeners. Large-scale organic farming operations practicing companion guidelines have also reported significant reductions in pest damage. Try repelling these widespread pests by planting plants proven to send them packing. (See the Pest-Discouraging Plants table on the opposite page.)

Applying a spray made from botanical extracts also contributes to a successful organic environment. All-natural sprays made from common plants further protect your plants as they contain compounds that insects and other pests find irritating or destructive to their bodies. Hot pepper extracts, garlic oil products, neem oil (extracted from the neem tree), and just plain soapy water, to name a few, all repel a variety of outdoor pests. Use caution with these,

These two dogs will deter deer better than this wrought-iron gate. To protect your yard, erect sturdy deer fencing.

Trumpet vines, like the ones on this wall, are both dog and deer proof.

Ornamental grass stands up to deer.

Deer don't like the lavender's odor.

and other sprays around your dog, as accidental ingestion could occur, resulting in irritation of your pet's eyes, nose, and mouth.

Barriers to Vertebrate Pests

Controlling four-legged pests presents special challenges in the backyard setting. Deer, moles, rabbits, squirrels, and other critters stop at nothing to nibble succulent young plants. Keeping them out while making your yard comfortable and safe for your own four-legged companion requires a little ingenuity.

Be aware that trying to control these pests can transform gardening from a mundane activity into an all-out war between man and nature. If control measures become exhausting and seemingly hopeless, allow nature to take its course—unleash the hounds. Dogs enjoy the spirit of a good chase. Let them do the work for you by doing what comes naturally.

DEER

Deer cause, by far, the most damage of any pest in your landscape. In a couple hours' time, they can wipe out an entire garden or strip your decorative landscape plants bare. With a taste for a wide variety of tender plant material, deer fatten up quickly thanks to your hard work. Not only do they make short work of the landscape, but deer also harbor deer ticks, which carry Lyme disease. For your health and that of your dogs,

Copper dashes across the yard, happy to chase away deer and other pests.

make it a priority to keep these critters out of the yard and garden.

The only sure-fire way to bar deer from entering the landscape is to erect deer fencing. Besides being the most costly solution, however, deer fencing's stockade appearance takes away from the beauty of your outdoor environment. So, before erecting any fencing, you may want to try choosing plants that deer won't eat, or you may want to consider some special sprays.

DEER-PROOF PLANTS

By removing temptation with unpalatable plants, you give deer no reason to browse on your property. Some of the plants, already discussed in chapter 2 for their durability and suitability for yards with dogs, also make great choices for deer control.

Grasses and vines: Many ornamental grasses and vines solve potential conflicts from dogs and deer. For grasses,

try any fescue or sea oats for vertical impact. For vines, choose clematis, honeysuckle, trumpet vine, or wisteria; they will grow out of your dog's reach while also repelling hungry deer.

Ground covers: Sturdy ground covers make excellent additions to yards with dogs and deer. Evergreen creeping junipers grow less than a foot off the ground, and they provide year-round color and interest with fast-growing branches. Deer won't eat them, and your dog can run roughshod over them without causing damage. Stonecrop and creeping thyme, also discussed as a great ground cover for dogs that like to lounge, presents a similar deer-proof solution.

Lavender: With its pungent odor, lavender makes a great addition to a landscape frequented by deer. While the plant's scent is treasured by humans, who appreciate its relaxing, aromatherapeutic benefits, deer seem not to care for.

Red twig dogwood and forsythia: Red twig dogwood, also called red osier dogwood, makes a striking bright red impression with its vibrant bark, while keeping deer at a distance. Forsythia, also a great durable plant for dogs, holds no appeal for deer.

Yarrow and aster: Yarrow and several varieties of aster, native to much of the United States, grow well in spite of heavy deer traffic. Their ability to ward off grazing animals makes them hearty and colorful choices.

DEER-REPELLING SPRAYS AND SOLUTIONS

Sprays and solutions designed to repel deer also contribute to organic control methods. Most contain either synthetic bobcat urine or hot pepper and/or garlic extracts. The goal is to frighten the animals away by indicating the presence of a predator or to make your plants unpalatable. Use care when applying irritants to ensure your dog doesn't suffer irritation of his mucous membranes.

GOPHERS

Gophers dig nearly as much as an active dog does, with one big difference. Their mission: to uncover and devour as many fleshy, tender roots as possible. Carrots and other root vegetables don't stand a chance against these critters. Shrubs and flowers with underground tubers also fall victim to hungry gophers that fail to discriminate when on the prowl.

You may be doing something to encourage these critters. Crabgrass, for instance, is a favorite gopher food. This weedy grass, found in most lawns, provides an excellent gopher habitat. Pull it quickly, and repair any bare patches with a fescue-ryegrass blend. You can also deal with gophers by putting down some physical barriers or enlisting the help of other animals.

GOPHER BARRIERS

As with other determined wildlife, barriers offer an effective control strategy for gophers. Try laying down hardware cloth or fine wire mesh beneath freshly installed sod. Wrap the mesh around the root balls of new perennials to keep incisors from damaging vital roots.

BIOLOGICAL GOPHER CONTROL

Minimizing, rather than eliminating, gopher populations may serve as the best course of action with such a pernicious pest. If your yard and garden seem infested, try biological controls that address the whole environment. Attempt to attract predators that effectively manage gopher populations.

The Great Horned Owl (shown here) and other owl species may eat the gophers in your yard.

Outdoor cats and birds of prey—such as hawks and owls—could rid an area of pesky yard-destroying rodents.

To attract hawks, owls, and American Kestrels, erect perching and nest platforms and boxes. Nest and perching platforms for hawks consist of simple 24-by-24-inch flat surfaces and can be mounted anywhere from 35 to 75 feet from the ground. Tree forks overlooking clearings or fields provide optimal sites to attract raptors. Platform plans may be offered by conservation organizations, such as a state's natural resources department or a local chapter of the National Audubon Society. Owl nest box plans—for Barn Owls, screech-owls, and American Kestrels—are on the U.S. Department of Agriculture Natural Resources Conservation Service Web site (www.nrcs.usda.gov); use the search phrase *owl nest box plans*.

RABBITS

Rabbits leave telltale calling cards with their characteristic nibbling habits. Freshly emerged seedlings cut off at the soil's surface have little chance of survival. Strips of bark removed at the base of the woody stems of landscape plants leaves those plants helpless against the elements.

Rabbit-proof fencing may be the only way to protect the vegetables you've worked so hard to grow. At a height of 36 inches, this fencing is less of an eye-sore than deer fencing. Try constructing a rabbit fence using chicken wire from your local hardware store. Make sure to bury at least 6 inches of the wire fencing below the soil surface. This prevents determined rabbits from tunneling their way to your garden's bounty. You can also try discouraging rabbits with certain herbs or ammonia.

RABBIT-REPELLING AROMATIC HERBS

Luckily for gardeners and landscaper, rabbits disdain aromatic herbs. Catni lavender, thyme, and others actually repel rabbits from your outdoor spac One, in particular, sends them scurry —garlic. Much like vampires, rabbits turn tail at the scent of this popular, easy-to-grow herb. Planted at the edg of a flower bed or among your favorit vegetables, garlic stops rabbits in thei tracks. Many rabbit-repellent sprays a made from garlic extracts. Exercise ca tion when using one, although genera considered safe for use around dogs, cessive ingestion of it can cause anem

DISCOURAGE RABBITS WITH AMMONIA

This household cleaner repels rabbits and many other creatures with a

licate sense of smell. Its strong odor
erwhelms their noses and sends them
cking. Make simple baits by soaking
tton balls in ammonia, placing them
reused, perforated plastic containers,
d then hanging the containers from
es and other plants. A word of cau-
on when using ammonia: the chemi-
l could send your own dog pack-
g—which may or may not be a good
ing. Be aware, however, that ammonia
n stimulate dogs to increase their
ent marking behaviors, which could
mage your landscape. For reasons yet
nknown, some dogs are drawn to the
ent, and some are repelled by it.

QUIRRELS

though most people associate these
imals with their bird-feeder-raiding
ays, squirrels can also cause significant
mage to the garden and landscape. By
gging up and feasting upon juicy bulbs,
uirrels undo the hard work of autumn
d prevent your favorite flowers from
er seeing the light of day. Squirrels can
ten be found in the garden, gnawing
les in fruits and vegetables to access
eir tasty seeds. To protect your garden
om ravaging squirrels, you can use
hysical barriers or sprays.

A diligent gardener has put down a black fabric weed barrier before spreading any mulch.

SQUIRREL BARRIERS

Squirrels can't eat what they cannot
reach, so you want to make sure that
no marauding paws can reach tender
bulbs buried beneath the soil. If not
protected properly, entire bulb gardens
can fall victim to hungry squirrels in a
few short days. For small bulbs, such as
crocus, grape hyacinth, and squill, you
can use overturned strawberry baskets
to prevent squirrels from reaching the
bulbs; the baskets will still allow the
bulbs to sprout in the spring. Place
the basket over groups of bulbs in the
bottom of the hole before burying. For
larger bulbs, like tulip and hyacinth
bulbs, place a sheet of chicken
wire over each of the bulbs
before burying them.
For an easier, though
less attractive, fix,
simply place a sheet of
plywood weighted with
rocks or bricks over
the area where you've
planted fresh bulbs.
In the spring, you can
remove the weights
and allow the bulbs
to sprout and flourish.

A wood basket can be placed over bulbs to
ward off squirrels.

SQUIRREL IRRITANTS

Squirrels have an acute sense of smell.
Because they respond so readily to irritants, a number of all-natural ingredients have proven successful in controlling their garden raids. The active
ingredient in hot peppers, capsaicin,
causes a highly unpleasant sensation
for squirrels and can be found in the
majority of products designed to repel
them. Predator urines (such as those
of bobcats, coyotes, and foxes) strike
fear into the hearts of skittish squirrels,
causing them to flee.

Weed-Control Methods

If pests present problems, weeds present crises. Unchecked, weeds easily
overtake an outdoor space, turning any
landscape from glamorous to ghastly in
a single growing season. Weed-infested
flower beds and gardens actually lower a
property's value, making enemies out of
neighbors and creating optimum habi-
tats for fleas and other pests. Rather than
starting from scratch by poisoning the
whole lot, do what's right for the health
of your pet and the environment. Learn
the basics of organic weed control.

WEED PREVENTION

By far the most important step, early prevention, saves countless hours of hard labor. Start by catching trouble spots early. Remove weeds before they bloom; when you let weeds flower and produce seed, you compromise weed control for the rest of the year. If you think weeds are difficult to control as it is, consider this: weeds produce enough seeds in their first year to deposit seven years' worth of seeds into the nearby soil. Their ability to produce—sometimes by the millions—seeds that will grow into the next generation is what makes weeds so successful. Take the following steps to prevent weed growth in your yard and garden.

Cover the entire area. Prevent weeds from getting the upper hand by avoiding large areas of exposed soil. Aim to cover 100 percent of your space with grass, landscape plants, or mulch. By removing the areas where opportunistic weeds can put down roots, you make it impossible for them to get established.

Use only reliable soil sources. Avoid bringing in large amounts of top soil or fill dirt from unreliable sources. Often, well-meaning gardeners, intending to improve their soil, obtain dirt from construction sites or fallow farmland. Soil from sources other than landscape suppliers may be riddled with weed seeds that set a lawn and garden up for years' worth of tough maintenance.

Kill roots before composting. Never throw weeds directly into your compost heap after you've pulled them from your lawn and garden. Allow them to dry in the sun first, thereby killing roots that could redevelop into weeds after you've spread the compost the following year.

Practice the sprinkle-and-pull method. Before adding new plants or sowing seed in the garden or landscap remove as many weeds as possible. Water the area, wait for weeds to sprout, and then pull them before they set seed. Repeat the sprinkle-pull sequence several times until weeds no longer sprout. By taking the seeds out of the soil in this way, you prevent late weed problems.

WEED REMOVAL

Regular weed removal is crucial, and there are different steps you can take depending on the type of weed you are dealing with.

Young weeds: Cultivate your soil regularly. Through the process of turning the soil under and exposing the roots of young weeds to the elements, you can destroy them without having

Lounging at his ease, this chocolate Lab enjoys the comfort and safety of an organic backyard.

Dead nettle (*Lamium maculatum*) borders a pathway of mulch.

o spend hours digging more mature weeds out of the ground.

Larger weeds: For larger weeds that appear to spring up overnight, some old-fashioned elbow grease, time, and hard work are the organic gardener's best tools for weed-pulling success. Grasp weeds firmly at the base, bend your knees, and use your leg strength to do the work to avoid injury to your lower back and arms. Make sure to remove the entire weed, including its fine feeder roots and its deep taproot. Many weeds quickly return if their underground parts remain.

Companion weeds: Some weeds spread by rhizomes, which are their underground roots that sprout more plants far from the originating plant. Make sure you search far and wide for a companion weed that looks similar to the one you just pulled. Pull that one, too, or you'll end up with recurring weeds. The underground rhizome between two identical weeds must also be removed to prevent more weeds from regenerating. If you can locate a rhizome, which is usually located not more than an inch below the surface, give it a tug, and it will lead you to the next weed that needs to be removed.

MULCH

Putting down mulch after weeds have been pulled accomplishes three things in an organic landscape. One, it smothers weeds, preventing them from germinating. Two, it preserves soil moisture by defusing sunlight and keeping the ground around your plants cool. Three, it adds nutrients to the soil as it decomposes. Mulch also acts as a design element, as it can be compiled of any number of materials. Wood chips, straw, pine needles, grass clippings, leaves, and compost all make great organic mulch.

Intensify your mulch's ability to block weeds by using a weed barrier underlayment. Simply spread a weed barrier over the soil and top with a layer of mulch to provide maximum control with minimal effort. Weed barriers allow water to penetrate down to the roots of your plants while at the same time preventing sun from reaching weed seeds. Use a roll of commercial weed fabric or plastic weed barrier designed for weed prevention, or make your own. Lay five or six layers of old newspaper over the soil, and wet it using a garden hose. Spread your mulch over the paper, and enjoy weed-free gardening.

Beware of Harmful Mulch

Beware of two types of mulch that can be harmful to your pet. Cocoa mulch, produced as a byproduct of the food industry, has become increasingly popular with home gardeners for its sweet scent and fine-textured appearance. Unfortunately, it contains the same toxic compounds found in processed chocolate and can be deadly if ingested by your dog. Coconut husks have also become a popular mulch option. Green enthusiasts are quick to spread the coconut-husk mulch—known for its ability to soak up and retain many times its weight in water—around thirsty plants. However, it will quickly swell in the digestive tract of any dog who consumes it and potentially cause blockage of the intestines.

Tolerate a Few Weeds and Pests

Organic gardening requires one more thing for naturally controlling the pests and weeds in your yard and garden areas—learning to live with a few dandelions and aphids. No yard, controlled naturally, can boast a 100 percent weed- and pest-free zone. If your goal is getting green with your outdoor space and making room to live in safety and harmony with your dog, tolerance of a less-than-perfect patch of flowers or vegetables is an absolute must.

CHAPTER 4

Recycling Home, Garden, and Yard Waste

What could be greener—and safer for your dog—than creating your very own fertilizer out of the waste found in and around your home? Rather than cluttering your curbside and the landfill with grass clippings and kitchen scraps; take those bags of trash and turn them into garden gold.

Environmentally friendly compost will fortify the plants in your yard like few other soil amendments can, and compost

is 100 pecent safe for your pet. Although keeping the process clean and tidy in a yard with an active dog can be a bit of challenge for you, making your own rich compost will give you peace of mind and will help you create a naturally gorgeous landscape and a bountiful garden full of fruits and vegetables.

Compelling Reasons to Compost

Why should you compost? Here are five good reasons for doing so:

Protect your dog. Commercial chemical fertilizers, particularly those formulated for flowering shrubs, can be downright

deadly when accidentally ingested by you pet. Dogs spend their lives on the ground lounging among plants and investigating the yard with their noses and mouths. Keeping them out of harm's way by creating your own all-natural, all-purpose fertilizer just makes sense.

Save your plants. It's easy to over-fertilize when you are using commercial products and adding large doses of chemicals to the soil can burn landscape plants. If you put compost around the bases of your garden and landscape plant several times throughout the year, they will receive small, consistent doses of nutrients, thus preventing burning while promoting lush growth.

Save the planet. Protecting our rivers streams, lakes, and even drinking water starts with what we use on our plants. By using organic compost instead of artificial fertilizers, you keep chemicals out of

Blue morning glories
hide an unsightly com-
post heap, located next to
blue rain barrels. Com-
posting areas can be
easily concealed.

A white Fox Terrier sprawls in a well-maintained backyard, one benefiting from rich compost.

your local watershed. Excess phosphorus and nitrogen (common chemicals in commercial fertilizers) promote algae growth in rivers, streams, and lakes. Algal blooms die and decompose, depleting the oxygen from water ways and choking out marine wildlife.

Over time, large-scale use of fertilizers increases the levels of nitrates and other harmful chemicals in the freshwater aquifers found deep beneath the ground. To preserve fresh drinking water for future generations, do your part by switching to compost.

Save money. Manufactured fertilizer products cost money. By composting with food items you have already purchased and waste you have lying around your yard and garden, you accomplish the same thing for free.

Reduce your carbon footprint. Reducing carbon footprints isn't just for celebrities. Understanding the mark you leave on the world and the destructive carbon you put into the air offers another opportunity to conserve and protect the environment. Commercial fertilizers, made by machines using fossil fuels, have large carbon footprints. Organic compost, made the low-impact way (using Mother Nature's power), significantly shrinks your carbon footprint.

Basic composting isn't rocket science. With a few rules in mind, you can do the right thing for your dog, your plants, and the environment. Backyard composting draws on the basic tenets of an eternal cycle of plant life, death, and decomposition. It's the natural way soil is made. On smaller scale, the process can be accelerated to produce enough rich, composted soil to nourish and revitalize all the plant in your yard and garden.

Dirt-Making Debunked

[Mi]sconceptions surrounding back[ya]rd composting abound. Most people [bel]ieve they need tons of space for [co]nstructing massive heaps of unsightly [ro]tting plant material that often smell [an]d draw insects and other pests. Noth[in]g could be further from the truth. [Co]mposting can be done in a neat and [tid]y space in any corner of your outdoor [sp]ace. Even a small composting opera[tio]n will provide plenty of nutrient-rich [fer]tilizer for your yard and garden. [W]hat's more, it should never draw an [ab]undance of insect or vertebrate pests [an]d has little to no offensive odor.

Fortunately for most backyard [ga]rdeners, several types of commercially available compost bins can be found at garden-supply stores. Cities and municipalities even give them away at little or no cost to gardeners who attend educational seminars on the benefits of composting. Contact your local government offices to find out if they host composting events. Most bins and tumblers that are recommended for small-scale composting are easy to use, take up minimal space, and are designed to contain and suppress odors while allowing for optimal air circulation. Many have lids, making them self-contained eco-units, impervious to curious animals.

If you have the space, a larger, true compost pile or heap may suit your needs. Just enclose it with a simple wire fence or wooden planking to contain the compost and keep your dog from getting too nosy.

What Not to Compost

The key to preventing wild vermin and the odors that attract them is keeping certain items out of your compost heap. As they decay, the items below offer temptation that is too seductive for coyotes, opossums, raccoons, skunks, and other critters to resist. Do not compost:

- meat and bones
- fats and cooking oils
- cooked fruits and vegetables
- manure from meat-eating animals (e.g., dogs, cats)

Small, contained composting units, such as this round one, offer a neat alternative to heaping, barely contained compost piles.

The Most Eco-Friendly Source

Composting provides the safest, most eco-friendly source of fertilizer for your lawn and garden. For the health of your dog, plants, and planet, this back-to-basics form of gardening represents the simplest alternative to chemical toxins that can kill. Any lawn or garden, particularly one with a dog, benefits from the addition of even a humble composting operation.

Perfect Pieces

Don't have time to cut your household waste into 1-inch pieces? Try this simple fix. Rather than purchasing a chipper to shred your waste, make your own. All you need is a garbage can and a string trimmer. Use a 40-gallon, or larger, round plastic trash can with a lid. Make a cut in the lid from the edge to the center. At the center, cut a round hole the size of the circumference of your string trimmer's neck.

To use, first fill the trash can with several inches of yard or kitchen waste; small twigs, vegetable peels, plant trimmings, and leaves work best. Then insert the string trimmer, and snap on the lid, which acts as a guard to prevent flying debris. Simply fire up your trimmer, and—voilà—you have perfectly diced compost material in a matter of minutes.

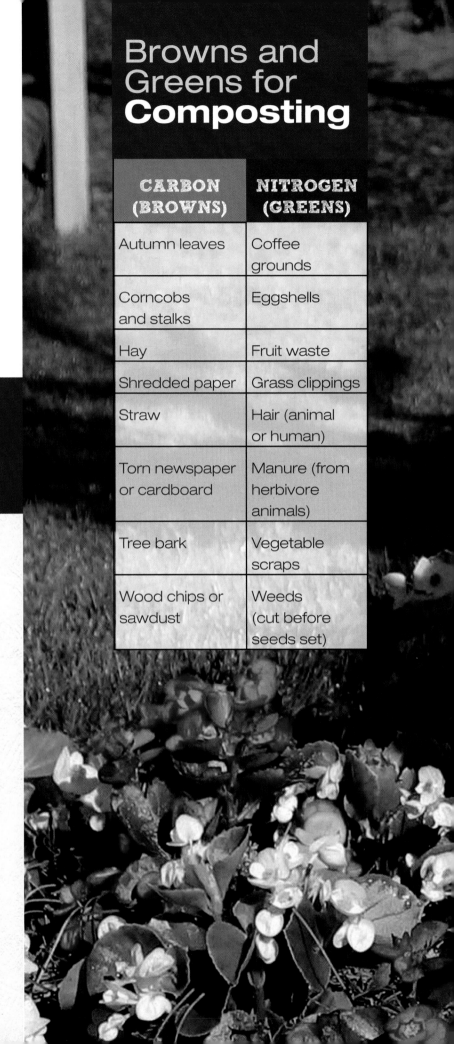

Browns and Greens for Composting

CARBON (BROWNS)	NITROGEN (GREENS)
Autumn leaves	Coffee grounds
Corncobs and stalks	Eggshells
Hay	Fruit waste
Shredded paper	Grass clippings
Straw	Hair (animal or human)
Torn newspaper or cardboard	Manure (from herbivore animals)
Tree bark	Vegetable scraps
Wood chips or sawdust	Weeds (cut before seeds set)

Like this Westie, your dog will benefit from a safer, back-to-basics approach to yard care.

Composting 101

The composting process consists of taking household and outdoor plant waste, encouraging the growth of bacteria and fungi, accelerating the decomposition process, and reaping the benefits of the end product. This self-contained process quickly and efficiently creates valuable fertilizer, provided the right conditions are maintained.

1 Mix

Composting starts with the right ingredients. The correct mix of carbon and nitrogen (often referred to as greens and browns, such as fallen leaves and grass clippings), creates the best environment for the beneficial bacteria and fungi that quickly digest plant waste. A 3:1 ratio by weight of carbon to nitrogen works best. Choose food and plant materials high in each of these elements from the table Browns and Greens on page 60.

Mix waste from the home and garden in the 3:1 proportion, and you're on your way. Too many browns or too many greens, and you'll achieve "cold" composting—the slower method for creating your own organic fertilizer, which could take several years. If your goal is a fresh crop of the good stuff inside a single year, aim for the right mix.

2 Chop

ay attention to the size of the waste you add to your
ompost pile. The smaller the piece, the faster the de-
omposition will happen. Aim for waste no larger than
quarter. Follow this 1-inch-or-less guide when prepar-
g your vegetable peelings and other yard waste for
omposting. It allows the bacteria to get into the center
the pieces, digesting them quickly and completely.

3 Inoculate

To speed up the process, try adding organic inocu-
lants (inactive forms of bacteria and fungi) found
at your local garden-supply store. When added to
your heap, they come to life and get to work on your
waste, converting it quickly into usable compost.

4 Turn

roducing oxy-
n to a compost
ap also speeds
e decomposi-
n process. The
cteria and fungi
at break down
aste require
equate oxygen
do their work at
speed. Turning
e compost heap
riodically helps

roduce this beneficial element. Using a pitchfork or
ovel, turn the pile from top to bottom, thoroughly mix-
g the layers. Most advocates of the quick composting
ethod recommend a thorough turning once a week.
hough it may seem like a chore, the solution to turning
ight be staring you in the face, or at least panting at the
or. If your dog likes to dig and you don't mind hosing
m down after he has finished, unleash him on your pile
d watch the fury of a four-legged gardener at work.

5 Sprinkle

Water is the final ingredient for any well-designed
composting operation. Water, along with the heat
that develops deep inside the pile, creates ideal
conditions for the growth of the bacteria and fungi
needed to quickly turn your plant waste into valuable
finished compost. Use the squeeze test to determine
whether it's time to sprinkle the pile. Grab a handful of
compost from just beneath the surface of the pile. If
it feels damp but not soggy, it contains the proper 40
to 60 percent moisture needed for composting. If it's
dry, give it a drink.

Organic Gardener, Organic Dogs

Johann and Gracie Tangled Up in Green

Blueberries are an important ingredient in Leslie May's homemade, all-natural frosty doggy treat.

Leslie May
Carmel, Indiana

When Leslie May bought her first home, she couldn't figure out what her neighbors were doing to their lawn. It seemed to her they were spreading a mysterious substance on the grass, an activity she'd never seen before. Having been raised in a green household before green was cool, she found the concept of commercial fertilizer totally foreign.

"I couldn't bear to put that stuff o[n] my lawn," May says. "I knew the dangers. I started investigating nonchemi[-]cal ways I could feed my lawn."

After much research and trial an[d] error, May settled on bone meal and blood meal—both readily available animal byproducts and equally effecti[ve] at giving landscape and garden plants [a] boost. Instead of harsh chemical weed killers, May started using corn gluten meal, which not only acts as a fertiliz[er] but also prevents the germination of weed seeds.

Later, when May adopted her dog[s] Johann and Gracie, from a shelter, th[e]

Leslie May enjoys the day with her dogs, Gracie (left) and Johann (right).

wo active Border Collies were easily integrated into her already organic lifestyle—something she takes pride in.

"I was just really glad I did what I did and kept to my core beliefs," May says. "I feel really comfortable that my animals are healthy out there."

May believes in promoting living green with canines—so much so that she started RaiseAGreenDog.com (http://blog.raiseagreendog.com/), a Web site and blog about all-natural dog care and products.

Enriching her dogs' diets with lots of organically grown fruits and vegetables and organic meats forms

the basis of her green canine regimen.

"Along with their kibble, they get organic vegetables [and] often organic yogurt," she says.

May even developed her own all-natural frosty treat recipe, perfect for a hot summer day packed with agility training—something both of her active dogs enjoy.

"It's yogurt, blueberries, bananas, and a little peanut butter. It's all frozen in an ice cube tray. It's an amazing summer treat. They love it."

On being green, May says it's easy. Dog ownership presents so many ways to be kind to the earth. One of the

simplest is how you choose to dispose of your own dog's waste. If left to decay on your lawn, dog feces can inadvertently spread harmful parasites into your local waterways, where they can infect wildlife as well as sully the local water supply.

Picking up the doo with biodegradable, organic waste bags (made of corn starch), instead of plastic grocery bags, keeps the environment clean while keeping trash out of the landfill. "[Plastic] bags take forever to go away, and they are made out of petroleum," May says. "On the front end, it's bad and on the back end, it's bad."

CHAPTER 5
Natural Fruits and Vegetables

All-natural fresh fruits and vegetables are great additions to your dog's already high-quality kibble. Adding fruits and vegetables gives you the opportunity to share the bounty of the garden in a manner that will ensure optimal nutrition for your furry companion. Most veterinarians agree that dogs benefit greatly from the supplementation of fresh fruits and fresh vegetables.

From an evolutionary standpoint, it makes sense. When dogs were wild, not all that long ago, they did not merely eat the meaty parts of their prey; they also ate the stomach contents. The herbivores that the wild dogs consumed most certainly feasted on a diet of fresh greens and fruits of the field. Clearly then, as grizzly as this explanation may seem to some people, fruits and vegetables have formed a part of the canine diet from the very beginning.

Supplementing your dog's meals with small amounts of fruits and vegetables from your garden could supply him with nutrients, such as vitamins, minerals, and amino acids, and other dietary components, such as fiber and enzymes, that once were a part of his ancestors' diet and should be a part of his, too.

By cultivating an organic garden through to production, you ensure that no traces of potentially toxic herbicides and pesticides make it into your pet's dinner bowl. Although science has yet to prove the full benefits of a diet rich in organic vegetables, many people believe that commercially grown produce found at the supermarket contains high levels of chemical residues that adversely affect our health and the health of our pets.

In most cases, organic gardening also saves you money and requires only a little extra effort. Eat the way Mother Nature intended, and feed your dog wholesome fruits and vegetables sure to make his coat shine.

Whole Foods Revolution

Fad diets come and they go, but since the beginning of time, human beings (and other animals) have stayed slim and healthy on a regimen of whole foods. This historical diet is no secret. Recently, however, people have rediscovered the benefits of a lifestyle that includes mostly whole foods.

The basis for a whole-foods diet is simple. Eat only foods that look just as

Beagle Chloe sits calmly amid a flourishing garden of lettuce, kale, and tomatoes, proving dogs and gardens can coexist peacefully.

Organically grown heirloom tomatoes are for sale at a farmer's market. Your dog can benefit from vegetables and fruits grown in your own garden.

they looked when they were harvested. If you can't tell by looking which fruit or vegetable you're about to eat, you shouldn't put it in your mouth say "whole foodies." The premise makes good sense. Processed foods contain artificial additives, preservatives, and colorings—man-made chemicals that have no business being in our foods and bodies.

When eaten at the height of freshness, unpreserved and free from chemicals (grown organically), fruits and vegetables give people and their dogs what nature intended; and they do so without the junk. When you are enriching your dog's diet with produce, play it safe. Go the whole organic nine yards.

Cooked without fats, sugar, or salt, lots of fruits and vegetables that you normally eat work just fine for your pet.

Remember to feed fruits and vegetables in moderation—a few berries here, a couple of tablespoons of pureed pumpkin there. Too much of a good thing can trigger stomach upset, particularly fruits, which contain certain acids your pet's digestive tract can only tolerate in small doses.

In the Fruit Orchard

Many foods we consider "vegetables" are actually fruits, by a botanical definition. To simplify matters here, however, we categorize them as fruits or vegetables as commonly understood.

APPLES

Most dogs love apples and, given the choice, would stand at the foot of any tree, gobbling them up as they fall to the ground. Although the leaves, stems, and seeds of apples contain trace amounts of cyanide poison, the fruit remains free from toxins. Because apples are high in sugar, dogs should be offered only a few slices at a time as treats. Try peeling the apples to lower the chances of your dog experiencing gastric upset.

BLUEBERRIES

Blueberries make most dogs drool. They're as tasty and as healthy as it gets when it comes to supplementing your dog's diet with fresh fruits. Even frozen blueberries will pack a powerful punch. Loaded with anthocyanin, the blue plant pigment, these little berries may be nature's wonder fruit. Scientists recently discovered that anthocyanins act as otent antioxidants, which boost the mmune system.

The sweet flavor of these berries makes them attractive to dogs who are looking for a quick treat. Veterinary research conducted with sled dogs in 2006 at the University of Alaska indicates that dogs who were regularly treated with blueberries recover more quickly and completely from rigorous activity. The sled dogs' muscles rebounded far more quickly than those of the dogs in control groups who didn't consume berries.

PEARS

As with apples, pears make great treats for dogs. They relish the sweetness and may eat the fruits whole if given the chance. Beware, however, of the seeds. As with other fruits, pear seeds contain low levels of poisons designed to keep insects and birds from eating the seeds in the wild. Feeding pears in large amounts will likely induce diarrhea, gastric upset, or both so offer your dog just a few pieces.

RASPBERRIES AND STRAWBERRIES

Plant raspberries and strawberries, and your only problem will be picking them before your pet does. Rabbits and birds are no match for a dog when it comes to cleaning out a ripe berry patch. Once dogs develop a taste for these juicy summer crops, they'll patrol your plants daily, looking for the choicest fruits. In moderation, this behavior poses no problems, but with a bumper crop of June-bearing plants, you may need to restrict your dog's access to the garden, too many berries may cause diarrhea.

In the Vegetable Garden

Here is a bushel of vegetables for you and your canine companion to enjoy. As with the fruits previously discussed, some of these veggie selections must be fed to your dog sparingly in order to avoid adverse reactions.

BELL PEPPERS

Red, green, orange, and yellow bell peppers in moderation add much-needed vitamins and minerals to a dog's diet. Steam, boil, or puree bell peppers to increase their digestibility; otherwise, they may cause gas or loose stools. The bright colors in red, yellow, and orange bell peppers are caused by carotenoids, plant pigments considered to act as powerful antioxidants for the humans and the animals that eat them. These peppers also contain more than three times the amount of vitamin C that is found in citrus fruit.

Avoid feeding your pet hot peppers. The capsaicin compound produced by the seeds of these vegetables causes

Garden's Bounty: Mixed Vegetables

Here are two healthy and tasty organic mixed-vegetable dishes: one for your dog and one for you!

Canine Curry (for Your Dog)	Hot Madras Curry over Rice (for You)
Ingredients: 1 ½ cup dry, yellow split peas 5 cups water ½ cup fresh green peas 1 cup sliced carrots ½ apple, cored and chopped 4 small red potatoes, diced 2 pinches of ground ginger 2 pinches of curry powder	**Ingredients:** Brown basmati rice 1 tablespoon hot Madras curry powder 2 teaspoons ground ginger Salt and pepper to taste Mixed vegetables, cooked
Directions: Add all ingredients to crock pot. Cook on high for 4 hours or on low for up to 6 hours or until vegetables are fork tender. Cool fully before serving over your pet's kibble.	**Directions:** Cook rice as directed. Season remaining portion of cooked vegetables with curry, ginger, and salt and pepper. Serve over rice.

vegetable garden lies just outside the back door of this French cottage. With planning and careful tending, you can have a flourishing organic garden for you and your dog.

ritation of the mucous membranes and dverse effects, such as upset stomach, diarrhea, and nausea.

BROCCOLI

Broccoli and other cruciferous (green and leafy) vegetables exhibit dramatic cancer-fighting properties. People and dogs alike appear to reap the benefits of

broccoli equally. As cancer is a leading cause of death in dogs, you may want to consider adding steamed broccoli to your dog's regular diet.

Keep in mind, however, that broccoli must be fed sparingly. It contains a weak toxin, called isothiocyanate, that causes gastric upset when fed in excess of 10 percent of your pet's daily diet. When given consistently in excess of 25 percent of the diet, broccoli has been shown to cause fatal toxicity. Broccoli toxicity was first observed in dairy cattle that were fed a high percentage of broccoli, which had been left over from a bumper crop in California. Further investigation found a correlation between the biological structures of ruminants (cattle, sheep, and so on) and those of some other animals, including dogs, and the absorption of isothiocyanate. So use caution when adding this vegetable to your dog's diet.

CABBAGE

Although cabbage is generally beneficial to your pet's digestive system, because of its high-fiber content, when is fed raw, it comes with an unpleasant side effect. Cook cabbage before adding it to your dog's daily diet, unless, of course, you don't mind smelly gas.

Garden's Bounty: **Carrots**

Carrot Snaps (for Your Dog)

Ingredients:

2 cups whole wheat flour

½ cup nutritional yeast

½ cup ground flax meal

1 cup steamed mashed carrots

4 tablespoons applesauce

4 tablespoons olive oil

1 teaspoon molasses

Directions:

Preheat oven to 325 degrees. Combine dry ingredients in a large bowl. Combine wet ingredients separately. Add wet to dry and stir just until dough comes together. Then drop teaspoon-size balls of dough on a greased cookie sheet and flatten with a fork. Bake 18 to 20 minutes or until crunchy. Cool before serving.

Dilled Maple Carrots (for You)

Ingredients:

2 cups sliced carrots

1 tablespoon butter

1 tablespoon brown sugar

2 tablespoons chopped fresh dill

Salt and pepper to taste

Directions:

Steam carrots until fork tender. Remove from heat and add remaining ingredients. Return to low heat until heated through. Serve warm.

CARROTS

Carrots make great treats for dogs, particularly those with a sweet tooth, as these vegetables contain a fair amount of natural sugars. Fresh carrots, with vitamins and other nutrients essential for healthy eyes and coats, makes a pleasant alternative to regular dog biscuits or chew toys. Because they contain lots of fiber, carrots help overweight dogs manage their cravings by keeping them full.

As with other high-fiber vegetables, cooking carrots first makes them easier for your pet to digest and lowers the chances of gas and stomach upset. Finely shredding raw carrots also enhances their digestibility by allowing your pet's stomach acids to access more nutrients directly.

CELERY

Celery makes another great high-fiber food for dogs. Many love to chew its stringy, crunchy stalks. Just be aware that long fibers may cause your dog to gag as he's snacking. To avoid unpleasant messes, cut stalks into smaller pieces before offering them to your pet.

For organic advocates, celery consistently rates high among the vegetables to watch for pesticide contamination. Its large water content makes it a "dirty" food by purist standards. It is thought that when the pesticides are sprayed onto the plant, they dissolve into the water the celery absorbs into its cells. Many gardeners believe that when the vegetable is eaten, small amounts of those same chemicals are ingested. For your sake and your dog's, make this addition to your table an organic one.

CUCUMBERS

Nothing beats a cool and juicy cucumber fresh from the garden on a summer day. The high water content in it makes it a great treat for your dog after a day of play in the backyard. A few slices suffice. Remove bitter, waxy peels before giving cucumber slices to your dog. Otherwise they may cause gastric upset, as their tough skins, tailor-made to keep out the summer sun, are difficult to digest.

GREEN BEANS

Many veterinarians prescribe cooked green beans as a supplement to a regular diet of low-cal kibble to manage canine obesity. Green beans contain high amounts of protein and fiber—both of which promote weight loss. Some veterinarians recommend a mixture as high as 50 percent green beans to 50 percent kibble, depending on the number of extra pounds a pet carries.

Start by adding a few beans to your dog's diet, and watch how his digestive system reacts. Gradually increasing the amount of beans in your portly pooch's dinner bowl may save him from obesity and all its related health issues.

PUMPKINS

Veterinarians love pumpkin—at least prescribing it—and so do most dogs. Dogs easily accept the addition of a few tablespoons of canned, or roasted, and pureed pumpkin. Luckily for them, it contains many health benefits. This filling, high-fiber addition to the diet not only helps with weight loss but also bulks up stool.

Veterinarians often recommend adding pumpkin to a dog's regular diet if the dog is experiencing loose or runny

tool, anal gland impaction, diminshed stool size, or constipation. A wonder drug you can grow yourself, pumpkin makes a great addition to any vegetable garden.

SPINACH

Spinach contains so many beneficial nutrients that it is often referred to as nature's powerhouse vegetable. It has high levels of beta-carotene, iron, calcium, and many other vitamins and minerals, so adding small amounts of it to the diet of a dog fuels him as few other fruits and vegetables are capable of doing.

Chop or blend this high-fiber, leafy green to enhance its absorption. Offer your dog small amounts once a week. There is a correlation between dogs prone to bladder stones who consume larger amounts spinach and the development of bladder stones.

SWEET POTATOES

Another veterinarian-approved (and often recommended) vegetable addition to your dog's diet, the sweet potato offers lots of health benefits. Loaded with vitamins, minerals, calcium, and fiber, this Thanksgiving Day staple grows quickly in most zones of the United States. Add sweet potatoes, cooked and mashed, to a dog's diet; their natural sweetness makes them irresistible.

For dogs with food allergies, sweet potatoes—on their own or in combination with a single protein source—provide balanced nutrition without irritation to the digestive tract, skin, and mucous membranes that other foods cause. Veterinarians often recommend an all-sweet-potato diet on a rotational

Garden's Bounty:
Sweet Potatoes

Here are two healthy and tasty organic sweet potato dishes: one for your dog and one for you!

Pup Potato Chips (for Your Dog)	Sweet Potato Fries (for You)
Ingredients: 1 medium sweet potato 2 tablespoons olive oil	**Ingredients:** 2 medium sweet potatoes Nonstick cooking spray 2 tablespoons sugar 1 tablespoon cinnamon
Directions: Preheat oven to 425 degrees. Cut sweet potato into 1/8-inch slices. Brush both sides with olive oil. Place on cookie sheet. Bake 15 to 20 minutes or until soft. Cool before serving.	**Directions:** Preheat oven to 425 degrees. Cut sweet potatoes into 1/8-inch slices. Spray both sides with nonstick cooking spray and sprinkle with sugar and cinnamon mixture. Bake 20 minutes or until crisp.

Secret to Success: Raised Beds

Active runners and diggers can reduce most vegetable gardens to rubbish in a short time. Protect your plants and the vegetables they produce by building raised garden beds. Elevating your garden, even just a few inches, is enough to ward off the bulk of your dog's undesirable behaviors. With your help, vegetable gardens and dogs will coexist peacefully. You'll appreciate the results of a full crop of healthy fruits and vegetables you and your pet can enjoy.

2 To build the frame, use 2 x 4s for smaller dogs; 2 x 6s or 2 x 8s for larger dogs. The board should reach the dog's knee or higher. Select "white" lumber (not pressure-treated wood, containing arsenic and other toxins). Assemble the lumber with screws, and drop the structure into place.

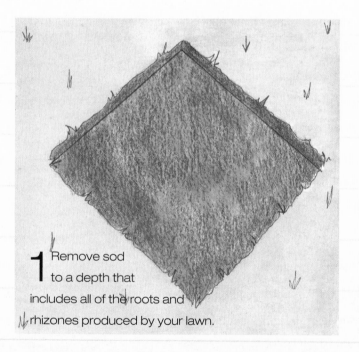

1 Remove sod to a depth that includes all of the roots and rhizones produced by your lawn.

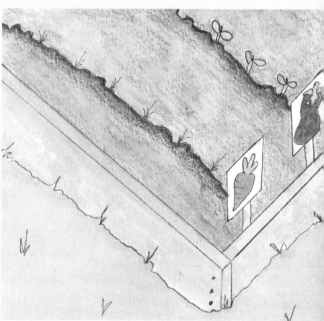

3 Fill the finished beds with high-quality compost or potting soil. Vegetables need lots of nutrients, particularly in a raised bed. If using cow manure, make sure it is thoroughly composted to remove any odors. Plant vegetables in your new bed.

A Word of Caution About Garlic

Many all-natural dog advocates praise the use of garlic as an anti-flea remedy. When given in small, regular doses, the pungent vegetable makes a dog's skin unpalatable to the persistent parasites. Garlic also contains high amounts of immune-boosting antioxidants. However, use caution when offering it to your dog. Although many animals seem to enjoy the flavor it adds to their food, too much of a good thing, as always, can lead to problems.

Onions, which have been shown to cause fatal anemia in dogs, and garlic come from the same botanical family. Although it's thought that garlic contains less of the riskier chemical compounds found in onions, high doses of garlic have resulted in canine health problems. Before sharing this year's garlic crop with your pet, make sure you consult a veterinarian regarding dosages appropriate for your dog.

basis in order to pinpoint a dog's particular food allergy. Adding sweet potatoes from your own garden provides a healthy and delicious treat.

TOMATOES

The current veterinary information on tomatoes suggests that they do not have any toxic effects on dogs. However, some consumer-based information warns that, at the very least, the leaves and stems of tomato plants, along with the unripe flesh, can be dangerous when consumed by your pet. The ripe flesh is said to contain the least amount of toxin. Play it safe by checking with your veterinarian before offering tomatoes to your dog and keeping a close eye on your pet while he's frolicking in the garden. Some dogs love the taste of tomatoes and will eat them as soon as they ripen.

The tomato, by the way, is one of foods that is classified as a fruit botani-

cally but that most people think of as a vegetable. References to tomatoes as vegetables irritate botanists and gardeners to no end!

ZUCCHINI

Zucchinis spring forth by the dozens from single plants, leaving gardeners wondering what to do with the leftover veggies at the end of the growing season. The perfect solution: Shred or puree them, freeze them in ice cube trays, and feed them to your dog through the fall and into the winter months. Chock full of vitamins, minerals, and fiber, zucchini enhances a dog's diet in so many ways by adding vital nutrients in a tidy little green package.

Toxic Produce

Not all fruits and vegetables enrich a dog's diet in healthy ways. Some of them can cause major health problems—or even death—when they are ingested.

Make sure your pet stays clear of certain vegetables and other plants in the garden. Onions cause canine anemia, a condition that can kill if it is not treated early. Grapes and raisins cause renal failure in some pets. The green leaves and stems of many common vegetables, including tomatoes and eggplants, also cause a wide range of health problems in animals. Never leave your dog unattended in your vegetable garden.

A World of Difference

Organic fruits and vegetables, grown in your own garden soil, make a world of difference in the way your food tastes and the superior nutritional value with which it fuels your body. Why not share the benefits of organically grown produce with your favorite pet? Even the smallest patch of earth or contained garden provides ample opportunity to go green, with your pet in tow.

CHAPTER 6

Soothing Water Features

Humans find themselves staring into pools of water, drawn to the sounds and movement of life-giving liquid—minds calmed, soothed, and relaxed amid life's hustle and bustle. Dogs similarly find themselves drawn to water, albeit for different reasons. Whether they are watching pond fish with amazement, wallowing in a cool muddy swamp on a hot day, or leaping with wild abandon into the family swimming pool, most dogs delight in the opportunity to experience water.

Backyard water features and ponds have grown tremendously popular among homeowners. As people discover how rewarding and easy it can be to bring water into their everyday lives, more and more of them are adding easy-to-install ponds and fountains to their yards and gardens.

However, dog ownership may or may not mesh well with a water-feature operation. Consider factors that may create conflict with your dog before you decide to add soothing water to your outdoor environment.

Water Hazards: Chemicals and Parasites

Any time you put a body of water in your backyard, be it swimming pool or lily pond, your dog is likely to take at least one dip and maybe a sip or two. Be aware that this may create any number of problems for your pet.

Swimming pools require a myriad of chemicals to keep them sparkling clean. Chlorine products cause stomach upset and potential gastric damage when regularly ingested. If your dog enjoys swimming with the family, a pool may do more harm than good, as the benefits of exercise take a backseat to skin irritations that are difficult to treat. A romp with the kids in the sprinkler creates a much healthier alternative.

A Soft Coated Wheaten Terrier approaches a backyard pond. Water features will help to keep your dog cool on a summer's day.

A hammock invitingly hangs by a pond, with the soothing murmur of a waterfall. Waterfalls also keep down the mosquito population in your pond.

Ponds don't have the chemicals that swimming pools do, but they often contain parasites such as flukes and microscopic worms, along with bacteria, that can infect your pet when exposed to skin or internal organs. Frogs, birds, and other animals will find their way to your pond, and their feces carry the majority of infectious agents. If your dog is prone to drinking from these ponds and eating tadpoles and fish, he may be at serious risk. To manage your pet's risk organically, you will need to limit his dips to brief cool-down sessions followed by a rinse with the garden hose. If your pet drinks from these living waters, monitor his health closely as this behavior puts him at risk of developing gastrointestinal infection.

Organic Mosquito Control

Larger bodies of backyard water or still pools present special health risks to your dog. Stagnant water, in particular, creates an ideal breeding ground for mosquitoes that carry West Nile virus and heartworm—both of which are bad news for your pet. If your backyard plans include a small garden pond, three simple strategies make all the difference and go a long way toward protecting your pet.

Add a bubbler or waterfall. First, look for areas on the surface of your pond where the water remains still.

Mosquitoes only lay eggs on the surface of water without waves. Ripples drown the pests and discourage them from depositing the next generation. Consider adding a simple bubbler or an attractive waterfall to stir things up a bit. Get the water moving, and you'll keep blood-suckers at bay.

Add fish. Next, consider introducing fish to your pond. Goldfish as well as common tadpoles supplement their diets with regular meals of developing pests. Gambusia (mosquito fish), guppies, and other species (often available free of charge from your local fish and wildlife department or vector control), gorge themselves on mosquito larvae as they hatch. Local game fish, such as

This terrier keeps a fascinated eye on a school of goldfish, which act as pest control, feeding on organisms that can damage the pond.

bluegills and bass, also dine on mosquitoes. Check with your local fish and wildlife office in order to find out whether the keeping of these fish in a backyard pond is legal. A number of states have ordinances that forbid the practice.

Add **Bacillus thuringiensis**. Next, try adding the natural enemy of mosquito larvae—*Bacillus thuringiensis* (also known as BT). The bacterium infects the soft-bodied larval stage of insects such as mosquitoes, flies, and moths, killing them before they grow into adults. BT is harmless to humans and pets. Available in convenient "dunks" that float on the water's surface and last from several weeks to months,

BT makes a safe and easy addition to any pond.

In the rest of your garden, the chemical-free way to control mosquitoes boils down to one simple strategy: don't let water collect anywhere around your house. Poor drainage spots, backed-up gutters, saucers under potted plants, mud puddles in the driveway, and other areas where water gathers provide opportune places for mosquitoes to lay their eggs. Take a quick walk around your yard to locate any problem areas that require your attention. Create a healthier, more enjoyable outdoor space for both you and your pet by taking a moment to reduce the risk of mosquito infestation.

Organic Algae Control

The number two scourge of the backyard pond and fountain—algae—creates just as many headaches as mosquitoes do. Nearly every quantity of water contains some algae spores; even a glass of water left on the counter for a couple of hours would contain a number of these free-floating single-cell plant organisms. Algae is simply everywhere, all the time. Under the right conditions, it blooms and reproduces rapidly, fouling pond water into a pea soup–like hue.

Dozens of chemicals marketed as "water clarifiers" and "algae control" water additives promise an easy fix for

Colorful koi swim about a well-
shaded pond. Koi will keep your
pond cleaner by eating algae.

exasperated pond owners. However, crystal-clear water comes at a price—both monetary and in the form of health risks associated with accidental canine ingestion. To control algae in your backyard pond or fountain the organic way, it helps to understand how and why algae develops. With this information, you can effectively control the causes, rather than poisoning a poorly managed body of water.

The right (or wrong) combination of food, heat, and light causes algae to bloom out of control. Full sun, excess nitrogen in the water, and warm temperatures together create a perfect storm for nuisance algae. If you manage these factors better, you will experience far fewer problems with algae—without resorting to harmful chemicals. Follow the steps below for organic, broad-spectrum algae control.

Provide shade. Shade your pond or water feature using a canopy of shade cloth, an attractive pergola, or a fast-growing shade tree. By limiting the sun that falls on the water's surface, you prevent water temperatures from soaring and take away a necessary element of photosynthesis.

Install a filter. Filter the water using even a simple sponge prefilter, attached to your pump's water intake, and you can remove a good deal of the algae manually with regular cleanings. Larger, more sophisticated filtration units for ponds remove even more problematic algae and need less frequent maintenance. Some units feature powerful ultraviolet lights that irradiate the water, killing algae spores before they multiply.

Add plants. Put underwater, marginal, or free-floating plants in your pond or in the bottom basin of a

Mixing Water and Electricity

When mixing water and electricity in or around water, make sure you know a few guidelines to keep you and your pet safe from harm. Using the two together without the proper safety equipment could cause painful injury or even death. Any component used to operate your water feature absolutely must be plugged into a ground fault circuit interrupter (GFCI) outlet. You know these devices from their installation in most bathrooms. The red and black "test" and "reset" buttons indicate their vital function.

Stray voltage from a frayed wire easily travels through water, charging every drop of liquid. One touch to the water's surface, and you or your pet could get the shock of your life. To prevent this from happening, install a simple GFCI where your outdoor electrical devices will be plugged in. At the first sign of stray voltage, which the GFCI detects as a power surge, the power is automatically cut. This safety feature has saved countless lives and should be an integral part of any water feature.

River rock in the bottom of a pond with a liner will protect that liner and help filter plant and fish waste.

fountain. Their roots remove nitrogen and other nutrients from the water that would otherwise fuel algae growth. They double their worth as beautiful, colorful additions to the outdoor environment.

Remove fallen plant matter. The debris dropped on the water's surface cause algae growth when they decay. Promptly remove dead plant matter, and you'll take away a key building block for algae.

Incorporate fish. Not only do fish, such as koi and goldfish, add color and movement to a water feature, but their omnivorous habits also mean they clean up stray algae. An added benefit to incorporating fish is their ability to fertilize plants with their waste, creating an environmentally friendly circle of life.

Clean up uneaten food. Clean up any uneaten pellet or flake food you may

have fed your pond fish. Excess food sinks to the bottom, where it rots and produces nitrogenous waste products—a favorite food of algae.

Organic water features go hand in hand with dog ownership. Keep the chemicals out, let the dogs in, and improve their quality of life and your own by forging a healing, restorative environment.

Secret to Success: Liner Savings

When building a custom splash pond for a large, water-loving dog, such as a retriever, you could save big by exploring alternative options for a liner. Consider using a low-cost stock tank from your local feed-and-seed store.

Originally designed as watering troughs for cows, horses, and pigs, these shallow, rigid tanks also work well as dog splash ponds. Stock tanks come in much larger sizes than do standard PVC preformed ponds and hold up far better under regular use than do flexible rubber and plastic sheeting liners. Choose one built from tough composite plastic or fiberglass for added durability and longevity that will keep your pet splashing season after season.

Protect Your Investment

Because most dogs find themselves so powerfully drawn to water, you may have considerable difficulty keeping their exuberant activities from tearing apart what you've worked so hard to construct. Dogs and flexible liners, in particular, don't mix. Claws easily tear holes in even the toughest ponds as dogs scramble into and out of the water. Your fish may not appreciate your dog either. When dogs plunge in on a hot day, terrorized goldfish and koi swim for cover, dashing themselves against stones and underwater potted plants. However, dogs and their people can enjoy well-stocked ponds—with a few modifications.

Preformed durable liners: Flexible-liner ponds offer affordable, versatile options for would-be water gardeners, but if you have an active dog, you may be better off with a different choice. Look into larger preformed fiberglass, sprayed concrete, or expandable foam options. These tougher liners cost more but mean you won't have to repeatedly replace shredded liners.

Gravel bottoms: Consider adding gravel to the bottom of your pond, which will create a layer of substrate, like in an aquarium, to act as a filter for plant and fish waste. Gravel also adds a layer of protection for your investment.

Gradual drop-offs: Gradual drop-offs entering your pond or a custom-built ramp give your dog controlled entry and exit points. Frantic scrambling to enter and exit the pond makes for a harmful situation for your pet and your liner. Note: gradual drop-offs increase the likelihood that fish predators will enjoy your water feature as well.

Overhangs and tunnels: Fish need a place to hide when your pet goes for a dip. Make sure your pond offers overhangs or tunnels that create a sense of security and safety for pond life.

A Doggy Oasis

A backyard with decorative water features provides a cool place for your pet. Whether you modify an existing koi pond or water garden or go the extra mile to build your dog an oasis of his very own, it is well worth the investment of time and money to satisfy your need (and your dog's) for a greener, more relaxed lifestyle.

Chloe enjoys her very own doggy oasis, complete with waterfall, in the backyard.

Do-It-Yourself Dog Pond

Sometimes the best cure for an excitable (and destructive) water dog is a pond of his very own—a place in which he can thrash about with reckless abandon. Consider building your dog a splash pond just for him. These shallow pools, designed with dogs in mind, offer an outlet for energy, while providing the peace and tranquility of a shallow reflecting pool.

Backyard watering holes for your dog used to come in one form—plastic kiddie pool. Banish that image. With the proliferation of the pond-keeping hobby, garden-supply, hardware, and pet stores contain all you need to create a beautiful, functional water feature that your dog will appreciate. All it takes is some form of durable liner, a small pump, and a piece or two of flexible tubing.

Start with a plastic pond shell. Pond shells come in a variety of preformed shapes and sizes. Models with edges, designed for potted aquatic plants, work best. Dogs use these as steps to enter and exit the water.

Most preformed ponds are between 18 and 24 inches deep, so if you have a smaller dog, you may want to add a safety ramp for entering and exiting the water. You can also make the pond shallower by stacking bricks or piling gravel on the bottom of it, which will give your pet a firm footing and prevent his head from dipping below the water's surface.

When choosing a pump, ask a qualified salesperson for help in selecting one appropriate for the size of pond you'll be building. The pump's functions will be to empty the pond for cleanings and to keep water moving to prevent mosquito proliferation. If you want to get creative, you can also use it to power a small waterfall or fountain. That's where the flexible tubing comes in. Use it to route water to a tranquil stone waterfall or elegant fountain made from your favorite piece of garden statuary.

Installing your dog-friendly water feature takes little time. Choose an area where your dog loves to hang out, dig a hole matching the feature's contours and depth, and drop in the liner. After concealing the edges with stone, burying any flexible tubing and cord, and plugging in your pump, you and your dog will have a new water feature to enjoy.

Organic Gardeners, Organic Dog

A Bear Among Vines

Sandy Pfister and Teddy Bear take a walk through their organic Pleasant View Vineyards.

Jerry Perrone and Sandy Pfister
Harbor Springs, Michigan

When Jerry Perrone and Sandy Pfister made the decision to retire from their careers, they knew it would be the perfect time to pursue a dream of theirs: opening a bed and breakfast and a vineyard. On a secluded piece of land, a stone's throw from Lake Michigan, in Harbor Springs, Michigan, they established Highland Hideaway Bed and Breakfast and the organic Pleasant View Vineyards Winery—protected, of course, by a feisty Shih-Tzu/Poodle mix named Teddy Bear.

With more than a dozen wines to offer, several acres of grapes and gardens, and a full-service bed and breakfast, this "retired" couple is fully engaged in a passion for the good life. The full richness of the latest chapter in their lives is made all the sweeter by the feeling they're doing it all with reverence for Mother Earth. For the sake of the environment and their treasured pet, they use green practices on their land.

Perrone, a former U.S. marine, oversees the cultivation of several varieties of grapes using a philosophy he feels is a step above organic.

"We're better than organic," Perrone says. "We're sustainable. Which means what we take out of the land, we put back in."

Teddy Bear guards the grapevines.

Treading lightly on the earth forms the basis of Perrone's horticultural practices. When most vintners furiously prune their vines in the summer for maximum yields, he lets the invasive and destructive Japanese beetle do the pruning for him. By observing the level of damage the beetles inflict on the flowers in his gardens, he knows when it's time to step out to the vineyard to mechanically remove the beetles before they go too far.

"I keep an eye on the roses," Jerry Perrone says. "If the beetles start to eat too much of them, I'll get a few guys together and head out to the grapes. We just pick off a few of the leaves that have the beetles on them, and that keeps their numbers down."

All the while, the pint-size Teddy Bear keeps a lookout for vermin on his daily patrols among the vines. Although normally sequestered in the innkeeper's apartment when the guest rooms are occupied, Teddy Bear accompanies Pfister on routine gardening chores around the inn and vineyard—sometimes disappearing for a quick nap beneath the thick green canopy created by row after row of prize-winning grapes.

Having left the technology industry to pursue life as an innkeeper, Pfister enjoys managing the business and working alongside "Teddy" in the luscious gardens—a far more rewarding pursuit, in her opinion.

The combined efforts of Perrone, Pfister, and their faithful companion have, over the past decade, brought many rewards. Their wines have earned regional and national awards and continue to showcase the versatility of new varieties of grapes developed on their property in conjunction with agricultural universities around the nation.

CHAPTER 7

Decks, Gazebos, Pathways, and Lights

O utdoor life with dogs means minimizing their risk of injury while maximizing their enjoyment with activities that will enhance their lives. At the same time, that outdoor life should provide a beautiful and relaxing environment for the people who work hard to maintain it. Creating a delicate balance between your needs and the needs of your dog does not have to be an enormous chore.

When you are dealing with landscape structures and with hardscape elements, for example, small modifications are all that you will need to make. Decks, patios, pathways, lighting, and other backyard necessities require just a handful of adjustments in order to accommodate life with dogs.

The core principle behind any landscaping project should be to allow both you and your pet to enjoy the great outdoors. Decks, pathways, and other structures enhance life in so many ways. Make them suitable for life with an active dog, and you will be able to enjoy paradise together.

Dog-Friendly Decks

Decks offer a focal point and center of activity for any outdoor environment. With platforms that allow for furniture, a grill, or an elevated fire pit, decks make outdoor living possible. They provide gathering spots for entertainment. What better way to include your pet in family life than by welcoming him onto your deck?

Your dog-friendly deck starts with material selection. Standard pressure-treated wood is neither your only—nor your best—option; there are plenty of great building materials that are better suited to life with dogs.

PRESSURE-TREATED LUMBER

Pressure-treated lumber remains one of the most popular materials for decks

When completely vine covered, this archway will provide this Golden Retriever with shade as well as adding a welcoming touch to the garden.

Pressure-treated wood is a popular choice for building because it is inexpensive; but it does contain toxins that could put your dog at risk.

and other outdoor structures. As the cheapest option for wood that will be exposed to the elements, it is often the first choice of many homeowners who are budget conscious. Pressure-treated wood contains significant amounts of arsenic, and it resists rot for up to fifteen years in most climates. When this poison is applied under pressure it is forced deep into the wood's grain where it deters wood-boring insects that would destroy traditional forms of lumber.

Clancy sits just outside the back door on a well-constructed deck.

Organically minded home-safety ↑vocates advise against the use of ₁essure-treated lumber around ₁ildren and pets. They claim sawdust ₁om construction sites causes the ₁ison to become airborne, and that, ↑er time, the arsenic leeches out of ↑e wood and into the environment. ₁r a little more money, all-natural op-₁ns resist rot even better than pres-↑re-treated lumber does and put your ₁ind at ease about risks to the health ↑ your family and your dog.

Safe Construction Techniques

When building with any material designed for use with dogs, you must choose the right equipment and materials and use the proper construction techniques. Below are some safety issues you need to keep in mind.

1 Fasteners

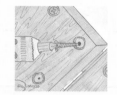

When building a deck, always use screws, never nails, on surfaces your pet will be using. Over time, as deck boards expand in the heat of summer and contract in the cold of winter, nails work themselves loose and protrude above a board's surface. An active dog enjoying the deck any time of year can easily catch a paw or skin on a loose nail.

Slivers, which make life unpleasant for owners and their dogs, can be avoided in decking board by countersinking the screws that fasten the board to the framing. Use a pilot bit designed to let the screws travel below the surface of the wood to prevent the surface from chipping. Finish the deck with a thorough sanding, and you'll lower the risk of injury to your dog.

2 Decking Gaps

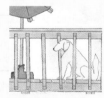

Gaps between boards can also present problems for dogs, especially small ones. As a dog runs across deck boards, his nails or feet may slip between a gap, resulting in a twisted ankle or a pinched toe. When securing boards, leave no gap between them greater than a 1/8-inch. Room is needed to allow for natural expansion and contraction, but too much makes the deck a hazard.

3 Balustrade Spacing

Spacing for balustrades is set by local city authorities. Check to make sure your plans meet the law. In most cities and municipalities, spacing of 4 inches or less is required. But if the width of your dog's head measures less than 4 inches, that standard may still present injury risks. A curious pet can easily get his head lodged between two balustrades. Use your pet's noggin as a measuring guide to ensure his safety and your sanity.

This composite decking (made of sawdust and recycled plastic) is durable, attractive, and environmentally—and Sheltie—friendly, as tested by Isabella.

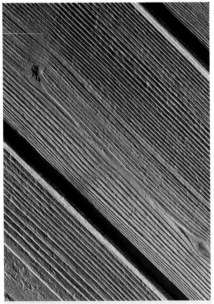

Unlike pressure-treated wood, cedar has naturally occurring oils that repel insects and are nontoxic to dogs.

CEDAR AND REDWOOD

Cedar and redwood naturally resist wood-damaging insects; they have evolved to produce their own plant-based pesticides. Although the pleasant odor given off by their essential oils makes these woods desirable to people, it repels insects, including fleas. Attractive and toxin free, cedar and redwood should last up to twenty years. With the application of a linseed oil–based sealant (to guard against sun and water damage) every three to five years, these woods look good long after pressure-treated options turn to sawdust.

For an added touch of green, make sure the forest from which your wood

came was managed properly. Most commercial logging companies participate in reforestation or patchwork harvesting that lowers their impact on the environment. Check out the brand names at your local home-improvement store and learn what you can about the companies' business practices before you buy.

EXOTIC HARDWOODS

For an even longer decking lifespan, and one without chemicals that could harm your pet, consider investing in tropical hardwoods such as red balau, teak, ipé, and ironwood. The grain in these woods is so dense that water and most insects are not able to penetrate the surface. With natural oils that repel water, these ods last more than twenty-five years. Though they cost significantly more than redwood and cedar do, hardwoods create durable surfaces that stand up even the most active dog. Equally impressive in style, hardwoods are sure catch the attention of party guests.

A word to the green when choosing ese woods: many of them come from ologically endangered areas of the rld, namely the Amazon River basin d Southeast Asian island nations. Be- e making the investment, make sure ese trees fell naturally and were not cut m forests. Several companies special- in importing these woods and should able to provide proof of their sources.

ECYCLED ATERIAL

ing true to the three Rs (reduce, reuse, ycle) of an all-natural household has ver been simpler or dog friendlier n now when it comes to your choice decking material. Thanks to advances manufacturing technology, indus- l wood scraps and empty milk jugs t would otherwise have ended up in dfills have found new uses as versatile lding materials. Composite decking de from sawdust and recycled plastic s longer, requires less maintenance, l stands up to dog damage better than other material on the market.

As it also happens to be one of the st expensive options, costing up to ce as much as traditional pressure- ated lumber, composite decking is not every budget. This material is, how- r, the most eco-friendly choice. Look a brand of decking made with at st 40 percent "postconsumer waste," you'll be responsible for saving lots rash from the dump.

Dakota stares through a screen door. A wise owner will make sure such screens are vinyl-coated fiberglass (pet proof).

Gazebos and Screen Porches

Other freestanding structures in the yard and garden fit well with your dog's needs and your own with a few simple modifications. You can have three seasons of outdoor enjoyment, courtesy of a screen porch or a gazebo. These structures afford people protection from mosquitoes, flies, and gnats and provide a safe haven for relaxation and recreation. Prevent the headaches of recurring costly maintenance by including a few dog-friendly features, and you and your pooch can enjoy the summer without worry.

Don't buy a screen for your porch or gazebo without finding these words somewhere on the product packaging: *vinyl-coated fiberglass*. Breakthroughs in technology using this material have led to the development of a new generation of extra-durable screen products. Many of them are guaranteed not

to tear or puncture, and they don't rust or fray. A number of screen products containing vinyl-coated-fiberglass technology are marketed for use with active cats and dogs—being touted as "pet-proof screens."

An active dog may burst right through a screen in a gazebo or a porch in pursuit of a passing critter. He will have considerable difficulty accomplishing that feat when surrounded by a tough-as-nails screen. As a consequence, your pet stays safe, and you're spared the cost and inconvenience of repeated trips to the hardware store.

Sturdy doors and windows also provide security and peace of mind when you include your pet during a summer afternoon on the porch. Surrounded by visual stimuli, dogs are likely to have a field day. A shattered window or broken door can lead to injury or escape. Look for durable options with sturdy construction.

Worry-Free Pathways

When constructing garden pathways to connect your home with any outdoor structures, keep in mind how your dog will use those functional highways and which areas of the yard he frequents the most. Constructing paths around your dog's needs, as well as your own, helps avoid conflict and unnecessary damage to the surrounding yard and garden environment.

When you let your dog designate where your pathways will be, you will virtually eliminate wear and tear marks on your lawn. By converting his normal roaming courses into permanent, paved paths, you turn what once were dirty ruts into functional and beautiful ways to move about your outdoor space.

Of course, if your particular dog crisscrosses your outdoor space, creating a spider web of paths to and fro, letting him determine pathways makes little sense. Try to strike a happy medium by matching a few of his patterns with your own, and you'll at least cut down on messes in the yard. For instance, if your dog consistently makes a beeline for the back fence as soon as he gets out the door, consider using at least part of that habitual course to lay down some paving stone, which could lead the way to a backyard entertainment area. Designing your pathways in this manner decreases conflict between your pet's needs and yours. Your choice of materials for garden pathways make all the difference if you'll be sharing your space with an active pet. Give some consideration to the options, and you'll save yourself the hassle of tedious maintenance chores later.

GRAVEL PATHS

Gravel paths convey a sense of Zen-like simplicity. Compounded with easy installation and a lower price point, gravel remains a popular choice with gardeners looking for instant gratification with eye-catching results. A leisure-oriented canine would be perfectly content to roam on a gravel highway, occasionally stopping for a snooze on the cool stones.

However, gravel pathways may not be the best option if you have a playful pet that is prone to digging and running. Gravel can be easily flung onto a nearby lawn by a rooting or frolicking dog, complicating mowing and other regular outdoor chores. If a gravel pathway backs up to an area that is regularly used by your pet for potty activities, it may also complicate waste removal, as feces tend to stick to smaller aggregate stones.

MULCH PATHS

Mulch makes another great choice for an easy-to-lay pathway. Simple sod removal followed by a weed barrier and a couple of cubic yards of chipped wood mulch instantly transforms a barren yard into a welcoming environment that encourages roaming and relaxing in the garden.

Caution should be exercised, though, when choosing this option for your pet. If, for instance, your dog enjoys chewing (and potentially ingesting) sticks and branches, mulch would not be a good choice. To avoid having to constantly monitor your pet and shouting the "leave it" command every five minutes, look into other options.

A Mulch **Warning**

This warning, given in chapter 3, bears repeating here: beware of cocoa mulch and coconut husk mulch. Cocoa mulch contains the same toxic compounds found in processed chocolate and can be deadly if ingested by your dog. Coconut husk mulch, known for its ability to soak up and retain many times its weight in water, is often spread around thirsty plants. However, it will quickly swell in the digestive tract of any dog who consumes it and cause potential blockage of the intestines.

A pet with a long or woolly coat may also attract small bits of mulch like a magnet, resulting in bothersome matting of the coat and indoor clean-ing hassles. Some dogs may even avoid mulch altogether, preferring grass or concrete to the rough texture of these pathways. Conversely, a nonchewer with a short coat may be well suited to an outdoor environment with several mulch pathways.

RECYCLED-MATERIAL PATHS

Recycled materials have grown in popularity for use in garden pathways. The added bonus is their "green" factor. By using pathway material that has been repurposed, you are doing your part to lessen the impact on the environment.

The philosophy of using recycled materials holds that any durable piece of material can be used to construct a pathway. Inventive gardeners construct their unique pathways out of a variety of "waste" products, all retrieved from the landfill.

■ Crushed glass, available in a wide range of colors, comes pretumbled to remove any sharp edges.

■ Salvaged concrete and bricks, reclaimed from building and renovation sites, are available at little cost and provide great alternatives to paving stones and flagstones.

■ Old tires make for an interesting pathway when cut into squares that can be laid just as paving stones would be. Their nonslip, durable characteristics make them perfect for yards with dogs.

PAVERS AND FLAGSTONES

Pavers and flagstones remain popular choices for homeowners. Although these are two of the most expensive and labor-intensive options to install in your outdoor environment, paving stones and flagstones make perfect sense for a life with dogs. They are 100 percent safe, easy to clean, and beautiful in their wide array of colors and textures.

Flagstones often come from local quarries, making them a greener choice than products shipped in from other locations at the expense of fossil fuels. Some gardeners with native-themed outdoor environments praise local flagstone for its ability to fit into the backyard naturally.

Paving stones have rapidly grown in popularity as their sizes, shapes, and colors have expanded, offering creative types more versatility with design choices. Their low-maintenance characteristics make them attractive, too. A simple soak using a garden hose will remove waste and debris.

Lighting the Landscape

Motion-sensor security lights and high-watt flood lamps are not the only options available for adding drama to your nighttime landscape. Lots of affordable, easy-to-install landscape lighting products quickly transform any ordinary backyard into a twenty-four-hour spot to enjoy the outdoors and keep an eye on your pet. For the safety and security of your home and your pet, consider shedding some light on plants and landscape features you've worked hard to install and maintain.

GO GREEN: SOLAR LIGHTING

At the beginning of this century, solar-powered landscape lighting exploded onto the lawn and garden scene. Now, nearly every major home-improvement store sports an impressive, and affordable, array of solar options. For the environmentally aware gardener, solar lighting presents an attractive option. Simply plant the light where you want it, and the sun takes care of the rest. No fossil fuels burned, no sweat

The only drawback is the sun's unreliability. A day or more of cloudy skies, and bulbs put out little more than a faint glow. Because the research and development of these products has yet to yield adequate storage batteries or brighter, more efficient bulbs, performance is spotty. Severe weather or a rambunctious

Star, a black Lab mix, paces along a strategically placed trail of flagstone

The Chicago Botanical Garden has used recycled, broken concrete to create this sun-dappled pathway.

pooch can also easily crack fragile solar cells, rendering lights useless.

LOW VOLTAGE = LOW IMPACT

Low-voltage landscape lighting offers a reliable source of outdoor light without the high operating cost of traditional incandescent lighting. Compact halogen bulbs last three to five years with moderate to constant use and create a warm, dramatic glow. Most kits come with instructions for easy installation and maintenance, and the lights take little time to put in. Get a model with a built-in timer, and your lights will greet you when you arrive home from work and then click off just before bed, saving even more electricity.

Although low-voltage lighting may cost only a couple of extra dollars per month to operate, consider the long-term cost of replacement bulbs and the rising cost of the kilowatt hour. These factors may make them cost prohibitive in the long run.

Spotlights

Using spotlights to light plants and structures from below allows you to chase away the shadows from the garden and enjoy your plants even after the sun goes down. Spotlights also allow you to see when your dog begins to uproot your favorite evergreen or decides to chew on your newly sprouted spring bulbs.

Chloe lies beside one of the solar lights that illuminate her yard at night.

CHAPTER 8

Organic Lawns

Lawns suffer most when dogs behave like, well, dogs; some damage is a given. No lawn where a dog treads will remain in pristine condition. The sooner you can accept that simple fact, the sooner you can take the steps necessary to achieve a more harmonious outdoor life. That is not to say that you have to allow your backyard to devolve into a muddy pit strewn with feces and ravaged by craters.

Plenty of organic strategies can help you to mitigate the damage caused by your pet. Although you may never win the best-lawn-on-the-block award, you can still enjoy the luxury of green between your toes with a lawn that will not upset the neighborhood association.

Tougher Turf

A lawn resistant to dog damage begins with the seed or sod from which your lawn grew. Certain varieties of grass simply perform better than others do under the pressure of life with dogs.

Consider overseeding your lawn with one of these varieties in early fall or spring to increase your lawn's overall vigor. Sprinkling the seed over existing lawns allows it to take root in bare patches, which improves the cosmetic appearance of your lawn until the grass you have has a chance to repair itself.

GRASSES SUITABLE FOR MOST AREAS

Two grasses suitable for most areas of the United States are rye grass and buffalo grass. Rye grass grows quickly,

which is helpful for filling in bare patches caused by urine spots and your dog's digging habit. Just keep your dog away from the area until the grass takes hold. Within a few weeks, your lawn should return to its pristine condition. A bonus: when seeded over the regular lawn in early spring, rye grass will crowd out opportunistic weeds before they have a chance to take hold.

Buffalo grass, a newly rediscovered U.S. native, grows wild as a prairie grass from Mexico to Canada and everywhere in between. It fares well with heavy foot (and paw) traffic and grows to a height of only 3 inches, therefore it never needs mowing. It thrives in droughtlike conditions or areas of standing water. Adaptable and maintenance free, it represents an environmentally friendly option your pet will love. However, buffalo grass can be slow to spread and doesn't compete well with other grasses. Before replacing your entire lawn with this grass, try it in a small area where your pet spends time to see how it responds to your local conditions.

A Greyhound sits in a well-maintained yard. You can create your own attractive organic lawn with the right grasses and techniques.

Moose, an energetic Great Dane, covers the backyard at a run. Be sure to choose the right grass to deal with your dog's daily activities.

In Idaho, a man examines the growth of tall fescue, an attractive cool-season grass. Easily damaged, it should be mixed with another grass, such as rye, in your lawn.

Frisbee clutched firmly, a dog scampers over a lawn of zoysia, a slow-growing, but tough, warm-season grass.

WARM-SEASON GRASSES

Two grasses suitable for areas with mild winters are Bermuda grass and zoysia. Bermuda grass, found most often in hot, wet areas of the United States, is classified as tropical and subtropical turf grass. It forms dense mats perfect for running, pacing, and other vigorous dog activities. Introduce this grass during the cool season by spreading its stolons (small pieces of surface roots). They take hold and send out more runners that root and spread quickly. The drawbacks of Bermuda grass are its high water requirement and aggressive growing habits. If you live in an area with heavy rainfall and don't mind having this grass invade your entire lawn, it just may be the solution to your dog-damage concerns.

The exotic-sounding zoysia grass, a recent addition to the world of turf grass, tolerates high traffic like a champ. However, it can take up to four years to become fully established and is slow to repair itself once damaged. It may be the best option if you're considering getting a second or third dog in a few years. Giving this grass time to grow deep roots makes a big difference in its suitability for yards with multiple dogs.

COOL-SEASON GRASSES

Kentucky bluegrass and tall fescue are two cool-season grasses, suitable for areas with harsh winters. Long valued for its rich blue-green color, Kentucky bluegrass works well for yards with dogs. Its ability to spread slowly means you don't have to replant or overseed your lawn. It simply creeps into areas damaged by your pet. You may, however, need to redirect your dog's activity from

Secret to Success: Earth-Friendly Lawn Care

Regular lawn-maintenance chores can, and should be, different when your yard is shared with a valued pet. Adopting a few simple modifications to the way you mow your grass makes your outdoor space kinder to Mother Earth and your pet.

- Mow your grass no shorter than 3 inches. Longer grass will stand up better to life with an active pet.
- Mow often. Cutting less of the grass blade more frequently causes less damage to the lawn, allowing it to grow healthier roots that survive without fertilizers.
- Switch to an old-fashioned, people-powered reel mower. Sparing fossil fuels and harmful greenhouse gas emissions, you do more to protect the environment. You also spare your pet the anxiety caused by loud machinery.

any damaged areas for several weeks to allow the lawn to repair itself.

Fescue, by contrast, doesn't spread well, so a lawn composed primarily of fescue won't repair itself once damaged. However, tall fescue does serve as an attractive base for a cool-season lawn. Its dark green color and compact growth create the lush look that most homeowners covet. Grass seed will have to be replanted in each area damaged by your pet, unless you mix a self-sustaining species of grass into your existing lawn (usually rye grass or Kentucky bluegrass).

Problems and Remedies

Tough grass can only get you so far. As dogs do what dogs do best, damage rears its ugly head. For each problem area, there's an organic solution—or at least a trick or two that will save your grass from ruin without poisoning your dog in the process.

URINE BURN

As discussed in chapter 2, damage to plants from dog urine occurs as a result of a dog's high-protein diet. When a dog metabolizes protein, one of the natural byproducts is excess nitrogen. Although nitrogen is often found in commercial fertilizers, the highly concentrated nitrogen in pet urine burns grass and other plants it comes into contact with. Contrary to popular belief, these burned patches in the lawn are not the result of the pH level of your pet's urine.

Many gimmicky pills and homespun food additives promise to "neutralize" dog urine when added to the pet's diet. Save your money—as noted above, acidity has nothing to do with what actually causes your pet's urine to kill your grass.

Instead, encourage your pet to drink more water. Clean, fresh water should always be available. Lots of fluid naturally dilute a dog's urine, lowering the nitrogen concentration, which in turn makes the urine less harmful to the lawn and other plants. More water, of course, means more trips to the backyard, so be sure you offer your pet enough opportunities to relieve himself. The longer a dog has to retain his urine, the more concentrated with nitrogen it becomes.

No matter how much water your dog takes in, a certain amount of spotty damage is bound to occur. To limit the aesthetic impact to your lawn, encourage your pet to potty in the same spot each time. Choosing a "potty spot" in an out-of-the-way corner of the yard hides the damage. Use a leash, if necessary, to walk your dog to the same spot each time he goes outdoors. It may take some time, but eventually he'll learn where to relieve himself.

Some owners swear by the use of "potty poles"—small wooden poles impregnated with canine pheromones thought to stimulate marking behaviors. Although less effective with female dogs and some neutered males, these devices have proven effective when used consistently with the above training technique.

DIGGING LARGE HOLES

Dogs dig holes; that is a fact of life. Although older dogs and less energetic breeds seem less likely to engage in the irksome habit, most dogs have been caught with mud on their noses at one point. There is one main reason dogs excavate large craters: to survive when temperatures begin to soar.

Nontoxic **Lawn Recipe**

When a dog spends so much time romping on the grass, nontoxic methods for greening up the yard are a must. Water and feed your lawn appropriately for a low-impact way to improve turf health. If you must water your lawn, water deeply and less frequently. Deep watering encourages strong root growth and improves the health of the lawn, plus it increases the time between watering.

In addition to the nontoxic herbicides and fertilizers discussed in chapter 3, make your own organic lawn fertilizer from ingredients already found in your pantry.

- 1 can of beer (not light)
- 1 can of soda (not diet)
- ½ cup molasses or corn syrup
- 1 cup Castile soap
- ½ cup liquid ammonia
- ½ cup mouthwash

Mix the ingredients, and pour into a hose-end sprayer. For best results, apply this to the lawn in early to midmorning every two to three weeks during your lawn's peak growing season or year-round in warmer climates. Apply the mixture on a rain-free day, and allow time for drying before your pet has access to the area.

Copper jumps to catch a ball. Give your dog enough exercise, and you might stop his digging habit.

Dog urine has burned this patch of fescue grass. To minimize damage, make sure your dog drinks lots of water and uses same area for eliminating.

Freshly dug dirt near the foundation of the house is evidence of a chronic canine digger. Dogs often dig to create cool spots, so providing shade may help prevent unsightly holes.

Most dogs have few sweat glands and must therefore rely on panting or wallowing to cool themselves. Body temperature regulation presents special challenges when you're covered in fur. Dirt is cool and often damp, particularly in the shade or next to a building's foundation. Lying with freshly turned dirt against their skin gives dogs the same relief a dip in the pool gives people.

Therein lies the solution to excavating. Keep your dog cool, and he'll have no need to crater the yard. Evaluate your outdoor space. Ask yourself these questions: Is there enough shade? Does my dog have sufficient drinking water? Can my pet find escape from the heat by going for a dip in a doggy pond? Is there an air-conditioned space my pet can go to when he has had enough of the heat? When you can answer yes to most of these, holes the size of Buicks in your lawn will be a thing of the past.

DIGGING SMALL HOLES

Smaller holes, too, often dot a landscape with an active dog. Understanding the reasons behind why many dogs dig small, widespread holes lawns helps address the root cause of the behavior. By offering your dog natural alternatives to his ingrained behaviors, you lower the impact on your lawn and create a more peaceful outdoor space for both you and your pet.

Most dogs dig small holes in the lawn for two reasons: frustration and (believe it or not) hunger. Pent-up energy causes some dogs to dig for the sheer thrill of it. The action, which engages most muscles in a dog's body,

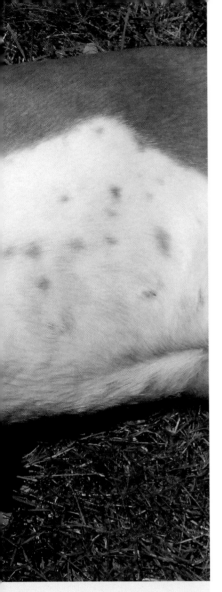

Mallory, a leisure-loving Bassett Hound, lounges in her favorite spot. Aerate packed earth to help grass regrow.

offers relief from tension that builds during a day of inactivity. Another, less obvious, cause of erratic lawn digging arises from a natural hunger for foods that are rich in protein. Dogs, whose acute senses of smell and hearing are many times more powerful than ours, hunt for bugs, grubs, and other creatures lurking underground. They can actually smell and hear insects and worms just beneath the soil. Watch your pet the next time you catch him digging. If you notice chewing, he's on the hunt.

Bugs and soft-bodied worms make an excellent source of protein-rich nourishment for your pet, plus they taste great. If it weren't for the damage your pet creates searching for them, these creepy crawlies would make excellent all-natural supplements to his diet. If your pet's digging habits have left you nursing sprained ankles and unable to grow anything but weeds, you may need to get a handle on this behavior. Start by adopting a comprehensive nontoxic pest-control regime, as outlined in chapter 3. By limiting the number of bugs in your lawn, you'll significantly reduce your pet's frequent digging behaviors.

Digging out of frustration can probably be cured with sufficient exercise; make sure your pet gets enough. You may need to add a brisk walk to your daily routine or make a special trip to your dog park a couple of times a week to allow your pet to blow off steam. A tired pooch is far less likely to litter the landscape with pits and trenches. Aim for at least thirty minutes a day in some sort of moderate to intense exercise, and you'll lower the likelihood of a hopelessly cratered lawn.

BARE PATCHES

Running, pacing, and lounging often create bare patches on the grass. These unsightly areas are simply a part of dog ownership, but there are organic ways you can help your grass recover from the damage caused by your pet. To remedy the situation, it helps to understand what causes the trails and spots to appear in the first place. The muddy, dirty areas of lawn your pet frequents aren't caused by his claws tearing up the blades of grass by the roots. In

reality, the grass dies because the soil below is compacted by the weight of your pet. When the soil doesn't drain properly or is not loose enough to allow the grass's roots to penetrate downward, the lawn dies.

By increasing the rainwater drainage in these trouble spots, you will increase the health of the lawn and make it easier for grass to survive in spite of an active pet. Loosening the soil is all it takes to let water percolate downward, where it can nourish the roots of your grass. Aeration of the lawn is the best way to solve this problem. Periodically stabbing a pitchfork or other sharp garden tool deep into the soil of any paths or lounging spots your pet uses breaks up soil clods and improves the health of your lawn. For larger areas, riding-mower attachments or special boot soles with aerating spikes accomplish the same thing.

When all else fails to get the grass growing in that often-trampled area of the lawn, consider simply disguising the area with a well-placed sturdy shrub. When grown as hedges, shrubs hide a multitude of doggy sins. For example, a hedge grown 2 to 3 feet back from a fence line, where your dog likes to pace, completely and beautifully conceals the area from view.

A Space for Joy

Whatever methods you choose to help keep your lawn looking its best, keep in mind how your dog uses the space and adapt your landscaping designs accordingly. Although it may mean surrendering part of your putting-green-quality lawn, giving your pet a space he can use to indulge his joy of the outdoors is sure to please both of you in the long run.

Organic Gardener, Organic Dog

Green Mountain State Goes Green

Roger, a Catahoula Leopard Dog, enjoys a sunny day on his owner's porch.

Laura McKenna
Burlington, Vermont

Vermont's largest and perhaps most cosmopolitan city, Burlington, is known for both its historic charm and its liberal, green mindset. Both reasons make Laura McKenna glad to be a part of a growing movement to pay homage to the environment by eating local foods and practicing organic gardening.

Together with her Catahoula Leopard Dog, Roger, McKenna tends her small yard and garden just a short distance from downtown and a few blocks from a picturesque New England waterfront. Her philosophies for protecting the environment and her pet are simple.

"We've done enough damage [to the environment]," says McKenna. "We don't need to spend money on chemicals to add to the water and soil. It just gets back to muscle. I prefer a hands-on involvement, as opposed to chemicals. I just don't think they're necessary."

McKenna works for a local dog-friendly communications firm, where she's allowed to bring Roger to the office

Laura McKenna buys from local farmers' markets to shrink Roger's and her carbon paw- and footprints.

with her every day. As part of a growing effort to respect pets as members of the family and members of a green society, McKenna takes Roger's role in her life seriously. Sharing her organic bounty with her constant companion just makes good sense.

"He hangs out with me in the garden," she says. "He eats carrots. We definitely share those."

The key to keeping her outdoor space chemical free involves daily chores and practicing a good lesson from the old-fashioned school of gardening.

"There's an overgrown area in my yard. Instead of dousing it with chemicals for mosquitoes, I just keep it cut and

dry," she says. "I use a reel mower instead of a real [gas] mower, as part of my commitment to be green. It has the least impact. It's basically sweat and muscle instead of any kind of chemicals."

To further reduce her carbon footprint, McKenna pledges that she will eat ingredients from close to home in a local initiative, the Eat Local Challenge. For an entire month each year, she only eats local foods that travel 100 miles or less to reach her dinner table.

Local food movements cite numerous green reasons for joining the cause that fit well with McKenna's main goals. Traveling shorter distances means the foods can be picked ripe and retain more

of their nutrients by the time they reach the consumer. Funding the local farming community helps family farms compete with larger commercial operations. In addition, by using less fossil fuel in their transport to the table, locally grown produce reduces greenhouse gas emissions.

Always on the lookout for ways to green up life with Roger, McKenna is encouraged by a growing trend toward products and lifestyles for pets that allow them to respect the environment.

"A lot of people are taking action, testing different pet foods and dog toys to be more proactive about bringing our green lifestyles to our pets," she says. "Why wouldn't I? [Roger's] half of the family."

CHAPTER 9

The Well-Behaved Organic Dog

Sometimes dogs need a little help when it comes to lawn and garden etiquette. Although for the most part they're bound to behave just as dogs have for thousands of years—romping, rolling, digging, and having a ball—they can learn which areas are off limits. Using a few basic techniques in behavior modification, you can help your dog learn the rules of the yard, while protecting your plants and your pet from harm.

The root causes of many problem canine behaviors are deeply ingrained in the animal's genetic code. However, much has been learned about the psychology that drives animals to carry out these sometimes destructive behaviors. Using what we know about how dogs think and respond to what their humans expect of them, you can show your own dog how to be a well-behaved, organic dog.

Basic Obedience

Basic obedience cues are a must for an outdoor lifestyle that is safe and enjoyable for you and your dog. Teaching a few basic cues to your pet ensures that you have all the tools to stop nearly every problem behavior you might encounter in the outdoor environment. Consider the following examples.

Rabbits, squirrels, gophers, and other vertebrate pests in the garden captivate a dog. As your pet locks on to his target with a steely gaze and gets ready to bolt, you have only a few seconds to get his attention. A well-timed *sit-stay* cue could mean the difference between a trampled vegetable patch and a bountiful harvest.

Fences and barriers in the garden can easily fall victim to a dog who likes to jump or lean to get a better view of what's on the other side. To protect a freshly planted or newly seeded area from certain destruction, the *off* cue teaches your dog what's expected. Over time, he will learn which structures are off limits.

Showing off his perfect garden manners, this well-trained Brittany sits calmly among the colorful flowers.

Dewey, happily rooting among the flowers, shows that he needs a little more training in garden etiquette.

Some dogs delight in helping themselves to fresh produce before you have the chance to pick it. Although eating from the vine can be a healthy habit, you may want first crack at your vegetables, before your dog starts to devour them.

A well-timed *leave it* cue reinforces the house rules when your dog is nosing through your garden. Just make sure to offer your pet a few freshly picked treats after you've had your fill.

A scenthound who catches a whiff of something irresistible while out in the yard can be gone in a flash if he's not taught to respect the *come* cue. Intervention that coincides with the first telltale lifting of the nose could save your pet from wandering too far from home.

The *drop it* cue works in many capacities with dogs who are enjoying the outdoors. Dogs, who explore the lawn and garden with their mouths, often pick up things that they shouldn't—such as a newly purchased pair of garden gloves. Train your pet to respect your belongings and to stay away from potentially hazardous objects around your yard and garden.

Training Techniques

Basic training techniques for all cues share the same principles: reward the behavior you want with food, praise, or both; reinforce your training with repetition and consistency. When you follow these rules, your dog soon learns to obey without rewards. Start small, keep it fun, and repeat the training process often. You'll soon discover that

A Golden Retriever receives a treat for responding correctly to a cue.

our pet does have the ability to respect our valued outdoor spaces. Just follow these easy steps.

Discover what motivates. Find out what your dog loves best. If he is motivated by food, use the treat that makes his mouth water the most. If he is motivated by praise or pats on the head, find a script of words and gestures that gets his tail wagging. Spend some time observing what your pet responds to most strongly.

Decide on the first cue. Which cue do you want to work on first? Practice one cue per training session. This works best with a dog's naturally short attention span and avoids confusing him. Build on other obedience skills one cue at a time—once your pet has mastered the first cue.

Start small. Limit your training sessions to ten to fifteen minutes at a time. If your pet doesn't grasp the concept of a simple cue, try again later. You can repeat training more than once a day, maybe after a long walk or other positive experience.

Control your emotions. Keep your own anxiety and frustration in check when working with your pet. Dogs sense changes in your mood and respond with similar anxiety or heightened activity level, cutting training sessions short.

Reward your pet appropriately. Failure to obey means no treats or no signs of affection. When your pet does respond well to cues, then you can praise him with a positive tone of voice and offer him his favorite tasty treat. When you reward good behavior during training sessions, you are increasing the likelihood of your dog's being able to repeat that behavior when you need him to do so the most.

Show your dog what you want. When you first begin training your dog to respond to a verbal cue, show him exactly what you want him to do. For example, take a long leash out to your yard or garden with you, and gently but firmly pull him your way when you give the *come* cue. Then, offer a reward. Eventually, you'll be able to take off his leash, and your dog will understand that you want him to move toward you when you issue the cue.

Repeat training exercises often. Repeating the training several times a day, several days a week, helps reinforce the desired behavior. After two to three weeks, you can begin phasing out the treats and praise. Following these initial weeks of practice, most dogs perform their cues under simple voice control.

Behavior modification through obedience training may solve many conflicts of interest between you and your dog, but for strong-willed pets something more may be needed.

Hands-Free Discipline

Combining obedience with aversion tactics maximizes the effectiveness of canine behavior modification. Your dog

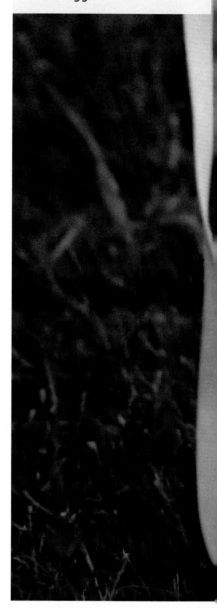

You can use aversion tactics to train a puppy, such as this Golden Retriever, to stay out of the flowers and veggies.

Secret to Success:
Canine Consequence

Discipline in or out of the garden requires eyes in the back of your head. You must catch your pet in the act for your consequential discipline to have the desired effect. With no concept of time or cause-and-effect relationships, dogs have no way of knowing after the fact if they've done something forbidden.

Only when caught in the act of digging up daisies will your dog respond and learn from disciplinary action. A stern "No!" or squirt of the hose ten minutes later only serves to confuse and aggravate your pet who has already long forgotten the activity that made you so frustrated. Unless you find your dog knee deep in compost, there's no sense in making a fuss.

may find a certain smell, taste, or sight unpleasant enough to discourage him from entering a forbidden area or from trampling your flower bed or vegetable garden full of tender young plants.

These organic strategies are not intended to harm your pet but to make him uncomfortable enough to go elsewhere in the yard or garden for entertainment. When you can't watch your dog every second that he has access to your outdoor environment,

an aversion tactic ensures that he will stay out of trouble. Consider it an insurance policy for your favorite plants and your dog's health.

NOISE AVERSION

Some dogs find certain noises unpleasant. They have sensitive hearing, which makes particular sounds overstimulating. Find out what noise your dog dislikes, and replicate that in the yard or garden environment. For instance, a

dog who jumps every time a paper bag is opened will likely stay clear of the ripe strawberries staked out with a shredded paper windsock. Anything that closely imitates a sound that awakens your dog's ingrained phobia can be used to your advantage.

Most dogs find sharp, unfamiliar sounds startling. Have a noisemaker at the ready so you can use it if you catch your pet engaging in a forbidden outdoor activity. You can create a noisemaker easily by filling a water bottle with a few rocks, a soda can with pennies, or a milk jug with a handful of marbles—whatever gets your dog's attention. Give the container a good shake when you observe the unwanted behavior. A bit of a spook will make him think twice before lying atop your bed of impatiens.

SMELL AVERSION

A dog's sense of smell ranks at the top of the list of animal superpowers. With noses many times more sensitive than ours, dogs pick up the smallest traces of odors from impressive distances. Thus, smell-aversion tactics may be just the way to convince your pooch to stay out of the marigolds. Although dogs like most smells, they do shy away from those they perceive as unnatural or potentially noxious. An all-natural solution found in many homes may hold the key to your behavior-modification woes.

Although not toxic or harmful to your pet, common white vinegar causes enough irritation of the nasal passages to send a curious dog in another direction. Make simple vinegar balls, and place them in areas you'd rather not have your pet walking or digging. Reuse small containers, such as plastic yogurt containers with lids, place cotton balls or rags inside, saturate with vinegar, and replace the lids. Poke holes in the top for the scent to escape, and place the containers in the desired area of your lawn or garden.

TASTE AVERSION

Dogs who chronically chew on forbidden items in the yard, from garden gloves and tool handles to fragile plants and shrubs, need to be trained—if not for your sanity,

then for your dog's health. Keeping your pet from chewing on inappropriate items takes dedication and persistence. When you can't be there to monitor and correct destructive chewing habits, consider using taste-aversion tactics to redirect your dog's activities.

Bitter-tasting plant extracts can be purchased at pet-supply stores and applied to a wide range of items, to make them unpalatable to dogs. However, the solution to your problem may already be in your spice rack. Ground black pepper, chili powder, and cayenne pepper taste highly unpleasant to animals that would normally eat anything. Dust plants and other objects regularly, and your dog will think twice before gnawing on them.

TEXTURE AVERSION

Dogs explore the world with their exquisitely sensitive noses and paws.

Teeming with touch receptors, your pet's front-and-center sense organs aren't that different from your own. Just as people dislike certain textures, so do dogs. Often, crushed stone, rough wood mulch, or pebbles and rocks irritate your dog enough to discourage him from regularly patrolling flower beds landscaped with these irregular materials.

Pine needles, juniper trimmings, and other common prickly yard waste also have the potential to keep your dog out of forbidden areas. Instead of putting them in the trash, try sprinkling a few in trouble spots to see how your pet reacts to the sensations they cause.

WATER AVERSION

Although most dogs have a positive relationship with water, some detest it. Use your dog's dislike of baths and rain to your advantage. By turning it into another tool you can use to shape your pet's

The rough texture of this juniper plant will keep a dog from patrolling any areas you want to protect.

To bar curious canines from parts of your garden, you can use a natural barrier, such as this attractive bamboo stand.

utdoor behavior. A quick spritz from a pray bottle or a shot or two from a water istol can send a dog with a dislike of ater running for cover—and away from he freshly planted vegetable garden.

For those times when you can't bserve what your dog is up to, try nstalling a motion-activated sprinkler. hese standard jet-style sprinklers are utfitted with motion sensors similar o the ones used for security porch ights. When your pet gets too close to he begonias, a surprise stream of water rupts in his direction. Eventually ssociating the begonias with bath ime, your dog learns to steer clear of he area altogether.

Divide and Conquer

Vhen behavior modification strate-ies fail to keep your dog at a distance, onsider interrupting his traffic patterns

with more surefire options. Attractive plantings of hedges or strategically placed fencing make great ways to curtail damage while providing the bonus of beautifying the yard.

FENCING AND PANELS

Anything, transparent or otherwise, that stops a dog in his tracks will prevent him from unwittingly damaging young,

tender plants. Galvanized hog wire and vinyl-coated garden fencing provide affordable, temporary structures that weather the elements and can easily be rolled up and stored when not needed. They let you monitor the health of new plants and see when it's time to allow your dog access. To minimize the appearance of these wire fences, try spray painting them black. Darker colors are more difficult to see from a distance, making them less of an eyesore while they're up.

Common chicken wire, available at your local feed or home-improvement store, also protects delicate plants effectively. Place it atop the soil anywhere you want to discourage digging. Tack it down using landscape staples, and cover it with mulch. When his claws hit the thin wires, your dog will soon discover that he can't get any farther. It protects areas near foundations and prevents sharp claws from reaching down into the soil where they will damage your plants' sensitive roots.

For more artistic barriers, try constructing a whimsical painted panel for the garden. These temporary, removable panels, placed in front of sensitive areas of the lawn and garden, give you something to look at while plants become established and keep your pets out of trouble. See Creating a Garden Panel at right. An outdoor screen will also work in these circumstances.

PLANTS THAT PROTECT

For more permanent solutions to chronic damage to sensitive plants, try simply putting in more plants. Choose species that quickly grow into thickets that prevent your pet from crashing through a tender flower bed. Choose from the following list, or experiment with your own favorite plants best suited for your local climate. Anything

Creating a Garden Panel

Made of wood or fabric stretched over simple frames, these devices brighten up your outdoor space and can be placed in corners, between structures, or anywhere you need to. They block pet traffic, while still allowing the sun to nourish the plants they protect.

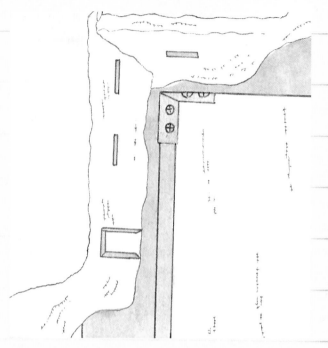

2 Secure canvas (or any fabric designed for exterior use) to the frame by stretching it firmly around the wood. Fasten the fabric to the frame using galvanized exterior staples with either a staple gun or hammer.

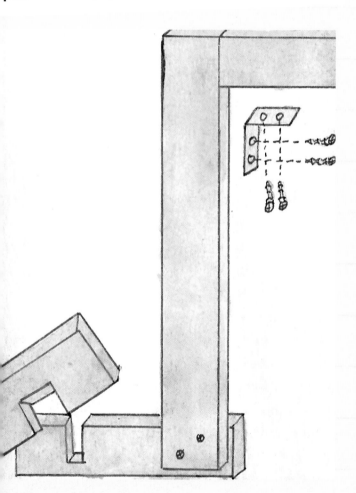

Using 1 x 6 or 2 x 6 lumber (depending on the size of your screen), cut simple "T" supports for supporting legs, like the ones shown here. Secure the upright frame with galvanized exterior screws and corner brackets.

3 Paint the resulting panel with any whimsical or traditional design you like. Oil-based or acrylic artist paints will stand up well to the environment for many years to come. Store it flat in the off season.

A juniper hedge, such as this one, growing at the Missouri Botanical Gardens can serve as a hardy, natural barrier.

that grows quickly and densely makes a good candidate for use as a living garden barrier.

Barberry: This makes an excellent choice for an attractive barrier against aggressive canine activity. Barberry can be found in a wide range of colors and grows anywhere from a few inches to several feet off the ground. Although the plant contains a fair number of thorns on each stem, they are softer and more flexible to the touch than they appear. Barberry branches provide enough of an irritation to discourage curious paws but prevent injury caused by thorns or needles lodged in the skin. Bright red berries, present on most cultivators, persist into the winter months and offer a splash of color during an otherwise drab season.

Junipers: These grow in hundreds of shapes and sizes. Choose one of the many versatile forms for a functional design that looks beautiful and keeps your dog from trampling more sensitive plants nearby. When planted close together, junipers form a suitably prickly barrier to discourage most paws from exploring any further. Junipers come in ground covers, pyramidal shrubs, neat mounds, and tall columns. These fast-growing, drought-tolerant, tough-as-nails plants present the perfect solution to outdoor life with dogs. Choose from blues, emerald greens, or yellows for an effective barrier that holds its appeal year round.

Mugo pine: This pine makes the perfect dog-friendly hedge. When planted closely together, mugo pines quickly grow into a 3- to 4-foot-high wall of green. The plant's attractive, round growing pattern makes it a

A well-planted garden and a well-behaved dog make for a beautiful landscape.

ersatile choice for formal and informal arden spaces. This evergreen grows ght to the ground, preventing curi- us pets from crashing through, and it quires little pruning to maintain its nape. For a year-round dose of green, nis plant is hard to beat.

Rugosa Rose: This plant—also nown as living fence—grows in most arts of the United States. Its fast- rowing, thorny canes spray branches every direction, creating an im- enetrable and beautiful screen that evens dogs from entering forbidden eas of the garden. The rugosa rose ooms in a wide array of colors, in- uding yellows, pinks, and reds. These

attractive plants even produce red fruits (or hips) that can be harvested to make tea or left as an attractive burst of color against the snow.

Yucca: Normally seen high and dry in arid areas of the United States, yucca also comes in a variety of cultivators suitable for cooler and wetter areas of the country. Try one in your garden, in an area you want to protect from damage your pet might cause. Mounds of this plant spread quickly under full-sun conditions, creating thick patches of dense foliage with sharp, pointed leaves. Yucca has a habit of sending out under- ground horizontal stems (or stolons) that quickly produce "daughter plants" in the

surrounding soil. Its dramatic white sum- mer flowers sit upon tall stalks and add "wow factor" to any outdoor space.

Show the Way

Once you have a working knowledge of your dog's behavior and basic training techniques, all you need is patience to complete the equation. A well- behaved, organic dog lives just beneath the surface of every digger, runner, and chewer. Your pet simply needs a dedicated owner willing to show him the way. For a more enjoyable outdoor lifestyle for you and your dog, invest a little time in behavior modification.

CHAPTER 10

Creating Doggy Nirvana

Picture an outdoor paradise for your pet, where each of his fundamental needs is addressed within a beautiful garden landscape. Imagine the delight experienced by your dog, free to roam amid a playground custom-built for him. Space permitting, and with love for and dedication to the pet who gives you so much joy and companionship, consider building him his own outdoor doggy nirvana.

As discussed in the previous chapters, there are certain elements to consider when tailoring a garden to your pet that will affect its design. They include:

Digging: Many dogs like the satisfaction of blowing off steam with a good dig. If your dog plays the role of chief excavator, you'll need to provide a special area where appropriate digging can be celebrated.

Exercise: A custom dog garden encourages roaming, bounding, and other activities that strengthen muscles and banish boredom. Make sure your pet's special area is large enough and offers objects to climb on and jump over.

Running: Most dogs love the exhilaration that comes from a full-speed gallop—if only for a few minutes a day. For a champion sprinter, make sure to include a long, narrow area of turf in his special area of the yard. Allowing your dog to run full throttle whenever he chooses indulges his natural need for speed.

Shade: A spot to keep cool is a must for dogs that enjoy time in the yard and garden. Without a spot to escape when the sun beats down, dogs tend to create their own microclimates by digging deep holes to collapse into. Worse yet, without an area that offers respite from the heat, your pet could easily succumb to heat exhaustion— a potentially fatal condition.

Water: Dogs who play hard are in need of a spot to rehydrate. Any garden built for your pet should contain a constant supply of fresh, cool water he can drink whenever the need arises. A source of water becomes vital during the hottest time of year, when failure to provide one could be detrimental to your dog's health.

Keep all of your dog's basic needs in mind, and get creative about planning your outdoor canine paradise. Concentrate on structures and planting techniques that fulfill each of your pet's requirements while addressing any aesthetic issues that you may have

A Golden Retriever puppy appears posed to spring into his personal paradise.

Chloe laps water from a bird bath. A dog needs a source of clean, fresh water in the yard to stay healthy.

Remember, building a custom space for your dog doesn't mean his corner of the yard has to look like a war zone. His garden can still offer a chance to indulge your sense of style.

Consider including the following structures and features in your dog's garden. Each one is designed to address his special needs while offering ample opportunity to exercise your own sense of creativity.

Pooch Pergola

Pergolas have grown increasingly popular in many areas of the United States, their simple construction techniques and Old World charm making them a good weekend project. Consider build- ing one so your dog can enjoy a good source of shade that gives structure to his space. Pergolas easily transform an otherwise stifling backyard into a shady spot to doze away a summer day.

Instead of building a traditional pergola, create a planted version, using planter boxes instead of roofing slats to provide shade below. As the plants

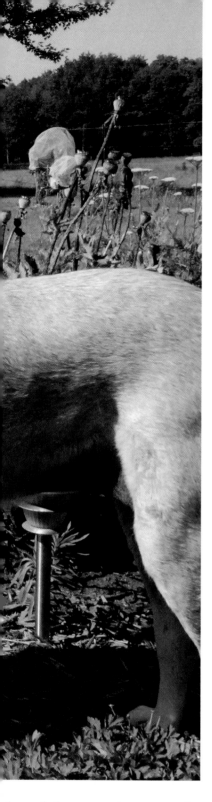

Hedges **for Hurdles**

If you've ever seen a dressage event, in which horses leap gracefully over manicured hedges, you have witnessed what could be a crown jewel of your dog's garden space, as well as an exercise tool to keep your pet strong and fit.

Dogs, too, can be trained to leap over hurdles, as many agility-trial spectators have witnessed. Replace those hurdles with formal English hedges, and you've added an element of sophistication to your pet's environment. These hurdle hedges can also be used to hide damage caused by your dog or unsightly features of his special space.

Take a few tips from agility pros. Start with low hurdles, which you can easily make from PVC pipes or wooden dowels and stacked blocks. Find the height your dog can effortlessly (and willingly) clear. Coax him with treats and praise. When jumping becomes second nature for him, look for a perennial, annual, or shrub that grows to the same comfortable height. Eventually, you can remove the man-made pole and leave Mother Nature to provide an attractive exercise tool.

Choose plants for the hedge based on their durability and suitability for your dog's behavior. Consult chapter 2 for easy-to-find selections that best fit your needs. Prune woody plants frequently throughout the growing season to contain their size and prevent injury to your pet.

the roof of your pergola mature and
rther block the sun, they provide an
-natural, green roof that shields your
t from the sun's heat.

You may also consider planting one
more dog-friendly vines (discussed in
apter 2) near each of the supporting
sts of your dog's pergola. As the vines
ature and climb the posts, they spread

A planted pergola provides colorful shade for your dog.

Building a Pooch Pergola

Build this special pergola according to the plans shown here; you can grow some of your favorite herbaceous annuals or even a few vegetables in the integrated planters. Elevated and protected from your dog's activities, a planted pergola serves both of your needs.

1 Simple planters can be made out of exterior-grade, 2 x 6 or 2 x 8 lumber, which can be fastened to decorate pergola trusses made from the same lumber.

2 Fasten the pergola to 4 x 4 posts, anchored a minimum of 3 feet into the ground. The planters can be filled and planted with favorite flowers or vegetables.

ver the planter boxes, further blocking
e sun. At the same time, the vines add
olor and fragrance to your dog's space
at you can also enjoy from a distance.

Another bonus: pergola construc-
on saves time and money in compari-
on to building a solid-roof structure.
ith only four corner posts and widely
aced roof slats, a low, dog-friendly
ergola goes up in a day with a short
st of materials. See Building a Pooch
ergola on the opposite page.

hady Sandbox

iving your dog a place to dig could be
e best gift you ever give him. Train-
g a digging-relishing dog to stay away
om foundations and freshly tilled
arden plots may prove impossible if
ou don't offer an alternative digging
ea. If you provide your dog with a
ace to burrow where he isn't scolded
r the activity, you may find that he will
g less often, or not at all, in forbidden
eas of the lawn and garden.

Dogs also dig to feel the cool, damp
il against their skins. Think of a cus-
m sandbox as a diminutive health spa
r your pet, one where he can get both
ercise and a chance to relax and cool
own. See Dig a Doggy Sandbox (right)
r instructions. Build the box frame out
f your favorite material, one you find
esthetically pleasing.

reshwater Fountain

nsure your dog has a fresh supply of
rinking water by creating a custom
ountain for him. With a few basic sup-
lies and simple instructions, you can
istall, in just an afternoon, an outdoor
howpiece that your dog also uses to

Dig a Doggy Sandbox

A sandbox amounts to nothing more than an edge raised just high enough to contain any sand flung back by your pet. You can choose to build it with a circle of fieldstone, landscape timbers, or an old tractor tire. Anything that helps contain the sand will work. A material that matches a theme or style of landscaping you may already have in the yard doubles as décor.

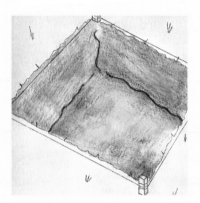

1 Start by removing 6 to 8 inches of top soil from the area where you'll be building your dog's digs. For larger dogs with more robust digging habits, you may want to remove as much as 12 inches.

2 Aggressive diggers may require that you construct a partially underground barrier to prevent an animal from digging into the surrounding lawn, as shown in the illustration at right.

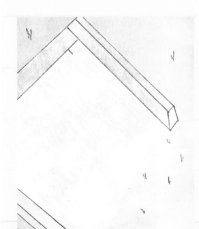

3 Now you can, backfill the hole with clean play sand—which can be purchased at most landscape supply stores—up to the surface of the surrounding soil. Then let your dog loose to dig to his heart's content.

This disappearing fountain, fashioned from a blue urn, provides beauty and tranquility.

stay hydrated. Thanks to the increasingly popular hobby of water gardening, nurseries, home-improvement stores, and pet stores are brimming with all the ingredients you'll need to create a healthy and beautiful water feature, like the one above, for your dog's own garden space.

First spend some time searching for your favorite piece of pottery. Choose one that fits your garden theme, something you'll enjoy for years to come. Then stock up on a few basic supplies, including: several bags of pea stone or other stone mulch; a piece of heavy-gauge plastic or rubber pond liner; a small recirculating pump with a prefilter for outdoor use; and several feet of flexible tubing. Now follow the instructions in Building a Disappearing Fountain on page 132 to assemble a dog-perfect fountain.

Your custom feature recirculates water from a retention basin and back up though the pottery, where it bubbles over the edges and cascades gently down the sides. Your pet can drink from the feature at his leisure, and you can enjoy the relaxing sound of moving water.

Faux Fetching Strip

A place to fetch, a patch to patrol—all dogs tend to make a habit out of using one area of the yard to perform their daily activities. Add a fetching strip into your dog's personal garden, and you'll satisfy his need to walk, return, and repeat, day after day. Better yet, make your dog's runway out of faux grass, and it will continue to look lush year after year, in spite of heavy paw traffic.

An environmentally friendly option for green dogs and their owners, artificial turf looks great without a drop of pesticide, fertilizer, or water. Imagine—no weed pulling or patching bare spots where your dog likes to run and play.

Before you pooh-pooh the idea of using artificial turf in your dog's garden

Mallory walks through the
backyard on her daily patrol.
This would be a good place
to install a fetching strip.

Building a
Disappearing Fountain

Once you have gathered the following materials and selected the site for your water feature, you can begin building the fountain.

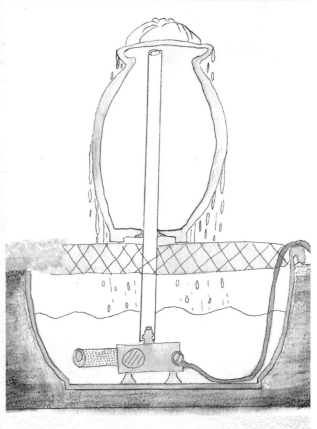

Materials:

• Glazed ceramic or container pot
• Pea stone or other stone mulch (several bags)
• Heavy-gauge plastic or rubber pond liner
• Recirculating pump with prefilter (small)
• Flexible tubing (several feet)

Building instructions:

1. Dig a hole with a diameter twice that of the piece of pottery you've chosen and half as deep as the pot is tall.

2. Cover the hole with the flexible liner of your choice.

3. Place the pump in the center of the hole with a piece of flexible tubing attached to the water outlet port.

4. Fill the hole with pebbles or stones, depending on the look you'd like to achieve.

5. Drill a hole in the bottom of the pot, matching the diameter of the tubing you have chosen. Be sure to select a drill bit made for penetrating masonry.

6. Thread the flexible tubing up through the bottom of your pot. Fill the pot and underground basin you've just created with clean water. Plug in the pump and enjoy.

Drain and change the water in your feature whenever it appears muddy or fouled. For an easy-to-install, healthy, beautiful feature in your dog's garden, a fountain is hard to beat. Consider adding one to your master plan for your doggy paradise. For even more luxury, consider installing a custom dog splash pond such as the one outlined in chapter 6.

space, consider new technologies that have created more realistic-looking faux grass than products of yesteryear. Banish the idea of plastic grass on a roll. Unnaturally bright, green synthetic turf has gone the way of leisure suits. In its place is a wide variety of durable and aesthetically pleasing products created to meet the needs of dog owners hoping to retain a bit of grass in the backyard.

Surrounded by the bounty of sniffable flowers, loungable ares of lawn, and other doggy delights, Mallory enjoys her very own backyard heaven.

Take your pick of fescue, Kentucky bluegrass, rye grass, or St. Augustine grass. Artificial grass now comes in every variety of the real thing. Just choose the type that matches your current grass species for a virtually seamless addition to your existing space.

Installing faux grass in your outdoor space requires little experience and should take no more than a weekend.

If you can install a weed barrier in a fresh garden bed or place patio stones for a pad or path, you can easily do this installation yourself.

Slice of Heaven

Integrating your dog into your outdoor life doesn't mean you have to surrender a large part of your yard or garden to his lawn-digging, plant-chewing, pond-splashing whims. Providing for your dog's outdoor needs won't turn your serene space into a mud bog filled with craters and littered with dog waste. Even a small corner of your space can be made more inviting for your pet. Give your dog his own little slice of heaven, and you provide a place for him to relax and exercise in appropriate and less destructive ways.

Organic Gardener, Organic Dogs

Green Family Matters

Gabriel and Evangeline Smith spend time with their dogs Scooby, Violet, and Belle and neighbor dog Suzzie.

Amanda Smith
Leesville, Louisiana

Life as a busy mom of two energetic kids and three rambunctious dogs leaves few dull moments for Amanda Smith of Leesville, Louisiana. Protecting her active family from harmful chemicals and outdoor toxins means getting back to basics with greener living—indoors and out.

Rural life with husband David and their two children, Evangeline, nine, and Gabe, six, just wouldn't be the same without generous landscaping, vegetables, and a rose garden. Keeping it all looking its organic best, with three dogs in tow, is no small feat.

"With my dogs, even if you go out to spray an ant's nest, they're going to want to walk all through it and want to be near you while you're out there. They're going to be covered in [poison] by the time you're done," Belle (a Rat Terrier mix) and Scooby Doo and Violet (both black Labrador Retrievers) do what dogs do best: hang out with the pack, dig in the shade, and chew the odd landscape plant or two. For the safety of her dogs and that of her children, Smith makes sure the plants around her home are not dangerous.

"I have very few plants that would make them sick," Smith says. "I love oleander. It's so pretty and smells good. But with kids and dogs, it's not worth it. You have to weigh the risk. Is it the pretty flowers your want or to be safe?"

Toads like this one enjoy the water feature in the Smith family's front yard and help control pests.

The secret, she says, is choosing plants that you know, frequently through trial and error, will fit with our furry family's lifestyle. "Mine like to chew on woody plants," Smith says. "Sometimes they'll dig up bulbs. If something has poisonous roots, I can't get it. You just have to watch them and see what they like to chew on and what they don't."

For the sake of her children and her pets, Amanda Smith controls pests using the most basic form of pesticide available—Mother Nature. Foundation plantings that surround her Louisiana home act as the perfect environment for beneficial biological weapons. Since we have a lot of plants around the house, we have a ton of green anoles everywhere," she says. "They help with the bugs quite a bit."

Toads baited by a front-yard water feature help control pests without chemicals. "The little water feature in front of the house has toads living all around it, because they know there's water there," she says. "Basically, it's the dog's water fountain, but it also encourages other things to come."

Controlling fleas amid the Louisiana wilderness is another struggle—one Smith tackles with natural alternatives. "In our area, sand fleas are terrible," Smith says. "Of course [the dogs'] favorite spot to lie is in the sand because it's cooler. I use eucalyptus oil, mixed into their flea and tick shampoo—just a few drops, so I can keep the bugs off."

Not relying on chemical-based flea control also gives Smith peace of mind where her children are concerned. "The kids play with the dogs and get greasy [medications] on themselves, and you don't know what's in it," she says. "And kids don't always wash their hands once they get into something."

By paying extra attention to her outdoor space, Smith has turned it into a kid and dog magnet—reinforcing the reason that she sticks to her green principles. "Every dog in the neighborhood comes to our house," Smith says. "So it's not just our dogs we have to watch out for—it's everybody else's too."

Appendix

The following maps indicate, by zone, what the temperature extremes are for your unique location. Use these two maps when selecting plants for your outdoor environment. Plant tags indicate which hardiness zone is ideal for planting the species you're considering. They also contain a minimum and maximum ideal air temperature in which a particular plant will thrive. Strong plants that have evolved to thrive in your climate will need less care and will be able to stand up to more of your dog's various activities than other species can. Plants that match your USDA Plant Hardiness Zone and your AHS Heat Zone will provide years of enjoyment for you and your pet.

American Horticultural Society Plant Heat-Zone Map

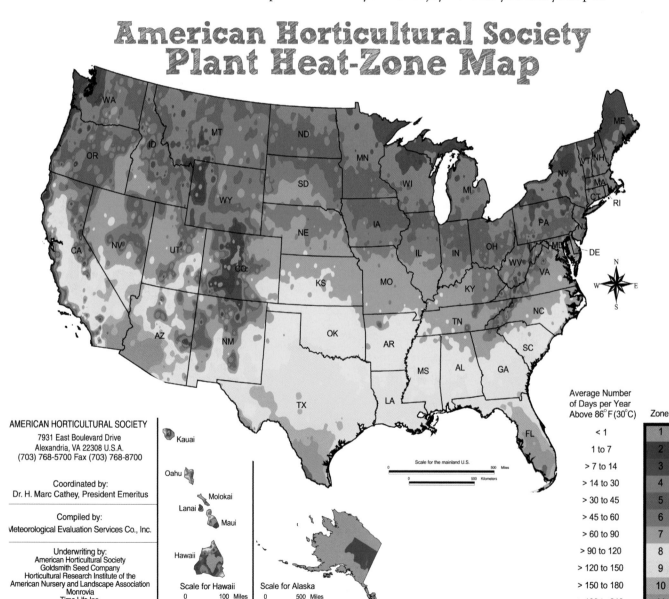

AMERICAN HORTICULTURAL SOCIETY
7931 East Boulevard Drive
Alexandria, VA 22308 U.S.A.
(703) 768-5700 Fax (703) 768-8700

Coordinated by:
Dr. H. Marc Cathey, President Emeritus

Compiled by:
Meteorological Evaluation Services Co., Inc.

Underwriting by:
American Horticultural Society
Goldsmith Seed Company
Horticultural Research Institute of the
American Nursery and Landscape Association
Monrovia
Time Life Inc.

Copyright © 1997 by the American Horticultural Society

Average Number of Days per Year Above 86°F (30°C)	Zone
< 1	1
1 to 7	2
> 7 to 14	3
> 14 to 30	4
> 30 to 45	5
> 45 to 60	6
> 60 to 90	7
> 90 to 120	8
> 120 to 150	9
> 150 to 180	10
> 180 to 210	11
> 210	12

Scale for the mainland U.S.
0 — 500 Miles
0 — 500 Kilometers

Scale for Hawaii
0 — 100 Miles
0 — 100 Kilometers

Scale for Alaska
0 — 500 Miles
0 — 500 Kilometers

USDA Plant Hardiness Zone Map

(USDA Miscellaneous Publication No. 1475—Issued January 1900)

AVERAGE ANNUAL MINIMUM TEMPERATURE

Temperature °C	Zone	Temperature °F
-45.6 & Below	1	Below -60
-42.8 to -45.5	2a	-45 to -50
-40.0 to -42.7	2b	-40 to -45
-37.3 to -40.0	3a	-36 to -40
-34.5 to -37.2	3b	-30 to -35
-31.7 to -34.4	4a	-26 to -30
-26.9 to -31.6	4b	-20 to -25
-26.2 to -28.8	5a	-15 to -20
-23.4 to -26.1	5b	-10 to -15
-20.6 to -23.3	6a	-6 to -10
-17.8 to -20.5	6b	0 to -5
-15.0 to -17.7	7a	5 to 0
-12.3 to -15.0	7b	10 to 5
-9.5 to -12.2	8a	15 to 10
-6.7 to -9.4	8b	20 to 15
-3.9 to -6.6	9a	25 to 20
-1.2 to -3.8	9b	30 to 25
1.6 to -1.1	10a	35 to 30
4.4 to 1.7	10b	40 to 35
4.5 and above	11	40 and above

Scale in Kilometers
0 100 200 300 400 500 600

Scale in Miles
0 100 200 300 400 500 600

Scale 1:6,000,000 (Approximately)

Resources

CANINE NUTRITION

Dr.. Kidd's Guide to Herbal Dog Care, by Randy Kidd, DVM (North Adams, Mass.: Storey Publishing, 2000).
A basic guide to herbal remedies for common dog ailments.

Yummy for Dogs: A Cook Book for Canines, by Veronica Noechel (LuLu .com, 2005).
A whole foods cookbook for dog treats and snacks.

COMPOSTING RESOURCES

Basic Composting: All the Skills and Tools You Need to Get Started, by Eric Ebeling (Mechanicsburg, Pa.: Stackpole Books, 2003).
A look at composting for beginners.

Texas A&M Department of Horticultural Sciences
AgriLife Extension
College Station, Texas
979-845-8565; http://aggie-horticulture .tamu.edu/
A good resource for an in-depth explanation of how composting works.

U.S. Environmental Protection Agency Waste Reduction and Resource Conservation Program
Washington, D.C.
Regional hotlines available Web site; www.epa.gov
Offers answers to frequently asked composting questions.

DIY CONSTRUCTION PLANS

Agriculture Natural Resources Conservation Service
www.nrcs.usda.gov
For owl nesting box plans, search *owl nest box plans* on this site.

Decks: Plan, Design, Build, by Steve Cory (Upper Saddle River, N.J.: Creative Homeowner, 2005).
Full of ideas and construction basics for the do-it-yourself crowd.

Decks.com
www.decks.com
Includes interactive design software, construction guidelines, and contractor directories.

DoItYourself.com
www.doityourself.com
Construction basics, including videos, on how to build a custom deck.

Gardeners' World.com
www.gardenersworld.com/how-to/ projects/cloche-seeds
Instructions for building a cloche.

University of Minnesota Extension Office
www.extension.umn.edu/yardand garden/ygbriefs/h137seasonextenders .html
Instructions for building cloches and cold frames in order to extend the growing season.

DOG-TRAINING RESOURCES

American Society for the Prevention of Cruelty to Animals
New York, N.Y.
212-876-7700; www.aspca.org
Offers "Virtual Pet Behaviorist" software that gives training tips based on whatever problem behavior you may be trying to solve.

The Big Book of Simple Solutions: Training Your Dog, by Kim Campbell Thornton (Irvine, Calif.: BowTie Press, 2004).
A good overview of the basics to redirect your dog's undesirable behaviors.

BowTie Press
www.bowtiepress.com; www.shopanimal network.com
A division of BowTie Inc. , the largest publisher of pet magazines, such as *Dog Fancy* and *Cat Fancy*. The BowTie collection is devoted to the joy, care, understanding and history of our companion animals.

DogChannel.com
www.dogchannel.com
Offers resources for dog owners from the people that bring you *Dog Fancy, Dog World, Dogs in Review, Popular Dogs, Popular Puppies, Dogs USA, Puppies USA.*

Humane Society of the United States
Washington, D.C.
202-452-1100; www.hsus.org

...ffers simple techniques for training ...ogs to follow commands.

GREEN LIFESTYLE RESOURCES

Low Impact Living
...ww.lowimpactliving.com
...alculate your personal impact on the ...nvironment and then find out how to ...ssen your impact by reviewing products ...r you and your dog.

OrganicAuthority.com
...ww.organicauthority.com
...he brainchild of organic-living guru ...aura Klein, with information on how to ... green in the garden and with pet care.

Raise a Green Dog
...ttp://blog.raiseagreendog.com
... blog about how to raise a green dog, ...ith lots of information on the earth-...iendliest ways to treat your dog, ...doors and out.

NATIVE PLANT RESOURCES

Colorado State University Extension Office
...ort Collins, Colo.
...70-491-6281; www.ext.colostate.edu
...rovides a comprehensive directory of ...rnamental grasses with photos.

PlantNative
...ortland, Ore.
...03-248-0104; www.plantnative.org
...A retail store and organization dedicated ...o promoting native plants. The Web site ...rovides a native-plant nursery finder by ...tate.

ORGANIC GARDENING RESOURCES

Capitol District Community Gardens
...roy, N.Y.
...18-274-868; www.cdcg.org
...A nonprofit community garden organiza-...ion offering basic organic gardening tips.

Maine Organic Farmers and Gardeners Association
PO Box 170
294 Crosby Brook Road
Unity, Maine
207-568-4142; www.mofga.org
The nation's oldest state organic organiza-tion for helping farmers and gardeners grow organic food.

Organic Gardening Magazine
Emmaus, Pa.
800-666-2206; www.organicgardening .com
A magazine dedicated to the latest infor-mation on organic gardening.

The Organic Gardener's Handbook of Natural Insect and Disease Control: A Complete Problem-Solving Guide to Keeping Your Garden and Yard Healthy Without Chemicals, edited by Fern Marshall Bradley and Barbara W. Ellis (Allenstown, Pa.: Rodale Press, 1996).
A comprehensive book on organic gar-dening, with a focus on pest control.

Rodale's Ultimate Encyclopedia of Organic Gardening: The Indispensable Green Resource for Every Gardener, edited by Fern Marshall Bradley, Barbara Ellis, and Ellen Phillips (Allenstown, Pa.: Rodale Press, 2009).
A comprehensive guide to going green in the garden.

PET POISONING RESOURCES

ASPCA Animal Poison Control Center
888-426-4435; www.aspca.org/pet-care/ poison-control/
Provides emergency assistance to owners with poisoned pets.

Cornell University
Department of Animal Science
Ithaca, N.Y.
607-255-2862; www.ansci.cornell.edu
Offers a comprehensive database of plants poisonous to dogs.

TURF RESOURCES

Kansas State University
Research and Extension Office
Manhattan, Kans.
785-532-5820; www.oznet.ksu.edu
Offering the latest information on turf-grass management to the public.

The Organic Lawn Care Manual,
by Paul Tukey (North Adams, Mass.: Storey Publishing, 2007).
A guide to organic lawn care.

SafeLawns.org
www.safelawns.org
A nonprofit organization dedicated to promoting chemical-free lawn care.

WATER GARDENING

All about Water Gardening, by Greg Speichert and Sue Speichert (New York: Meredith Books, 2001).
A basic guide for the novice pond keeper.

The American Horticultural Society: Water Gardening, by Peter Robinson (New York: Covent Garden Books, 2005).
A more advanced guide to building and maintaining a water garden.

Garden Ponds: Basic Pond Setup and Maintenance, by Dennis Kelsey-Wood and Tom Barthel (Irvine, Calif.: BowTie Press, 2006).
A comprehensive guide on setup and maintenance of a backyard water feature.

Ponds & Fountains: Step-by-Step Proj-ects, by Jim Barrett (Upper Saddle River, N.J.: Creative Homeowner, 2003).
A good, illustrated guide to installing custom water features and fountains.

Ponds USA
www.shopanimalnetwork.com; www .pondsmagazine.com
Offers valuable resources and information for building and maintaining ponds and water gardens in your backyard.

Index

Index

ABOUT THE AUTHOR

An avid naturalist and certified master gardener, Tom Barthel has written hundreds of articles on pets and gardening over the past decade. He is also coauthor of the book *Garden Ponds* (BowTie Press, 2006). He lives in Lansing, Michigan with his wife, Rachel, and their Labradoodle, Dakota. The author's main ambitions center on fostering a greater respect for the earth and the pets we share it with. As a means to that end, he promotes lifestyle choices that lessen carbon footprints, conserve natural resources, and rely on organic options whenever possible.

RUN DATE 03/15/1-- MM DD YY	ACCOUNTS RECEIVABLE FILE MAINTENANCE Input Form	Problem No. 8-S FORM AR-1

	CUSTOMER NUMBER	CUSTOMER NAME	
1	050	Linda's Fitness Center	1
2	110	Marsha's Auto Repair	2
3			3
4			4
5			5
6			6
7			7
8			8
9			9
10			10
11			11
12			12
13			13
14			14
15			15
16			16
17			17
18			18
19			19
20			20
21			21
22			22
23			23
24			24
25			25

Figure 8.15   Accounts Receivable File Maintenance Input Form (Problem 8-S)

09 Sold merchandise on account to Marsha's Auto Repair, $72.00, plus 6 percent sales tax (Sales Invoice No. 452).

Marsha's Auto Repair is a new customer and does not appear on the current customer list. Therefore, the account is recorded on the Accounts Receivable File Maintenance input form as Customer No. 110. Sales Invoice No. 452 is recorded on the Accounts Receivable input form using the customer number for Marsha's Auto Repair.

10 Received cash on account from Robert Fox, $1,033.50, covering Sales Invoice No. 443 (Customer Check No. 917).
11 Sold merchandise on account to Harmon Furniture Co., $106.86, plus 6 percent sales tax (Sales Invoice No. 453).
12 Sold merchandise on account to Dakota County Inquirer, $270.00, plus 6 percent sales tax (Sales Invoice No. 454).
15 Sold merchandise on account to Linda's Fitness Center,

RUN DATE _03 / 15 / - -_ MM DD YY

BATCH NO. _5_

ACCOUNTS RECEIVABLE
Input Form

Problem No. _8-S_

FORM AR-2

		SALES					CASH RECEIPTS		
	SALES INVOICE NO.	CUST. NO.	DATE MO. DAY YR.	GEN. LEDGER ACCT. NO.	INVOICE AMOUNT	SALES TAX %	DATE MO. DAY YR.	DOC. NO.	CASH RECEIVED
1	447	020	03 01 --	410	297 20	6			
2	448	080	03 02 --	410	826 00	6			
3	449	050	03 03 --	410	100 50	6			
4	442						03 03 --	1585	2660 07
5	450	040	03 04 --	410	48 00	6			
6	451	030	03 05 --	410	2123 20	6			
7	447						03 08 --	2306	315 03
8	452	110	03 09 --	410	72 00	6			
9	443						03 10 --	917	1033 50
10	453	070	03 11 --	410	106 86	6			
11	454	010	03 12 --	410	270 00	6			
12	455	050	03 15 --	410	104 50	6			
13	451						03 15 --	1428	2250 59
14	448						03 15 --	1145	875 56
15									
16									
17									
18									
19									
20									
21									
22									
23									
24									
25									

BATCH TOTALS   3948 26   7134 75

Figure 8.16   Accounts Receivable Input Form (Problem 8-S)

$104.50, plus 6 percent sales tax (Sales Invoice No. 455).

15   Received cash on account from Superior New and Used Autos, $2,250.59, covering Sales Invoice No. 451 (Customer Check No. 1428).

15   Received cash on account from Galactic Insurance, $875.56, covering Sales Invoice No. 448 (Customer Check No. 1145).

Step 2   Bring up the System Selection Menu according to the instructions for your microcomputer.

Step 3   Select Option C, *Load Data from Disk*, from the System Selection Menu.

Step 4   Select Problem 8-S from the *Load Data from the Program Disk* option (if using an Apple with 5 1/4-inch disk, select *Load Data from the Template Disk*) by key-entering **AA8-S** when the directory list appears.

Step 5 Select Option D, *Company Information*, from the System Selection Menu. Verify that the *Problem Number* field contains **Problem 8-S**, that the *Company Name* field contains **Hardware Plus**, and that the *Type of Business* field is set to **P**. If these data fields are correct, set the run date to **March 15** of the current year and proceed to Step 6. If these data fields are not correct, the wrong file has been loaded into your computer's memory and you should repeat Steps 3 and 4 above.

Step 6 Select Option H, *Accounts Receivable*, from the System Selection Menu.

Step 7 Select Option F, *Customer File Maintenance*, from the Accounts Receivable Main Menu. Key-enter the customer file maintenance transactions from the Accounts Receivable File Maintenance input form in Figure 8.15.

Step 8 Select Option G, *Customer List*, and display or print a customer list. Verify that the data you key-entered is correct. The correct customer list is shown in Figure 8.17.

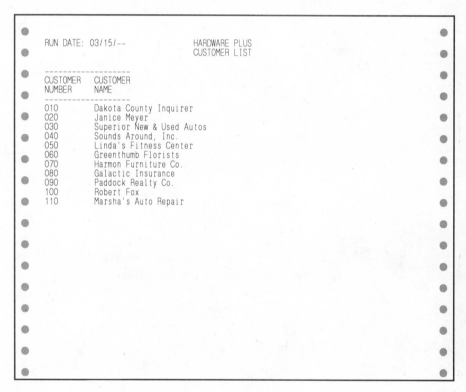

```
RUN DATE: 03/15/--              HARDWARE PLUS
                               CUSTOMER LIST


--------------------
CUSTOMER   CUSTOMER
NUMBER     NAME
--------------------
010        Dakota County Inquirer
020        Janice Meyer
030        Superior New & Used Autos
040        Sounds Around, Inc.
050        Linda's Fitness Center
060        Greenthumb Florists
070        Harmon Furniture Co.
080        Galactic Insurance
090        Paddock Realty Co.
100        Robert Fox
110        Marsha's Auto Repair
```

Figure 8.17   Revised Customer List after File Maintenance (Problem 8-S)

Step 9 Select Option H, *Set Run Date and Batch Number*, from the Accounts Receivable Main Menu. Verify that the run date has been set to **March 15** of the current year and that the batch number has been set to **5**. If not, make the necessary changes and strike **R** to record this data.

Step 10 Select Option I, *Enter/Correct Sales and Cash Receipts*, from the Accounts Receivable Main Menu.

Step 11 Key-enter and post the sales and cash receipt transactions from the Accounts Receivable input form in Figure 8.16.

Step 12   Select Option J, *Sales on Account Report*, from the Accounts Receivable Main Menu, and display or print the Sales on Account report. Compare your Sales on Account report with the correct one shown in Figure 8.18. The computer total of the *Invoice Amount* column should be the same as the calculator total for the Invoice Amount column on the Accounts Receivable input form. If your Sales on Account report is correct, proceed to Step 14.

```
RUN DATE: 03/15/--                    HARDWARE PLUS
                               SALES ON ACCOUNT BATCH #5
---------------------------------------------------------------------
CUSTOMER                      INVOICE           G.L.    INVOICE    SALES
NO. NAME                      NO.    DATE     ACCOUNT    AMOUNT     TAX
---------------------------------------------------------------------
020 Janice Meyer              447  03/01/--    410       297.20    17.83
080 Galactic Insurance        448  03/02/--    410       826.00    49.56
050 Linda's Fitness Center    449  03/03/--    410       100.50     6.03
040 Sounds Around, Inc.       450  03/04/--    410        48.00     2.88
030 Superior New & Used Autos 451  03/05/--    410      2123.20   127.39
110 Marsha's Auto Repair      452  03/09/--    410        72.00     4.32
070 Harmon Furniture Co.      453  03/11/--    410       106.86     6.41
010 Dakota County Inquirer    454  03/12/--    410       270.00    16.20
050 Linda's Fitness Center    455  03/15/--    410       104.50     6.27
                                                       --------- ---------
   TOTALS                                               3948.26   236.89
                                                       ========= =========
```

Figure 8.18   Sales on Account Report (Problem 8-S)

Step 13   If your Sales on Account report is in error, select Option I, *Enter/Correct Sales and Cash Receipts*. Key-enter and post the corrections, and then display or print another Sales on Account report. Repeat this step until your Sales on Account report is correct.

Step 14   Select Option K, *Cash Receipts Report*, from the Accounts Receivable Main Menu, and display or print a Cash Receipts report. Compare your Cash Receipts report with the correct one shown in Figure 8.19. The Total Cash Receipts should agree with the calculator total of the Cash Received column on the Accounts Receivable input form. If your Cash Receipts report is correct, proceed to Step 16.

Step 15   If your Cash Receipts report is in error, select Option I, *Enter/Correct Sales and Cash Receipts*. Key-enter and post the corrections and then display or print another Cash Receipts report. Repeat this step until your Cash Receipts report is correct.

Step 16   Select Option L, *General Ledger Posting Summary*, and display or print a general ledger posting summary. The correct general ledger posting summary is shown in Figure 8.20. Notice that this report is for

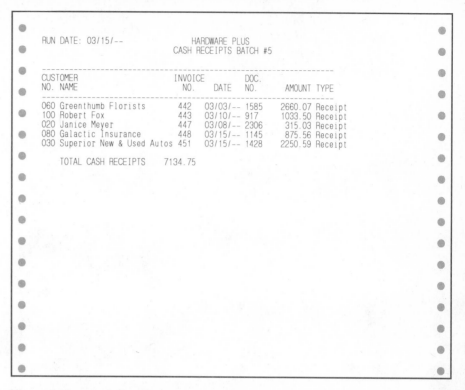

```
RUN DATE: 03/15/--                    HARDWARE PLUS
                                 CASH RECEIPTS BATCH #5

------------------------------------------------------------------
CUSTOMER                        INVOICE        DOC.
NO. NAME                          NO.   DATE   NO.       AMOUNT TYPE
------------------------------------------------------------------
060 Greenthumb Florists           442  03/03/-- 1585   2660.07 Receipt
100 Robert Fox                    443  03/10/-- 917    1033.50 Receipt
020 Janice Meyer                  447  03/08/-- 2306    315.03 Receipt
080 Galactic Insurance            448  03/15/-- 1145    875.56 Receipt
030 Superior New & Used Autos 451 451  03/15/-- 1428   2250.59 Receipt

    TOTAL CASH RECEIPTS    7134.75
```

Figure 8.19   Cash Receipts Report (Problem 8-S)

```
RUN DATE: 03/15/--                    HARDWARE PLUS
                          GENERAL LEDGER POSTING SUMMARY BATCH #5

----------------------------------------------------------
ACCOUNT ACCOUNT
NUMBER  TITLE                          DEBIT      CREDIT
----------------------------------------------------------
110     Cash                          7134.75
120     Accounts Receivable           4185.15
120     Accounts Receivable                       7134.75
220     Sales Tax Payable                          236.89
410     Sales                                     3948.26
                                      ---------  ---------
        TOTALS                        11319.90   11319.90
                                      =========  =========
```

Figure 8.20   General Ledger Posting Summary (Problem 8-S)

all transactions in Batch No. 5. Therefore, if you enter transactions or make corrections during more than one work session, your general ledger posting summary will still reflect all the transactions in a particular batch number.

Step 17   Select Option M, *Schedule of Accounts Receivable*, from the Accounts Receivable Main Menu, and display or print a schedule of accounts receivable. The correct schedule of accounts receivable is shown in Figure 8.21.

```
RUN DATE: 03/15/--                   HARDWARE PLUS
                          SCHEDULE OF ACCOUNTS RECEIVABLE

-----------------------------------------------------------
CUSTOMER                        INVOICE
NO. NAME                        NO.   DATE        AMOUNT
-----------------------------------------------------------
010 Dakota County Inquirer      454  03/12/--      286.20
    CUSTOMER TOTAL                                 286.20

040 Sounds Around  Inc.         438  02/18/--     1219.00
040 Sounds Around  Inc.         450  03/04/--       50.88
    CUSTOMER TOTAL                                1269.88

050 Linda's Fitness Center      449  03/03/--      106.53
050 Linda's Fitness Center      455  03/15/--      110.77
    CUSTOMER TOTAL                                 217.30

070 Harmon Furniture Co.        440  02/21/--     1661.78
070 Harmon Furniture Co.        453  03/11/--      113.27
    CUSTOMER TOTAL                                1775.05

110 Marsha's Auto Repair        452  03/09/--       76.32
    CUSTOMER TOTAL                                  76.32

                                                -----------
    FINAL TOTAL                                   3624.75
                                                ===========
```

Figure 8.21   Schedule of Accounts Receivable (Problem 8-S)

Step 18   Select Option N, *Customer Statements*, and display or print the customer statements. If you are using preprinted statement forms, insert them into your printer and align them so that the print head is centered in the box on the upper left corner of the statement form. The box is printed at the left edge of the paper, over one of the tractor feed holes. The statements shown in Figure 8.22 are printed on preprinted statement forms.

Step 19   Return to the System Selection Menu.

Step 20   Select Option F, *General Ledger*, from the System Selection Menu.

Step 21   Select Option K, *Trial Balance*, from the General Ledger Main Menu and display or print a trial balance. The correct trial balance is shown in Figure 8.23 (page 248). Notice that the general ledger accounts that were affected by accounts receivable transactions have been updated through the integration that has taken place. The Accounts Receivable balance should be the same as the final total on the schedule of accounts receivable prepared in Step 17.

Step 22   Return to the System Selection Menu.

Step 23   Save your work as a work in progress file on your own data disk (recommend file name **AA8-S**) and shut down the computer. Then complete the student exercise and transaction problem which follow.

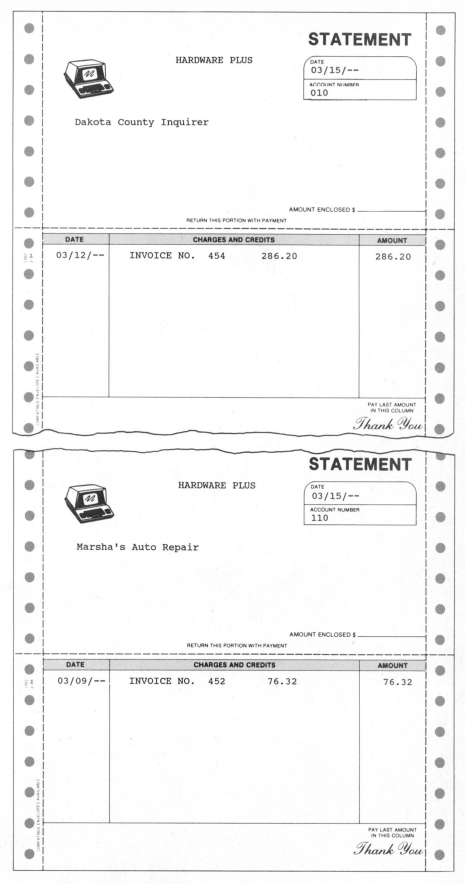

Figure 8.22   Customer Statements on Preprinted Forms (Problem 8-S)

```
RUN DATE: 03/15/--                      HARDWARE PLUS
                                        TRIAL BALANCE

       ----------------------------------------------------------------
       ACCOUNT      ACCOUNT
       NUMBER       TITLE                   DEBIT AMOUNT      CREDIT AMOUNT
       ----------------------------------------------------------------
       110          Cash                      13376.50
       120          Accounts Receivable        3624.75
       130          Merchandise Inventory    108639.42
       140          Supplies                    655.20
       150          Prepaid Insurance           380.00
       210          Accounts Payable                            4095.00
       220          Sales Tax Payable                           1074.18
       310          Dennis Siegel, Capital                     58811.98
       330          Ruth Hines, Capital                        58746.45
       410          Sales                                       3948.26
                                             --------------    --------------
                    TOTALS                    126675.87         126675.87
                                             ==============    ==============
```

Figure 8.23   Trial Balance (Problem 8-S)

Name _____

Class _____ Date _____

CHAPTER 8
STUDENT EXERCISE

I. Matching   For each of the following definitions, write the letter of the term which best fits that definition in the space provided.

a. Sales on account
b. Customer file maintenance
c. Cash receipts report
d. Sales on account report
e. Schedule of accounts receivable

f. Cash receipt
g. Customer list
h. General ledger posting summary
i. Customer statement
j. Sales invoice number

1. _____ A number assigned to each sale on account for the purpose of identification. (Obj. 11)

2. _____ The process of adding, changing, or deleting customer data. (Obj. 1)

3. _____ Accounts receivable transactions involving the sale of merchandise or services for which the customer will pay in the future. (Obj. 4)

4. _____ An accounts receivable transaction that indicates payment on account has been received. (Obj. 4)

5. _____ A report which shows in summary form all journal entries which are automatically generated and posted to the general ledger *only* from the current batch of accounts receivable transactions. (Obj. 7)

6. _____ A report which shows the customer data and which is used to verify customer file maintenance data that has been entered into the Accounts Receivable System. (Obj. 2)

7. _____ A report which lists all transactions in which cash has been received and applied to open items in the accounts receivable data file. (Obj. 6)

8. _____ A report which shows the customer number and name, invoice number, date, and amount of each outstanding sales invoice or open accounts receivable item for that customer. (Obj. 9)

9. _____ A report which lists all transactions, by batch, for which cash is to be received. (Obj. 5)

10. _____ A report which lists all outstanding or open sales invoices by customer, the total amount due from each customer, and the total amount due from all customers. (Obj. 8)

II. Short Answer

1. Explain the purpose of the general ledger account number on the Accounts Receivable input form. (Obj. 11)

_____

_____

_____

2. Explain the Accounts Receivable System/General Ledger System integration process in the following situations: (Obj. 11)

   A new sales transaction is entered. _____

   _____

   A cash receipt is entered. _____

   _____

3. Why must the *Save Data to Disk* be the last option selected prior to shutting down the computer system or selecting another file from disk? (Obj. 10)

   _____

   _____

   _____

   _____

4. Identify the procedures used by this automated accounting system to perform accounts receivable processing. (Obj. 11)

   _____

   _____

   _____

   _____

   _____

   _____

ACCOUNTS RECEIVABLE TRANSACTIONS AND REPORTS TRANSACTION PROBLEM 8-1

Problem 8-1 is a continuation of the Chapter 8 sample problem. The sample problem contained the accounts receivable transactions for the first half of March. Problem 8-1 contains the accounts receivable transactions for the second half of March. Therefore, if you did not complete the sample problem, you must load the opening balances for Problem 8-1 from disk. (Obj. 1-11)

Instructions

Step   1   Remove the blank input forms and the Chapter 8 Audit Test at the end of this chapter. Complete the questions on the audit test as you work through the following steps.

Step   2   The following accounts receivable transactions for Hardware Plus occurred during the last half of March. Record the transactions on the proper input forms.

March 16   Received cash on account from the Dakota County Inquirer, $286.20, covering Sales Invoice No. 454 (Customer Check No. 1487).

19   Sold merchandise on account to Sounds Around, Inc., $465.18, plus 6 percent sales tax (Sales Invoice No. 456).

20   Received cash on account from Marsha's Auto Repair, $76.32, covering Sales Invoice No. 452 (Customer Check No. 769).

21   Received cash on account from Sounds Around, Inc., $1,219.00, covering Sales Invoice No. 438 (Customer Check No. 2560).

21   Received cash on account from Sounds Around, Inc., $50.88, covering Sales Invoice No. 450 (Customer Check No. 2566).

23   Sold merchandise on account to Robert Fox, $251.70, plus 6 percent sales tax (Sales Invoice No. 457).

26   Sold merchandise on account to Dakota County Inquirer, $500.00, plus 6 percent sales tax (Sales Invoice No. 458).

27   Sold merchandise on account to Southtown TV Repair (Customer No. 120), $1,338.54, plus 6 percent sales tax (Sales Invoice No. 459).

29   Sold merchandise on account to Linda's Fitness Center, $285.00, plus 6 percent sales tax (Sales Invoice No. 460).

30   Received cash on account from Linda's Fitness Center, $106.53, covering Sales Invoice No. 449 (Customer Check No. 1052).

31   Changed the name of Paddock Realty Co. to Key City Realty Co.

Step   3   Bring up the System Selection Menu.

Step   4   If you did not complete the sample problem, select the *Load Data from*

Disk option, select *Load Opening Balances from the Program Disk*, and choose Problem 8-1 by key-entering the file name **AA8-1** when the directory list appears. If you did complete Problem 8-S, load the data from your work in progress file.

Step 5   Set the run date to **March 31** of the current year. Set the problem number to **Problem 8-1**.

Step 6   Select the *Accounts Receivable* option from the System Selection Menu.

Step 7   Key-enter and record the customer file maintenance transactions from the Accounts Receivable File Maintenance input form.

Step 8   Display or print a customer list and verify the entries key-entered in Step 6.

Step 9   Set the batch number to **6**.

Step 10   Key-enter and post the sales and cash receipts transactions from the Accounts Receivable input form.

Step 11   Display or print the Sales on Account report and check the computer total against the total on your input form.

Step 12   Display or print the Cash Receipts report and check the computer total against the total on your input form.

Step 13   Verify that the data key-entered is correct. If errors are found, make the necessary corrections and print new Sales on Account and Cash Receipts reports.

Step 14   Display or print a general ledger posting summary.

Step 15   Display or print a schedule of accounts receivable.

Step 16   Display or print the customer statements.

Step 17   Return to System Selection Menu.

Step 18   Select the *General Ledger* option from the System Selection Menu.

Step 19   Display or print a trial balance. The Accounts Receivable account balance should be the same as the final total on the schedule of accounts receivable prepared in Step 15.

Step 20   Return to the System Selection Menu.

Step 21   Save your work as a work in progress file (recommend file name **AA8-1**). Then shut down the computer.

Step 22   Hand in your completed student exercise sheets, input forms, the audit test, and any printouts to your instructor.

You have now completed the computer exercise for Chapter 8.

Name _____

Class _____ Date _____

	ACCOUNTS RECEIVABLE FILE MAINTENANCE Input Form	Problem No. _____
RUN DATE __/__/__ MM DD YY		FORM AR-1

	1		2	
	CUSTOMER NUMBER		CUSTOMER NAME	
1				1
2				2
3				3
4				4
5				5
6				6
7				7
8				8
9				9
10				10
11				11
12				12
13				13
14				14
15				15
16				16
17				17
18				18
19				19
20				20
21				21
22				22
23				23
24				24
25				25

Part 3   Accounts Receivable

ACCOUNTS RECEIVABLE
Input Form

RUN DATE ___/___/___
MM DD YY

BATCH NO. [ ]

Problem No. _____

FORM AR-2

	1	2	3	4	5	6	7	8	9	
	SALES INVOICE NO.	SALES					CASH RECEIPTS			
		CUST. NO.	DATE MO. DAY YR.	GEN. LEDGER ACCT. NO.	INVOICE AMOUNT	SALES TAX %	DATE MO. DAY YR.	DOC. NO.	CASH RECEIVED	
1										1
2										2
3										3
4										4
5										5
6										6
7										7
8										8
9										9
10										10
11										11
12										12
13										13
14										14
15										15
16										16
17										17
18										18
19										19
20										20
21										21
22										22
23										23
24										24
25										25

BATCH TOTALS [ ]   [ ]

Name _____

Class _____ Date _____

CHAPTER 8
AUDIT TEST

1. What is the new name of Customer No. 090?

   _____

2. What is the gross amount of Sales Invoice No. 456?

   _____

3. What is the amount of the sales tax for Sales Invoice No. 458?

   _____

4. What were the total sales on account for the last half of March?

   _____

5. What was the amount of cash received in payment of Sales Invoice No. 449?

   _____

6. What was the total cash received on account during the last half of March?

   _____

7. What was the net amount of change in the Accounts Receivable account as a result of the accounts receivable transactions during the period of March 15 through March 31?

   _____

8. What are the numbers of the unpaid sales invoices for Linda's Fitness Center on March 31?

   _____

9. What is the total amount owed to Hardware Plus by Harmon Furniture Co. on March 31?

   _____

10. What is the total amount owed to Hardware Plus by all customers on March 31?

    _____

Part 4

ADVANCED ACCOUNTS PAYABLE AND ACCOUNTS RECEIVABLE

9 DISCOUNTS, DEBIT MEMORANDUMS, AND CREDIT MEMORANDUMS (EXPANDED VERSION)

LEARNING OBJECTIVES

Upon completion of this chapter, you will be able to:

1. Record and process purchases discounts.
2. Record and process debit memorandums.
3. Record and process sales discounts.
4. Record and process credit memorandums.
5. Complete the accounting cycle using all three integrated accounting systems (the General Ledger, Accounts Payable, and Accounts Receivable Systems).

INTRODUCTION

In this chapter, you will learn how purchases discounts and debit memorandums are processed through the Accounts Payable System and how sales discounts and credit memorandums are processed through the Accounts Receivable System. In addition, you will learn how to complete the accounting cycle by processing transactions using all three integrated systems (the General Ledger, Accounts Payable, and Accounts Receivable Systems). In the previous chapters, you have learned how to complete the accounting cycle for each of these systems individually. For example, you first worked with the General Ledger System, then the General Ledger and Accounts Payable Systems, and finally the General Ledger and Accounts Receivable Systems. The procedure followed in *Automated Accounting for the Microcomputer* to integrate the three systems together (with discount, debit memorandum, and credit memorandum transactions) is illustrated in Figure 9.1.

The various transactions that occur during the month must be recorded on the appropriate input forms. The table in Figure 9.2 shows the form on which each type of transaction is recorded.

Four major steps must be performed in order to complete the accounting cycle using all three integrated systems and their reporting capabilities. First, the General Ledger System is selected, and the general ledger file maintenance and general ledger journal entries are key-entered into the computer. Second, the Accounts Payable System is selected, and the vendor file maintenance, purchases, cash payments, and debit memorandum transactions are key-entered into the computer. Third, the Accounts Receivable System is selected, and the customer file maintenance, sales, cash receipts, and credit memorandum transactions are key-entered into the computer. Finally, the Gen-

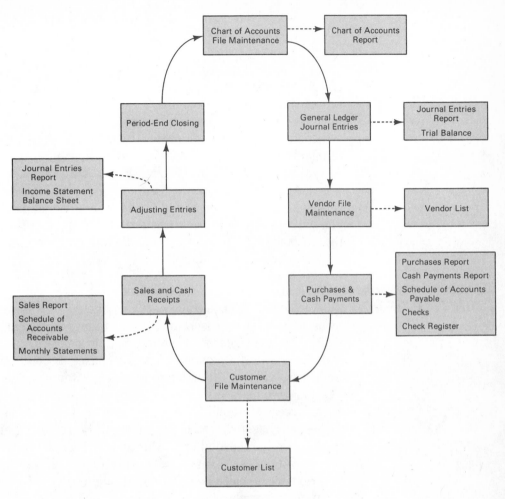

Figure 9.1   General Ledger, Accounts Payable, and Accounts Receivable
Transaction Processing Procedure

TYPE OF TRANSACTION	INPUT FORM
Additions, Changes, & Deletions to the Chart of Accounts	General Ledger File Maintenance Input Form (Form GL-1)
General Ledger Journal Entries	General Ledger Input Form (Form GL-2)
Additions, Changes, & Deletions to Vendor Data	Accounts Payable File Maintenance Input Form (Form AP-1)
Purchases, Purchases Discounts, Cash Payments, & Debit Memorandums	Accounts Payable Input Form (Form AP-3)
Additions, Changes, & Deletions to Customer Data	Accounts Receivable File Maintenance Input Form (Form AR-1)
Sales, Sales Discounts, Cash Receipts, & Credit Memorandums	Accounts Receivable Input Form (Form AR-3)
Adjusting Entries	General Ledger Input Form (Form GL-2)

Figure 9.2   Input Form Used for Each Type of Transaction

eral Ledger System is selected again. Adjusting entries are key-entered into the computer, the financial statements are printed or displayed, and the period-end closing is performed.

COMPLETING THE INPUT FORMS

As shown in Figure 9.2, purchases discounts and debit memorandums are recorded on an Accounts Payable input form (Form AP-3). This form is identical to Form AP-2 except that a Debit Memos section and a Discount Percent column have been added to record additional data. Similarly, sales discounts and credit memorandums are recorded on an Accounts Receivable input form (Form AR-3). This form is identical to Form AR-2 except that a Credit Memos section and a Discount Percent column have been added to record additional data. In this chapter, you will learn how these forms are used to record the data required by the computer to process discounts, debit memorandums, and credit memorandums.

Accounts Payable Input Form (Form AP-3)

Buyers are often given a deduction on the invoice amount of credit sales in order to encourage early payment. This deduction is referred to as a **purchases discount.** If the purchase invoice amount is paid within the time period specified on the invoice, the discount may be deducted from the payment. The purchases discount is recorded on the Accounts Payable input form as a percentage of the invoice amount. The percentage is recorded in decimal format (for instance, 5 1/2 percent is recorded as 5.50, and 6 percent is recorded as 6).

The purchases discount percent may be recorded either at the time the invoice is recorded or at the time of the cash payment. To be consistent with most manual accounting texts, all purchases discounts in this text-workbook are recorded at the time the invoice is paid.

Buyers may also be granted credit for returned or damaged merchandise. Since this type of transaction results in a deduction from the accounts payable account, it is referred to as a **debit memorandum**. In this automated accounting system, the debit memorandum is applied to the original purchase invoice unless it has already been paid. If the invoice has been paid, the debit memorandum is applied to the oldest unpaid purchase invoice for that vendor. To record a debit memorandum on the Accounts Payable input form (Form AP-3), the following information must be recorded: (1) the purchase invoice number, (2) the debit memo date, (3) the debit memorandum number (in the Memo Number column), and (4) the debit memorandum amount. The Accounts Payable input form in Figure 9.3 contains three transactions involving purchases discounts and debit memorandums.

The first transaction is a purchase of merchandise on account involving a purchases discount.

October 1, 19--
Purchased merchandise on account from DataPro Paper Supply, $13,500.00, Vendor No. 010 (Purchase Invoice No. 560).

The entry to record this transaction is shown on line 1 of the input form in Figure 9.3.

The second transaction is an example of a purchase invoice which is released for payment after the discount period.

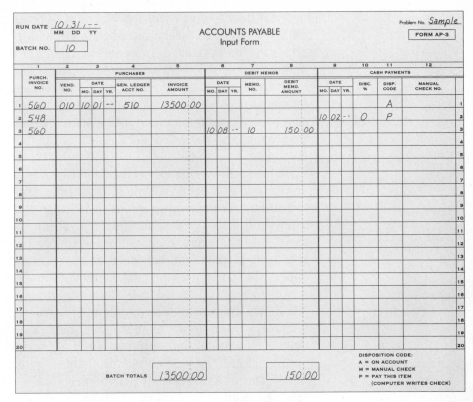

Figure 9.3   Accounts Payable Input Form Showing Purchases Discount and Debit Memorandum Transactions

October 2, 19--
Released Purchase Invoice No. 548 to Vendor No. 040 for payment, no discount.

The entry to record this transaction is shown on line 2 of the input form. Because this purchase invoice was not paid within the discount period, the discount percentage is recorded with a zero to inform the computer that no discount is to be deducted. If this purchase invoice had been paid within the discount period, the discount percent would have been recorded.

The third transaction is a debit memorandum which applies to a previous unpaid purchase invoice.

October 8, 19--
DataPro Paper Supply granted us credit for damaged merchandise, $150.00 (Purchase Invoice No. 560, Debit Memorandum No. 10).

The entry to record this transaction is shown on line 3 of the input form. Note that only the purchase invoice number, debit memorandum date, debit memo number, and debit memorandum amount are required. The rest of the information is not required because this debit memorandum applies to a previously recorded unpaid purchase invoice.

Accounts Receivable Input Form (Form AR-3)   Businesses often give customers a deduction on the invoice amount of sales on account in order to encourage early payment. This deduction is referred to as a **sales discount.** If the sales invoice amount is paid within the time period specified on the invoice, the customer may deduct the discount from the payment. The sales discount is recorded on the Accounts Receivable input form as a percentage of the invoice amount. The percent is recorded in decimal format (for instance, 5 1/2 percent is recorded as 5.50, and 6 percent is recorded as 6).

The sales discount percent may be recorded either at the time the invoice is recorded or later at the time of the cash receipt. To be consistent with most manual accounting texts, all sales discounts in this text-workbook are recorded at the time the cash is received from the customer.

Businesses may grant credit to customers for returned or damaged merchandise. Since this type of transaction results in a deduction from the accounts receivable account, it is referred to as a **credit memorandum**. In this automated accounting system, the credit memorandum is applied to the original sales invoice unless payment has already been received. If payment has been received, the credit memorandum is applied to the oldest open sales invoice for that customer. To record a credit memorandum on the Accounts Receivable input form (Form AR-3), the following information must be recorded: (1) the sales invoice number, (2) the credit memorandum date, (3) the credit memorandum number (in the Memo Number column), and (4) the credit memorandum amount. The Accounts Receivable input form in Figure 9.4 contains three transactions involving sales discounts and credit memorandums.

The first transaction is a sale of merchandise on account involving a sales discount.

RUN DATE 10 / 31 / -- (MM DD YY) Problem No. Sample

ACCOUNTS RECEIVABLE
Input Form

FORM AR-3

BATCH NO. 10

	1	2	3			4	5	6	7			8	9	10			11	12	13	
	SALES INVOICE NO.	SALES							CREDIT MEMOS					CASH RECEIPTS						
		CUST. NO.	DATE			GEN. LEDGER ACCT. NO.	INVOICE AMOUNT	SALES TAX %	DATE			MEMO. NO.	CREDIT MEMO. AMOUNT	DATE			DOC. NO.	DISC. %	CASH RECEIVED	
			MO.	DAY	YR.				MO.	DAY	YR.			MO.	DAY	YR.				
1	780	010	10	04	--	410	1160 50	6												1
2	746													10	05	--	1597	0	2963 87	2
3	780								10	10	--	92	110 00							3
4																				4
5																				5
6																				6
7																				7
8																				8
9																				9
10																				10
11																				11
12																				12
13																				13
14																				14
15																				15
16																				16
17																				17
18																				18
19																				19
20																				20
						BATCH TOTALS	1160 50						110 00						2963 87	

Figure 9.4 Accounts Receivable Input Form Showing Sales Discount and Credit Memorandum Transactions

October 4, 19--

Sold merchandise on account to Dakota County Inquirer, $1,160.50, plus 6 percent sales tax, Customer No. 010 (Sales Invoice No. 780).

The entry to record this transaction is shown on line 1 of the input form in Figure 9.4.

The second transaction is an example of a cash receipt on account which was received after the discount period.

October 5, 19--

Received cash on account from Customer No. 060, $2,963.87, covering Sales Invoice No. 746, no discount (Customer Check No. 1597).

The entry to record this transaction is shown on line 2 of the input form. Because the cash was not received within the discount period, the discount percentage is recorded with a zero to inform the computer that no discount is to be granted. If the cash had been received within the discount period, the discount percent would have been recorded.

The third transaction is a credit memorandum which applies to a previously recorded unpaid sales invoice.

October 10, 19--

Issued credit memorandum to Universal Insurance, $110.00, for merchandise returned (Sales Invoice No. 780, Credit Memorandum No. 92).

The entry to record this transaction is shown on line 3 of the input form. Note that only the sales invoice number, credit memorandum date, credit memo number, and credit memorandum amount are required. The rest of the information is not required because this credit memorandum applies to an existing unpaid sales invoice.

ACCOUNTS PAYABLE AND ACCOUNTS RECEIVABLE INTEGRATION

As accounts payable and accounts receivable transactions are entered or corrected, the journal entries resulting from those transactions are automatically integrated into the General Ledger System by the computer. To integrate these entries, the computer must know the account numbers you have assigned to the general ledger accounts involved. You must provide the computer with these control account numbers by entering them using the *Set Control Accounts* option of both the Accounts Payable Main Menu and the Accounts Receivable Main Menu. The additional accounts required in order to process purchases discounts, sales discounts, credit memorandums, and debit memorandums are: (1) Sales Discounts, (2) Purchases Discounts, (3) Sales Returns & Allowances, and (4) Purchases Returns & Allowances. The expanded chart of accounts for Hardware Plus shown in Figure 9.5 includes these additional accounts.

In the Accounts Payable System, the control account numbers for Accounts Payable, Purchases Discount, and Purchases Returns & Allowances must be provided. The account number to be debited is provided at the time a purchase invoice is entered. When a new purchase invoice is key-entered into the computer, the computer will (1) debit the account number which is entered as part of the transaction and (2) credit the vendor's account and Accounts Payable in the general ledger. When a purchase invoice is released for payment, the com-

Acct No.	Account Title
ASSETS	
110	Cash
120	Accounts Receivable
130	Merchandise Inventory
140	Supplies
150	Prepaid Insurance
LIABILITIES	
210	Accounts Payable
220	Sales Tax Payable
CAPITAL	
310	Dennis Siegel, Capital
320	Dennis Siegel, Drawing
330	Ruth Hines, Capital
340	Ruth Hines, Drawing
350	Income Summary
REVENUE	
410	Sales
420	Sales Discounts
430	Sales Returns & Allowances
COST OF MERCHANDISE	
510	Purchases
520	Purchases Discounts
530	Purchases Returns & Allowances
EXPENSES	
605	Delivery Expense
610	Insurance Expense
620	Legal & Professional Fees Expense
630	Miscellaneous Expense
640	Rent Expense
650	Salary Expense
660	Supplies Expense

Figure 9.5   Hardware Plus Expanded Chart of Accounts

puter will (1) debit the vendor's account and Accounts Payable, (2) credit Cash, and (3) credit Purchases Discounts (if there is a cash discount). If a debit memorandum is entered, the computer will: (1) debit the vendor's account and Accounts Payable and (2) credit Purchases Returns & Allowances. (If a Purchases Returns and Allowances account is not used, then the Purchases account will be credited.) If a correction is necessary, the computer will automatically remove the incorrect data and replace it with the correct data you key-enter.

In the Accounts Receivable System, the control account numbers for Accounts Receivable, Sales Discounts, Sales Returns & Allowances, and Sales Tax Payable must be provided. The account number for Sales is provided at the time a sales invoice is entered. When a sales invoice is key-entered into the computer, the computer will: (1) debit the customer's account and Accounts Receivable in the general ledger,

(2) credit the sales account entered as part of the transaction, and (3) credit Sales Tax Payable. When cash is received, the computer will: (1) debit Cash, (2) debit Sales Discounts, and (3) credit the customer's account and Accounts Receivable. If a credit memorandum is entered, the computer will: (1) debit Sales Returns & Allowances, (2) debit Sales Tax Payable, and (3) credit the customer's account and Accounts Receivable. If a correction is necessary, the computer will automatically remove the incorrect data and replace it with the correct data you key-enter.

EXPANDED ACCOUNTS PAYABLE AND ACCOUNTS RECEIVABLE OPERATIONAL PROCEDURES

Once the transactions have been recorded on the Accounts Payable and Accounts Receivable input forms, they must be key-entered into the computer. Various reports may then be printed or displayed in order to complete the accounting cycle for the fiscal period. Since most of the operational procedures for processing transactions through the Accounts Payable and Accounts Receivable Systems have been covered in earlier chapters, this section will cover only those procedures that are unique to discounts, debit memorandums, and credit memorandums.

Accounting System Setup Option B (System Selection Menu)

Option B of the System Selection Menu, *Accounting System Setup*, allows you to choose between the simplified and expanded versions of the General Ledger, Accounts Payable and Accounts Receivable Systems. In order for the computer to process discounts, debit memorandums, and credit memorandums, Accounts Payable and Accounts Receivable must be set to **E** (for expanded version), as illustrated in Figure 9.6.

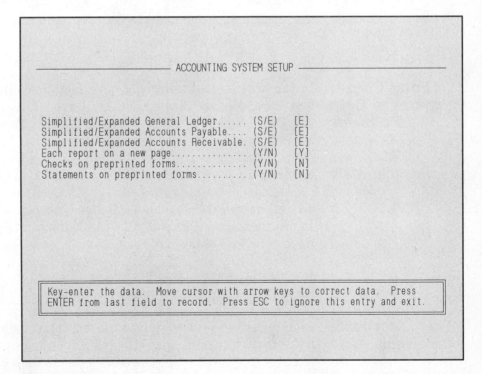

Figure 9.6   Accounting System Setup Data Entry Screen for Expanded General Ledger, Accounts Payable and Accounts Receivable Systems

Set Control Accounts Option C (Accounts Payable Main Menu)

In order to process purchases discounts and debit memorandums, the computer must know the account numbers assigned to Accounts Payable, Purchases Discounts, and Purchases Returns & Allowances. These control account numbers are required by the computer to perform the integration with the General Ledger System. The Accounts Payable Set Control Accounts data entry screen is shown in Figure 9.7.

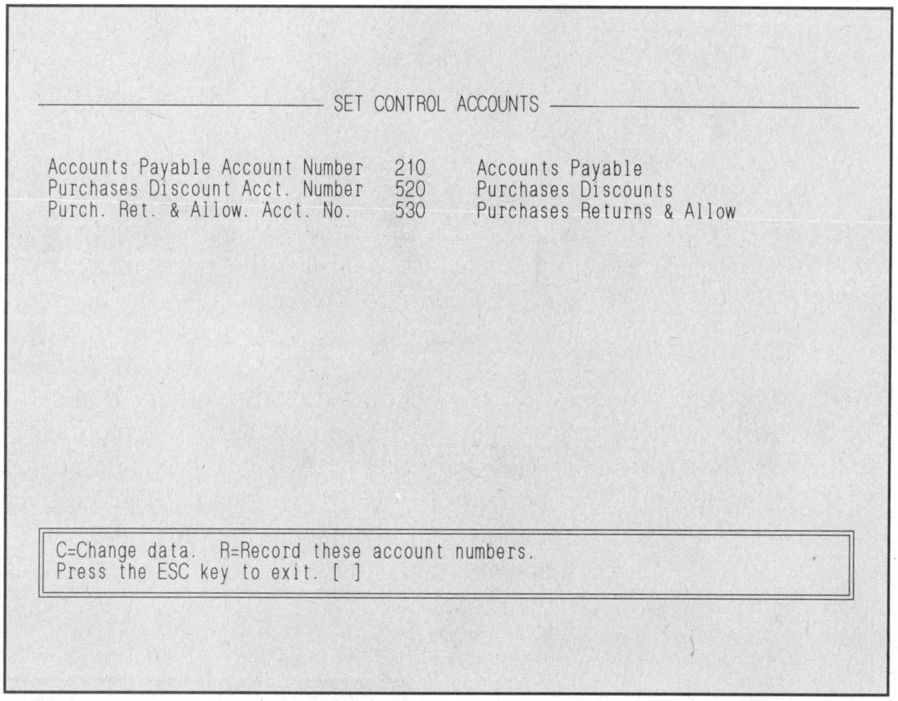

```
┌──────────────────────────────────────────────────────────────────┐
│                                                                    │
│                                                                    │
│                                                                    │
│  ──────────────────── SET CONTROL ACCOUNTS ─────────────────────   │
│                                                                    │
│   Accounts Payable Account Number   210    Accounts Payable        │
│   Purchases Discount Acct. Number   520    Purchases Discounts     │
│   Purch. Ret. & Allow. Acct. No.    530    Purchases Returns & Allow│
│                                                                    │
│                                                                    │
│                                                                    │
│                                                                    │
│                                                                    │
│                                                                    │
│                                                                    │
│                                                                    │
│  ┌──────────────────────────────────────────────────────────┐    │
│  │ C=Change data.  R=Record these account numbers.           │    │
│  │ Press the ESC key to exit. [ ]                             │    │
│  └──────────────────────────────────────────────────────────┘    │
│                                                                    │
└──────────────────────────────────────────────────────────────────┘
```

Figure 9.7   Set Control Accounts Data Entry Screen for the Expanded Accounts Payable System

Enter/Correct Purchases & Cash Payments Option J (Accounts Payable Main Menu)

In the previous chapters, you have seen and worked with the simplified version of the Enter/Correct Purchases & Cash Payments data entry screen. The expanded version of this data entry screen includes an additional Debit Memo Information section for the following fields: *Debit Memo Date*, *Debit Memo Number*, and *Debit Memo Amount*. In addition, a *Discount Percent* field is included in the Payment Information section of the data entry screen. Data entered into these fields will also appear on the Accounts Payable Transaction reports. Figure 9.8 shows the expanded version of the Enter/Correct Purchases & Cash Payments data entry screen.

Set Control Accounts Option C (Accounts Receivable Main Menu)

In order to process sales discounts and credit memorandums, the computer must know the account numbers assigned to Accounts Receivable, Sales Tax Payable, Sales Discounts, and Sales Returns & Allowances. These control account numbers are required by the computer to perform the integration with the General Ledger System. The Accounts Receivable Set Control Accounts data entry screen is shown in Figure 9.9.

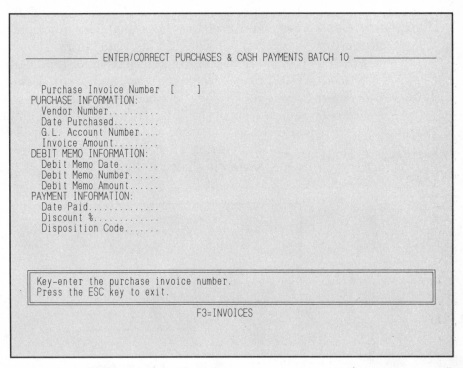

Figure 9.8   Expanded Enter/Correct Purchases & Cash Payments Data Entry Screen

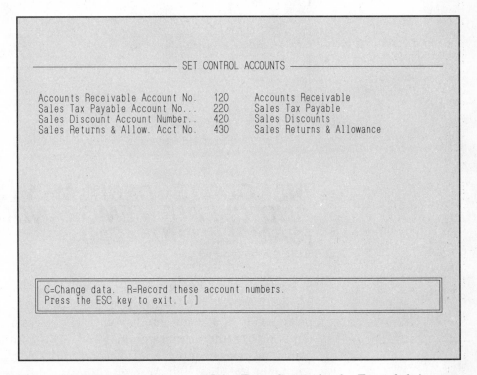

Figure 9.9   Set Control Accounts Data Entry Screen for the Expanded Accounts Receivable System

Enter/Correct
Sales and Cash
Receipts
Option I
(Accounts
Receivable Main
Menu)

In the previous chapters, you have seen and worked with the simplified version of the Sales and Cash Receipts data entry screen. The expanded version of this data entry screen includes an additional Credit Memo Information section for the following fields: *Credit Memo Date, Credit Memo Number,* and *Credit Memo Amount*. In addition, a *Discount Percent* field has been included in the Cash Receipt Information section of the data entry screen. Data entered into these fields will also appear on the Accounts Receivable Transaction reports. The expanded version of the Enter/Correct Sales and Cash Receipts data entry screen is shown in Figure 9.10.

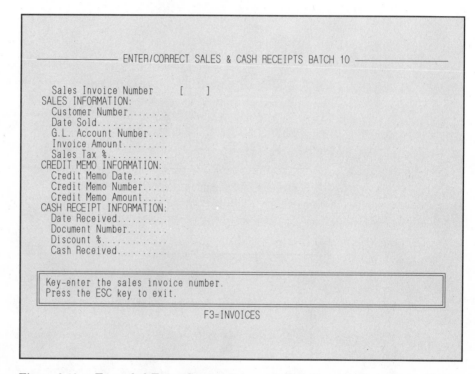

Figure 9.10   Expanded Enter/Correct Sales and Cash Receipts Data Entry Screen

DISCOUNTS, DEBIT MEMORANDUMS, AND CREDIT MEMORANDUMS (SAMPLE PROBLEM)

The sample problem which follows will take you through the complete accounting cycle for Hardware Plus. The purpose of this problem is to permit you to become familiar with (1) discounts, (2) debit memorandums, (3) credit memorandums, and (4) a complete accounting cycle using all three integrated accounting systems (General Ledger, Accounts Payable, and Accounts Receivable).

The chart of accounts, vendors, customers, and opening balances for Hardware Plus as discussed and prepared in the previous chapters have been stored on disk under the file name **AA9-S**. The following sections provide step-by-step procedures for completing the accounting cycle for the fiscal period ending October 31 of the current year.

Instructions

Step   1   The following transactions for Hardware Plus occurred during October of the current year. The necessary changes in general ledger, accounts payable, and accounts receivable account titles and numbers have been recorded on the appropriate file maintenance input forms (Figures 9.11, 9.12, and 9.13). The transactions have been analyzed and recorded as Batch No. 19 on the General Ledger input form (Figure 9.14), as Batch No. 10 on the Accounts Payable input form (Figure 9.15), and Batch No. 10 on the Accounts Receivable input form (Figure 9.16). These six figures are shown below and on the following pages.

	ACCOUNT NUMBER	ACCOUNT TITLE	
1	650	D	1
2	601	Advertising Expense	2
3			3
4			4
5			5
6			6
7			7
8			8
9			9
10			10
11			11
12			12
13			13
14			14
15			15
16			16
17			17
18			18
19			19
20			20
21			21
22			22
23			23
24			24
25			25

RUN DATE 10/31/-- (MM DD YY)

GENERAL LEDGER FILE MAINTENANCE Input Form

Problem No. 9-S   FORM GL-1

Figure 9.11   General Ledger File Mainentance Input Form (Problem 9-S)

Oct 01   Purchased merchandise on account from DataPro Paper Supply, $13,500.00 (Purchase Invoice No. 560).

02   Released Purchase Invoice No. 548 to Computer Distribution Co. for payment, 2 percent discount to be taken.

	VENDOR NUMBER	VENDOR NAME	
	1	2	
1	170	*Digital Discount Depot*	1
2	090	*D*	2
3			3
4			4
5			5
6			6
7			7
8			8
9			9
10			10
11			11
12			12
13			13
14			14
15			15
16			16
17			17
18			18
19			19
20			20
21			21
22			22
23			23
24			24
25			25

ACCOUNTS PAYABLE
FILE MAINTENANCE
Input Form

RUN DATE 10 / 31 / -- MM DD YY

Problem No. 9-S

FORM AP-1

Figure 9.12   Accounts Payable File Mainentance Input Form (Problem 9-S)

03   Released Purchase Invoice No. 550 to Computer Executive Ltd. for payment, no discount.

04   Sold merchandise on account to Dakota County Inquirer, $1,160.50, plus 6 percent sales tax (Sales Invoice No. 780).

05   Received cash on account from Greenthumb Florists, Inc., $2,963.87, covering Sales Invoice No. 746, no discount (Customer Check No. 1597).

08   DataPro Paper Supply granted us credit for damaged merchandise, $150.00 (Purchase Invoice No. 560, Debit Memorandum No. 10).

08   Deleted the account titled *Salary Expense* (Account No. 650) from the chart of accounts.

08   Sold merchandise on account to Greenthumb Florists, Inc., $382.00, plus 6 percent sales tax (Sales Invoice No. 781).

09   Received cash on account from Harmon Furniture Co.,

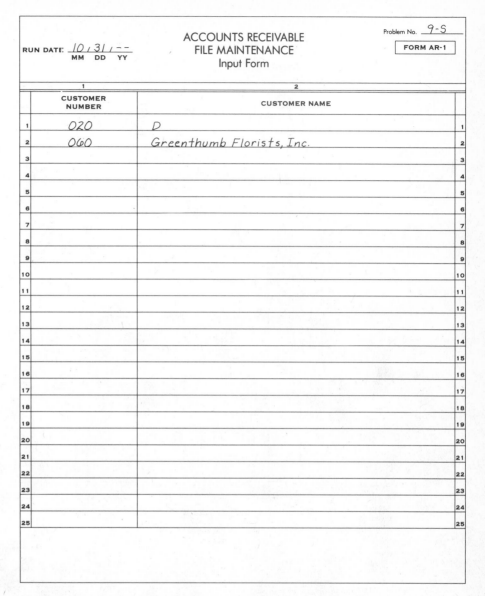

Figure 9.13   Accounts Receivable File Mainentance Input Form (Problem 9-S)

$2,960.58, covering Sales Invoice No. 750, less 2 percent discount and credit memorandum (Customer Check No. 1880).

09   Added Digital Discount Depot to the vendor list. Assigned Vendor No. 170.

10   Issued credit memorandum to Dakota County Inquirer, $110.00, for merchandise returned (Sales Invoice No. 780, Credit Memorandum No. 92).

10   Released Purchase Invoice No. 552 to Quality Ribbon Co. for payment, 2 percent discount to be taken.

13   Deleted Tri-State Telephone (Account No. 090) from the vendor master file.

14   Cash sales, $6,100.00, plus sales tax, $366.00. Total, $6,466.00 (Cash Register Tape No. 15).

17   Purchased merchandise on account from Digital Electronics Co., $5,605.00 (Purchase Invoice No. 561).

RUN DATE _10 , 31 , - -_
MM   DD   YY

BATCH NO. ___19___

GENERAL LEDGER
Input Form

Problem No. _9-S_

FORM GL-2

	DAY	DOC. NO.	ACCOUNT NUMBER	DEBIT AMOUNT	CREDIT AMOUNT	
1	14	T15	110	6466 00		1
2			220		366 00	2
3			410		6100 00	3
4	28	T16	110	7314 00		4
5			220		414 00	5
6			410		6900 00	6
7						7
8						8
9						9
10						10
11						11
12						12
13						13
14						14
15						15
16						16
17						17
18						18
19						19
20						20
21						21
22						22
23						23
24						24
25						25

BATCH TOTALS   13780 00   13780 00

Figure 9.14   General Ledger Input Form (Problem 9-S)

18   Sold merchandise on account to Harmon Furniture Co., $6,500.00, plus 6 percent sales tax (Sales Invoice No. 782).

19   Recorded Purchase Invoice No. 562 to A & K Advertising Co. for advertising, $370.50. Released this purchase invoice for payment, no discount.

Advertising Expense is recorded on the General Ledger File Maintenance input form as Account No. 601. Purchase Invoice No. 562 is recorded as a payment for advertising expense.

20   Recorded Purchase Invoice No. 563 to Etter and Panozza for legal services, $116.98. Released this purchase invoice for payment, no discount.

21   Digital Electronics Co. granted us credit for merchandise returned, $200.00 (Purchase Invoice No. 561, Debit Memorandum No. 11).

ACCOUNTS PAYABLE — Input Form

RUN DATE 10/31/-- (MM DD YY)   BATCH NO. 10   Problem No. 9-S   FORM AP-3

	PURCH. INVOICE NO.	VEND. NO.	DATE MO.	DAY	YR.	GEN. LEDGER ACCT NO.	INVOICE AMOUNT	DATE MO.	DAY	YR.	MEMO. NO.	DEBIT MEMO. AMOUNT	DATE MO.	DAY	YR.	DISC. %	DISP. CODE	MANUAL CHECK NO.	
1	560	010	10	01	--	510	13500.00										A		1
2	548												10	02	--	2	P		2
3	550												10	03	--	0	P		3
4	560							10	08	--	10	150.00							4
5	552												10	10	--	2	P		5
6	561	100	10	17	--	510	5605.00										A		6
7	562	050	10	19	--	601	370.50						10	19	--	0	P		7
8	563	160	10	20	--	620	116.98						10	20	--	0	P		8
9	561							10	21	--	11	200.00							9
10	564	110	10	24	--	640	1150.00						10	24	--	0	P		10
11	565	040	10	24	--	510	11500.00										A		11
12	566	020	10	24	--	510	285.00										A		12
13	567	070	10	25	--	150	190.00						10	25	--	0	P		13
14	568	120	10	27	--	605	200.00						10	27	--	0	P		14
15	561												10	28	--	2	P		15
16	569	130	10	31	--	320	1150.00						10	31	--	0	P		16
17	570	140	10	31	--	340	1150.00						10	31	--	0	P		17

BATCH TOTALS 35217.48   350.00

DISPOSITION CODE:
A = ON ACCOUNT
M = MANUAL CHECK
P = PAY THIS ITEM (COMPUTER WRITES CHECK)

Figure 9.15   Accounts Payable Input Form (Problem 9-S)

ACCOUNTS RECEIVABLE — Input Form

RUN DATE 10/31/-- (MM DD YY)   BATCH NO. 10   Problem No. 9-S   FORM AR-3

	SALES INVOICE NO.	CUST. NO.	DATE MO.	DAY	YR.	GEN. LEDGER ACCT. NO.	INVOICE AMOUNT	SALES TAX %	DATE MO.	DAY	YR.	MEMO. NO.	CREDIT MEMO AMOUNT	DATE MO.	DAY	YR.	DOC. NO.	DISC. %	CASH RECEIVED	
1	780	010	10	04	--	410	1160.50	6												1
2	746													10	05	--	1597	0	2963.87	2
3	781	060	10	08	--	410	382.00	6												3
4	750													10	09	--	1880	2	2960.58	4
5	780								10	10	--	92	110.00							5
6	782	070	10	18	--	410	6500.00	6												6
7	783	030	10	26	--	410	5810.69	6												7
8	784	090	10	26	--	410	402.00	6												8
9	785	010	10	26	--	410	1050.70	6												9
10	782													10	26	--	1894	2	6752.20	10

BATCH TOTALS 15305.89   110.00   12676.65

Figure 9.16   Accounts Receivable Input Form (Problem 9-S)

24   Recorded Purchase Invoice No. 564 to Park Ave. Developers for rent, $1,150.00. Released this purchase invoice for payment, no discount.

24   Purchased merchandise on account from Computer Executive Ltd., $11,500.00 (Purchase Invoice No. 565).

24   Purchased merchandise on account from Computer Distribution Co., $285.00 (Purchase Invoice No. 566).

25   Recorded Purchase Invoice No. 567 to Inntouch Marketing for insurance, $190.00. Released this purchase invoice for payment, no discount.

26   Sold merchandise on account to Superior New & Used Autos, $5,810.69, plus 6 percent sales tax (Sales Invoice No. 783).

26   Sold merchandise on account to Key City Realty Co., $402.00, plus 6 percent sales tax (Sales Invoice No. 784).

26   Sold merchandise on account to Dakota County Inquirer, $1,050.70, plus 6 percent sales tax (Sales Invoice No. 785).

26   Received cash on account from Harmon Furniture Co., $6,752.20, covering Sales Invoice No. 782, less 2 percent discount (Customer Check No. 1894).

27   Deleted Janice Meyer (Account No. 020) from the customer master file.

27   Recorded Purchase Invoice No. 568 to Rocket Delivery Service for delivery services, $200.00. Released this purchase invoice for payment, no discount.

27   Changed the customer name for Greenthumb Florists to Greenthumb Florists, Inc.

28   Released Purchase Invoice No. 561 to Digital Electronics Co. for payment, less 2 percent discount.

28   Cash sales, $6,900.00, plus sales tax, $414.00. Total, $7,314.00 (Cash Register Tape No. 16).

31   Dennis Siegel, partner, wishes to withdraw $1,150.00 for personal use (Purchase Invoice No. 569). Released this purchase invoice for payment.

31   Ruth Hines, partner, wishes to withdraw $1,150.00 for personal use (Purchase Invoice No. 570). Released this purchase invoice for payment.

Step 2   Bring up the System Selection Menu according to the instructions for your microcomputer.

Step 3   Select Option C, *Load Data from Disk*, from the System Selection Menu.

Step 4   Select Problem 9-S from the *Load Opening Balances from the Program Disk* option by key-entering **AA9-S** when the directory list appears.

Step 5   Select Option D, *Company Information*, from the System Selection Menu. Verify that the *Problem Number* field contains **Problem 9-S**, that the *Company Name* field contains **Hardware Plus**, and that the *Type of Business* field is set to **P**. If these data fields are correct, set the run date to **October 31** of the current year and proceed to Step 6. If these data fields are not correct, the wrong file has been loaded into your computer's memory, and you should therefore repeat Steps 3 and 4 above.

Step 6 Select Option F, *General Ledger*, from the System Selection Menu.

Step 7 Select Option F, *Chart of Accounts File Maintenance*, from the General Ledger Main Menu.

Step 8 Key-enter and record the general ledger file maintenance transactions from the General Ledger File Maintenance input form in Figure 9.11.

Step 9 Select Option G, *Chart of Accounts Report*, and display or print a revised chart of accounts. Verify that the data you key-entered is correct. The revised chart of accounts is shown in Figure 9.17.

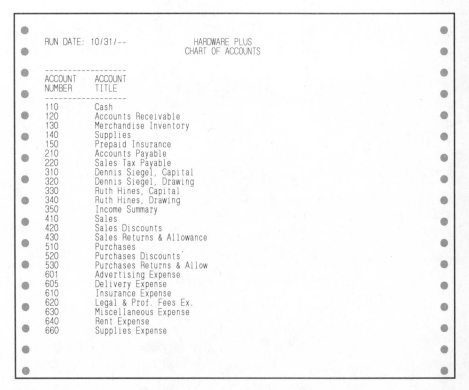

RUN DATE: 10/31/--   HARDWARE PLUS
                                      CHART OF ACCOUNTS

ACCOUNT   ACCOUNT
NUMBER   TITLE
----
110   Cash
120   Accounts Receivable
130   Merchandise Inventory
140   Supplies
150   Prepaid Insurance
210   Accounts Payable
220   Sales Tax Payable
310   Dennis Siegel, Capital
320   Dennis Siegel, Drawing
330   Ruth Hines, Capital
340   Ruth Hines, Drawing
350   Income Summary
410   Sales
420   Sales Discounts
430   Sales Returns & Allowance
510   Purchases
520   Purchases Discounts
530   Purchases Returns & Allow
601   Advertising Expense
605   Delivery Expense
610   Insurance Expense
620   Legal & Prof. Fees Ex.
630   Miscellaneous Expense
640   Rent Expense
660   Supplies Expense

Figure 9.17   Revised Chart of Accounts after File Maintenance (Problem 9-S)

Step 10 Select Option H, *Set Run Date and Batch Number*, from the General Ledger Main Menu. Verify that the run date has been set to **October 31** of the current year and that the batch number has been set to **19.** If not, make the necessary changes and strike **R** to record this data.

Step 11 Select Option I, *Enter/Correct Journal Entries*, from the General Ledger Main Menu. Key-enter and post the general ledger transactions from the General Ledger input form in Figure 9.14.

Step 12 Select Option J, *Journal Entries Report*, from the General Ledger Main Menu, and display or print a Journal Entries report. Compare your Journal Entries report with the correct one shown in Figure 9.18. The computer totals of the Debit Amount and Credit Amount columns should be the same as the calculator batch totals of these columns on the General Ledger input form. If your Journal Entries report is in error, key-enter and post the corrections, and then display or print another Journal Entries report. Repeat this step until your Journal Entries report is correct.

```
RUN DATE: 10/31/--                    HARDWARE PLUS
                                JOURNAL ENTRIES BATCH #19

----------------------------------------------------------------------------
JE#   DATE     ACCOUNT NUMBER & TITLE          DEBIT AMOUNT  CREDIT AMOUNT
----------------------------------------------------------------------------
0001  10/14/-- 110    Cash                        6466.00
               220      Sales Tax Payable                       366.00
               410      Sales                                  6100.00
               DOCUMENT: T15

0002  10/28/-- 110    Cash                        7314.00
               220      Sales Tax Payable                       414.00
               410      Sales                                  6900.00
               DOCUMENT: T16


               TOTALS                            13780.00     13780.00

               IN BALANCE

Cash Receipts        13780.00
Cash Payments             .00
```

Figure 9.18   Journal Entries Report (Problem 9-S)

Step 13   Return to the System Selection Menu.

Step 14   Select Option G, *Accounts Payable*, from the System Selection Menu.

Step 15   Select Option C, *Set Control Accounts*, from the Accounts Payable Main Menu, and verify that the control accounts are set as follows. If not, make the necessary changes and strike **R** to record this data.

Accounts Payable Account No................. 210
Purchases Discounts Account No. 520
Purchases Returns & Allowances Account No. ... 530

Step 16   Select Option G, *Vendor File Maintenance*, from the Accounts Payable Main Menu. Key-enter and record the vendor file maintenance transactions from the Accounts Payable File Maintenance input form in Figure 9.12.

Step 17   Select Option H, *Vendor List*, and display or print a revised vendor list. Verify that the data you key-entered is correct. The revised vendor list is shown in Figure 9.19.

Step 18   Select Option I, *Set Run Date and Batch Number*, from the Accounts Payable Main Menu. Verify that the run date has been set to **October 31** of the current year and that the batch number has been set to **10**. If not, make the necessary changes and strike **R** to record this data.

Step 19   Select Option J, *Enter/Correct Purchases & Cash Payments*, from the

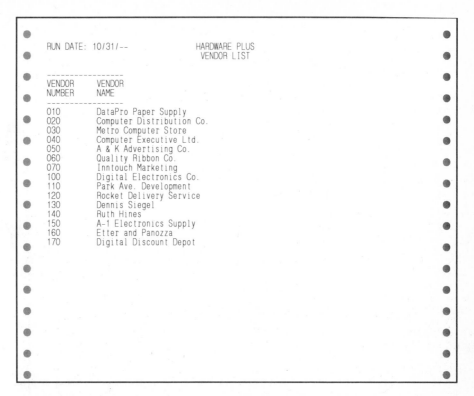

```
RUN DATE: 10/31/--              HARDWARE PLUS
                                VENDOR LIST

   ------------------
   VENDOR   VENDOR
   NUMBER   NAME
   ------------------
   010      DataPro Paper Supply
   020      Computer Distribution Co.
   030      Metro Computer Store
   040      Computer Executive Ltd.
   050      A & K Advertising Co.
   060      Quality Ribbon Co.
   070      Inntouch Marketing
   100      Digital Electronics Co.
   110      Park Ave. Development
   120      Rocket Delivery Service
   130      Dennis Siegel
   140      Ruth Hines
   150      A-1 Electronics Supply
   160      Etter and Panozza
   170      Digital Discount Depot
```

Figure 9.19   Revised Vendor List after File Maintenance (Problem 9-S)

Accounts Payable Main Menu. Key-enter and post the purchases and cash payments transactions from the Accounts Payable input form in Figure 9.15.

Step 20   Select Option K, *Purchases on Account Report*, from the Accounts Payable Main Menu. Display or print a Purchases on Account report. Compare your Purchases on Account report with the correct one shown in Figure 9.20. The computer total of the Amount column should be the same as the calculator batch total of the Invoice Amount column on the Accounts Payable input form. If your Purchases on Account report is in error, key-enter and post the corrections, and then display or print another Purchases on Account report. Repeat this step until your Purchases on Account report is correct.

Step 21   Select Option L, *Cash Payments Report*, from the Accounts Payable Main Menu. Display or print a Cash Payments report. Compare your Cash Payments report with the correct one shown in Figure 9.21. If your Cash Payments report is in error, key-enter and post the corrections, and then display or print another Cash Payments report. Repeat this step until your Cash Payments report is correct.

Step 22   Select Option M, *General Ledger Posting Summary*, and display or print a general ledger posting summary. The correct general ledger posting summary is shown in Figure 9.22 (page 279).

Step 23   Select Option N, *Schedule of Accounts Payable*, and display or print a schedule of accounts payable. The correct schedule of accounts payable is shown in Figure 9.23 (page 279).

```
RUN DATE: 10/31/--                    HARDWARE PLUS
                           PURCHASES ON ACCOUNT BATCH #10

--------------------------------------------------------------
VENDOR                         PURCH.      G.L.
NO. NAME                       INV. DATE   ACCOUNT    AMOUNT
--------------------------------------------------------------
010 DataPro Paper Supply       560  10/01/--  510     13500.00
100 Digital Electronics Co.    561  10/17/--  510      5605.00
050 A & K Advertising Co.      562  10/19/--  601       370.50
160 Etter and Panozza          563  10/20/--  620       116.98
110 Park Ave. Development       564  10/24/--  640      1150.00
040 Computer Executive Ltd.    565  10/24/--  510     11500.00
020 Computer Distribution Co.  566  10/24/--  510       285.00
070 Inntouch Marketing         567  10/25/--  150       190.00
120 Rocket Delivery Service    568  10/27/--  605       200.00
130 Dennis Siegel              569  10/31/--  320      1150.00
140 Ruth Hines                 570  10/31/--  340      1150.00

    TOTALS                                           35217.48
                                                    ==========
```

Figure 9.20   Purchases on Account Report for Batch No. 10 (Problem 9-S)

```
RUN DATE: 10/31/--                    HARDWARE PLUS
                            CASH PAYMENTS BATCH #10

------------------------------------------------------------------------
VENDOR                      INVOICE                            DOC. MAN.
NO. NAME                    NO. DATE    DISCOUNT  AMOUNT TYPE   NO.  CHK.
------------------------------------------------------------------------
020 Computer Distribution Co. 548 10/02/--   37.00  1850.00 Payment
040 Computer Executive Ltd.   550 10/03/--     .00  1050.00 Payment
060 Quality Ribbon Co.        552 10/10/--   24.80  1240.00 Payment
010 DataPro Paper Supply      560 10/08/--           -150.00 Dr Memo 10
100 Digital Electronics Co.   561 10/21/--           -200.00 Dr Memo 11
100 Digital Electronics Co.   561 10/28/--  108.10  5605.00 Payment
050 A & K Advertising Co.     562 10/19/--     .00   370.50 Payment
160 Etter and Panozza         563 10/20/--     .00   116.98 Payment
110 Park Ave. Development      564 10/24/--     .00  1150.00 Payment
070 Inntouch Marketing        567 10/25/--     .00   190.00 Payment
120 Rocket Delivery Service   568 10/27/--     .00   200.00 Payment
130 Dennis Siegel             569 10/31/--     .00  1150.00 Payment
140 Ruth Hines                570 10/31/--     .00  1150.00 Payment

    TOTAL DEBIT MEMOS     350.00
    TOTAL DISCOUNTS       169.90
    TOTAL CASH PAYMENTS 13702.58
```

Figure 9.21   Cash Payments Report for Batch No. 10 (Problem 9-S)

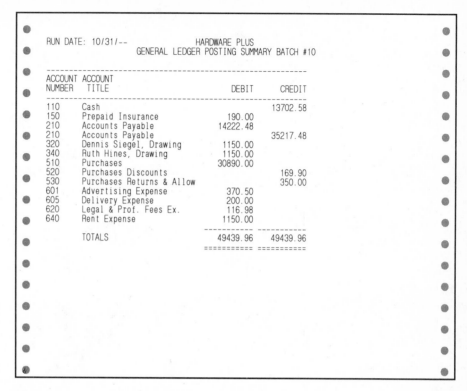

```
RUN DATE: 10/31/--                  HARDWARE PLUS
                      GENERAL LEDGER POSTING SUMMARY BATCH #10

---------------------------------------------------------------
ACCOUNT ACCOUNT
NUMBER  TITLE                        DEBIT      CREDIT
---------------------------------------------------------------
110     Cash                                    13702.58
150     Prepaid Insurance            190.00
210     Accounts Payable           14222.48
210     Accounts Payable                        35217.48
320     Dennis Siegel, Drawing      1150.00
340     Ruth Hines, Drawing         1150.00
510     Purchases                  30890.00
520     Purchases Discounts                       169.90
530     Purchases Returns & Allow                 350.00
601     Advertising Expense          370.50
605     Delivery Expense             200.00
620     Legal & Prof. Fees Ex.       116.98
640     Rent Expense                1150.00
                                  ----------  ----------
        TOTALS                     49439.96    49439.96
                                  ==========  ==========
```

Figure 9.22   General Ledger Posting Summary for Accounts Payable Transactions (Problem 9-S)

```
RUN DATE: 10/31/--                  HARDWARE PLUS
                        SCHEDULE OF ACCOUNTS PAYABLE

------------------------------------------------------------------
VENDOR NUMBER AND NAME                         DEBIT MEMO
         INVOICE   DATE    AMOUNT  DISCOUNT   DATE   NUMBER  AMOUNT
------------------------------------------------------------------
010  DataPro Paper Supply
        560   10/01/--   13500.00    .00  10/08/--   10    150.00
        VENDOR TOTALS    13500.00    .00                   150.00

020  Computer Distribution Co.
        566   10/24/--     285.00    .00
        VENDOR TOTALS      285.00    .00                      .00

040  Computer Executive Ltd.
        565   10/24/--   11500.00    .00
        VENDOR TOTALS    11500.00    .00                      .00

                        ---------- ----------         ----------
FINAL TOTALS             25285.00    .00                   150.00
                        ========== ==========         ==========

GROSS ACCOUNTS PAYABLE   25285.00
      LESS DEBIT MEMOS     150.00
                        ----------
NET ACCOUNTS PAYABLE     25135.00
                        ==========
```

Figure 9.23   Schedule of Accounts Payable (Problem 9-S)

Step 24   Select Option O, *Check Register*, and display or print a check register. The correct check register is shown in Figure 9.24.

```
RUN DATE: 10/31/--                    HARDWARE PLUS
                                CHECK REGISTER BATCH #10

-------------------------------------------------------------------
CHECK  VENDOR VENDOR                              CHECK
NUMBER NUMBER NAME                                AMOUNT
-------------------------------------------------------------------
4410   020    Computer Distribution Co.          1813.00
4411   040    Computer Executive Ltd.            1050.00
4412   050    A & K Advertising Co.               370.50
4413   060    Quality Ribbon Co.                 1215.20
4414   070    Inntouch Marketing                  190.00
4415   100    Digital Electronics Co.            5296.90
4416   110    Park Ave. Development              1150.00
4417   120    Rocket Delivery Service             200.00
4418   130    Dennis Siegel                      1150.00
4419   140    Ruth Hines                         1150.00
4420   160    Etter and Panozza                   116.98
                                                 ---------
              FINAL TOTAL                        13702.58
                                                 =========
```

Figure 9.24   Check Register (Problem 9-S)

Step 25   Select Option P, *Checks*, and display or print the checks. If you have informed the computer that you are using preprinted check forms (during accounting system setup), insert the forms into the printer and align them properly. The checks shown in Figure 9.25 are printed on preprinted check forms.

Step 26   Return to the System Selection Menu, from the Accounts Payable Main Menu.

Step 27   Select Option H, *Accounts Receivable*, from the System Selection Menu.

Step 28   Select Option C, *Set Control Accounts*, from the Accounts Receivable Main Menu, and verify that the control accounts are set as follows. If not, make the necessary changes and strike **R** to record this data.

Accounts Receivable Account No. 120
Sales Tax Payable Account No. 220
Sales Discounts Account No. 420
Sales Returns & Allowances Account No. 430

Step 29   Select Option F, *Customer File Maintenance*, from the Accounts Receivable Main Menu. Key-enter the customer file maintenance transactions from the Accounts Receivable File Maintenance input form in Figure 9.13.

Step 30   Select Option G, *Customer List*, from the Accounts Receivable Main

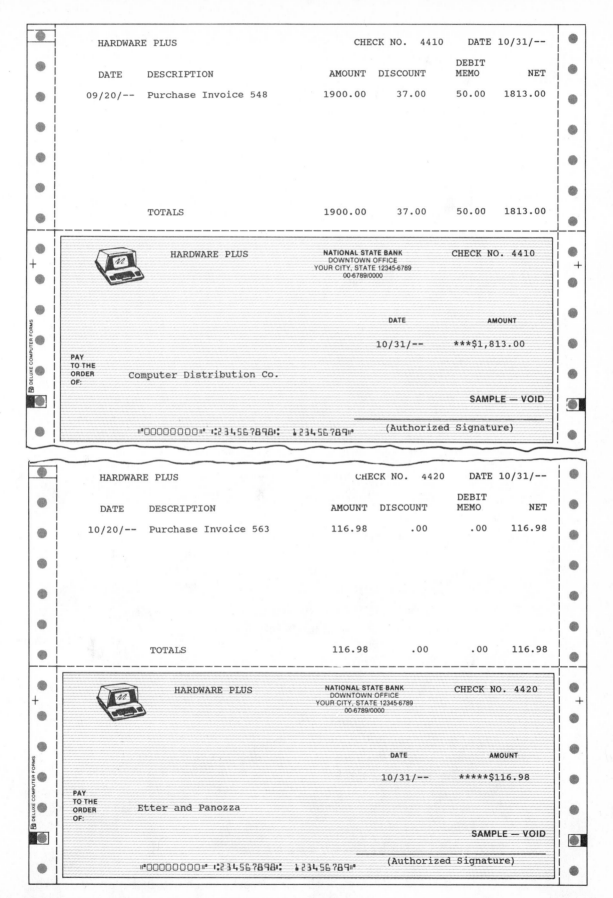

| | HARDWARE PLUS | | CHECK NO. 4410 | DATE 10/31/-- |

DATE	DESCRIPTION	AMOUNT	DISCOUNT	DEBIT MEMO	NET
09/20/--	Purchase Invoice 548	1900.00	37.00	50.00	1813.00
	TOTALS	1900.00	37.00	50.00	1813.00

HARDWARE PLUS
NATIONAL STATE BANK
DOWNTOWN OFFICE
YOUR CITY, STATE 12345-6789
00-6789/0000
CHECK NO. 4410

DATE	AMOUNT
10/31/--	***$1,813.00

PAY TO THE ORDER OF: Computer Distribution Co.

SAMPLE — VOID

⑆00000000⑆ ⑆23456789⑆ 123456789⑈

(Authorized Signature)

| | HARDWARE PLUS | | CHECK NO. 4420 | DATE 10/31/-- |

DATE	DESCRIPTION	AMOUNT	DISCOUNT	DEBIT MEMO	NET
10/20/--	Purchase Invoice 563	116.98	.00	.00	116.98
	TOTALS	116.98	.00	.00	116.98

HARDWARE PLUS
NATIONAL STATE BANK
DOWNTOWN OFFICE
YOUR CITY, STATE 12345-6789
00-6789/0000
CHECK NO. 4420

DATE	AMOUNT
10/31/--	*****$116.98

PAY TO THE ORDER OF: Etter and Panozza

SAMPLE — VOID

⑆00000000⑆ ⑆23456789⑆ 123456789⑈

(Authorized Signature)

Figure 9.25   Checks on Preprinted Check Forms (Problem 9-S)

Menu, and display or print a revised customer list. Verify that the data you key-entered is correct. The revised customer list is shown in Figure 9.26.

```
RUN DATE: 10/31/--              HARDWARE PLUS
                                CUSTOMER LIST

----------------------
CUSTOMER   CUSTOMER
NUMBER     NAME
----------------------
010        Dakota County Inquirer
030        Superior New & Used Autos
040        Sounds Around, Inc.
050        Linda's Fitness Center
060        Greenthumb Florists, Inc.
070        Harmon Furniture Co.
080        Galactic Insurance
090        Key City Realty Co.
100        Robert Fox
```

Figure 9.26   Revised Customer List after File Maintenance (Problem 9-S)

Step 31   Select Option H, *Set Run Date and Batch Number*, from the Accounts Receivable Main Menu. Verify that the run date has been set to **October 31** of the current year and that the batch number has been set to **10**. If not, make the necessary changes and strike **R** to record this data.

Step 32   Select Option I, *Enter/Correct Sales and Cash Receipts*, from the Accounts Receivable Main Menu. Key-enter and post the sales and cash receipts transactions from the completed Accounts Receivable input form in Figure 9.16.

Step 33   Select Option J, *Sales on Account Report*, from the Accounts Receivable Main Menu. Display or print a Sales on Account report. Compare your Sales on Account report with the correct one shown in Figure 9.27. The computer total of the Invoice Amount column should be the same as the calculator batch total of the Invoice Amount column on the Accounts Receivable input form. If your Sales on Account report is in error, key-enter and post the corrections, then display or print another Sales on Account report. Repeat this step until your Sales on Account report is correct.

Step 34   Select Option K, *Cash Receipts Report*, from the Accounts Receivable Main Menu. Display or print a Cash Receipts report. Compare your Cash Receipts report with the correct one shown in Figure 9.28. The computer total of the Cash Receipts should be the same as the calcula-

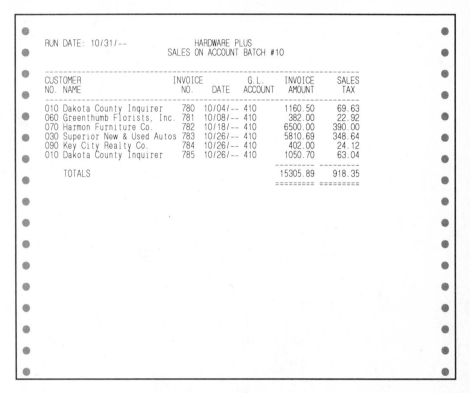

```
RUN DATE: 10/31/--                 HARDWARE PLUS
                           SALES ON ACCOUNT BATCH #10

-------------------------------------------------------------------
CUSTOMER                      INVOICE         G.L.    INVOICE    SALES
NO. NAME                        NO.    DATE  ACCOUNT   AMOUNT     TAX
-------------------------------------------------------------------
010 Dakota County Inquirer      780  10/04/--  410    1160.50   69.63
060 Greenthumb Florists, Inc.   781  10/08/--  410     382.00   22.92
070 Harmon Furniture Co.        782  10/18/--  410    6500.00  390.00
030 Superior New & Used Autos   783  10/26/--  410    5810.69  348.64
090 Key City Realty Co.         784  10/26/--  410     402.00   24.12
010 Dakota County Inquirer      785  10/26/--  410    1050.70   63.04
                                                     --------- --------
    TOTALS                                           15305.89  918.35
                                                     ========= ========
```

Figure 9.27   Sales on Account Report for Batch No. 10 (Problem 9-S)

```
RUN DATE: 10/31/--                 HARDWARE PLUS
                           CASH RECEIPTS BATCH #10

-------------------------------------------------------------------
CUSTOMER                      INVOICE        DOC.
NO. NAME                        NO.    DATE   NO.    AMOUNT TYPE    DISCOUNT
-------------------------------------------------------------------
060 Greenthumb Florists, Inc.   746  10/05/-- 1597  2963.87 Receipt     .00
070 Harmon Furniture Co.        750  10/09/-- 1880  2960.58 Receipt   57.00
010 Dakota County Inquirer      780  10/10/--   92  -110.00 Cr Memo
070 Harmon Furniture Co.        782  10/26/-- 1894  6752.20 Receipt  130.00

    TOTAL CREDIT MEMOS     110.00
    TOTAL DISCOUNTS        187.00
    TOTAL CASH RECEIPTS  12676.65
```

Figure 9.28   Cash Receipts Report for Batch No. 10 (Problem 9-S)

tor batch total of the Cash Received column on the Accounts Receivable input form. If your Cash Receipts report is in error, key-enter and post the corrections, then display or print another Cash Receipts report. Repeat this step until your Cash Receipts report is correct.

Step 35 Select Option L, *General Ledger Posting Summary*, and display or print a general ledger posting summary. The correct general ledger posting summary is shown in Figure 9.29.

```
RUN DATE: 10/31/--                     HARDWARE PLUS
                       GENERAL LEDGER POSTING SUMMARY BATCH #10

-----------------------------------------------------------------
ACCOUNT ACCOUNT
NUMBER  TITLE                              DEBIT      CREDIT
-----------------------------------------------------------------
110     Cash                            12676.65
120     Accounts Receivable             16224.24
120     Accounts Receivable                        12991.47
220     Sales Tax Payable                  17.82
220     Sales Tax Payable                            918.35
410     Sales                                      15305.89
420     Sales Discounts                   187.00
430     Sales Returns & Allowance         110.00
                                        ---------- ----------
        TOTALS                          29215.71   29215.71
                                        ========== ==========
```

Figure   9.29   General   Ledger   Posting   Summary   for   Accounts   Receivable Transactions (Problem 9-S)

Step 36 Select Option M, *Schedule of Accounts Receivable*, from the Accounts Receivable Main Menu. Display or print a schedule of accounts receivable. The correct schedule of accounts receivable is shown in Figure 9.30.

Step 37 Select Option N, *Customer Statements*, and display or print the customer statements. If you informed the computer that you are using preprinted statement forms (during accounting system setup), insert the forms into the printer and align them properly. The statements shown in Figure 9.31 (page 286) are printed on preprinted statement forms.

Step 38 Return to System Selection Menu.

Step 39 Select Option F, *General Ledger System*, from the System Selection Menu.

Step 40 Select Option K, *Trial Balance*, from the General Ledger Main Menu, and display or print a trial balance. The correct trial balance is shown in Figure 9.32 (page 287). Notice how the general ledger accounts that were affected by accounts receivable and accounts payable transactions have been updated through the integration process. The Accounts Receivable balance (Account No. 120) should be the same as the final total on the schedule of accounts receivable prepared in Step 36. The

```
RUN DATE: 10/31/--                    HARDWARE PLUS
                               SCHEDULE OF ACCOUNTS RECEIVABLE

------------------------------------------------------------------------
CUSTOMER                          INVOICE                           CREDIT
NO. NAME                          NO.    DATE     AMOUNT  DISCOUNT    MEMO
------------------------------------------------------------------------
010 Dakota County Inquirer        780  10/04/--   1223.53     .00   110.00
010 Dakota County Inquirer        785  10/26/--   1113.74     .00      .00
    CUSTOMER TOTALS                                2337.27     .00   110.00

030 Superior New & Used Autos     783  10/26/--   6159.33     .00      .00
    CUSTOMER TOTALS                                6159.33     .00      .00

060 Greenthumb Florists, Inc.     781  10/08/--    404.92     .00      .00
    CUSTOMER TOTALS                                 404.92     .00      .00

080 Galactic Insurance            760  09/30/--    416.28     .00      .00
    CUSTOMER TOTALS                                 416.28     .00      .00

090 Key City Realty Co.           784  10/26/--    426.12     .00      .00
    CUSTOMER TOTALS                                 426.12     .00      .00

                                                ---------- ---------- ----------
    FINAL TOTALS                                   9743.92     .00   110.00
                                                ========== ========== ==========

GROSS ACCOUNTS RECEIVABLE                 9743.92
    LESS CREDIT MEMOS                      110.00
                                       ----------
EQUALS NET ACCOUNTS RECEIVABLE            9633.92
                                       ==========
```

Figure 9.30   Schedule of Accounts Receivable (Problem 9-S)

Accounts Payable balance (Account No. 210) should be the same as the final total on the schedule of accounts payable prepared in Step 23.

Step 41   Select Option L, *General Ledger Report*, and display or print a General Ledger report to prove cash. When prompted to do so, choose the **S** option (*Specific Account*), and enter the Cash account number (110). Verify that the ending cash balance is equal to the checkbook balance of $18,995.82. Cash may also be proven by using the cash balance from the preceding trial balance.

Step 42   The information needed to complete the adjusting entries for October for Hardware Plus is listed below. The completed General Ledger input form for the adjusting entries is shown in Figure 9.33 (page 288). Examine these adjusting entries to make sure you understand them.

Adjustment Information for October 31

Ending Merchandise Inventory $118,417.50
Supplies Inventory $502.00
Value of Insurance Policies $475.00

Step 43   Select Option H, *Set Run Date and Batch Number*, from the General Ledger Main Menu. Set the batch number to **20** and strike **R** to record the information.

Step 44   Select Option I, *Enter/Correct Journal Entries*, and key-enter and post the adjusting entries from the General Ledger input form in Figure 9.33.

Step 45   Select Option J, *Journal Entries Report*, from the General Ledger Main Menu. Print or display a Journal Entries report for the adjusting

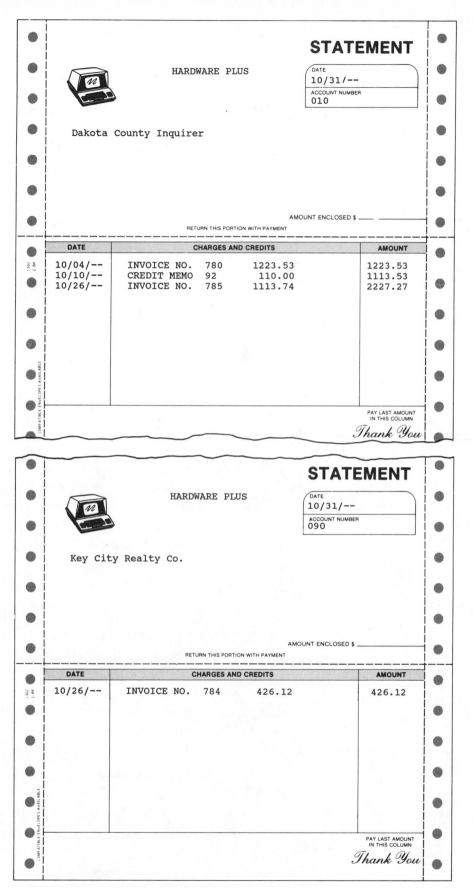

Figure 9.31   Customer Statements on Preprinted Statement Forms (Problem 9-S)

```
RUN DATE: 10/31/--              HARDWARE PLUS
                                TRIAL BALANCE

-----------------------------------------------------------------
ACCOUNT      ACCOUNT
NUMBER       TITLE                   DEBIT AMOUNT    CREDIT AMOUNT
-----------------------------------------------------------------
110          Cash                       18995.82
120          Accounts Receivable         9633.92
130          Merchandise Inventory     109088.96
140          Supplies                     655.69
150          Prepaid Insurance            570.00
210          Accounts Payable                           25135.00
220          Sales Tax Payable                           2749.67
310          Dennis Siegel, Capital                     58811.98
320          Dennis Siegel, Drawing      1150.00
330          Ruth Hines, Capital                        58746.43
340          Ruth Hines, Drawing         1150.00
410          Sales                                      28305.89
420          Sales Discounts              187.00
430          Sales Returns & Allowance    110.00
510          Purchases                  30890.00
520          Purchases Discounts                          169.90
530          Purchases Returns & Allow                    350.00
601          Advertising Expense          370.50
605          Delivery Expense             200.00
620          Legal & Prof. Fees Ex.       116.98
640          Rent Expense                1150.00
                                      -------------   -------------
             TOTALS                     174268.87       174268.87
                                      =============   =============
```

Figure 9.32   Trial Balance after October Transactions (Problem 9-S)

entries. The correct report is shown in Figure 9.34 (page 289). If your Journal Entries report is in error, make the necessary corrections. Then print or display another Journal Entries report. Repeat this step until your Journal Entries report for the adjusting entries is correct.

Step 46   Select Option K, *Trial Balance*, and print or display a trial balance. Compare your trial balance with the correct one shown in Figure 9.35 on page 289).

Step 47   Select Option M, *Income Statement*, from the General Ledger Main Menu. Display or print an income statement and compare it with the one shown in Figure 9.36 on page 290. If your income statement is different, make the necessary corrections using Option I, *Enter/Correct Journal Entries*. Repeat this step until your income statement is correct. *Remember that it is much more difficult to make corrections after performing period-end closing.*

Step 48   Select Option N, *Balance Sheet*, and display or print a balance sheet. Compare your balance sheet with the one shown in Figure 9.37 on page 290. If your balance sheet is different, make the necessary corrections using Option I, *Enter/Correct Journal Entries*. Repeat this step until your balance sheet is correct.

Note: When a balance sheet is generated using the expanded version of the general ledger, Net Working Capital and Current Ratio information appears at the end of the report. The current ratio shows the relationship between current assets and current liabilities. It is computed by dividing the total current assets ($148,024.24) by the total current liabilities ($27,884.67). The result of the computation (current ratio =

	DAY	DOC. NO.	ACCOUNT NUMBER	DEBIT AMOUNT	CREDIT AMOUNT	
1	31	ADJ ENTR	130	9328 54		1
2			350		9328 54	2
3	31	ADJ ENTR	660	153 69		3
4			140		153 69	4
5	31	ADJ ENTR	610	95 00		5
6			150		95 00	6

RUN DATE 10/31/-- BATCH NO. 20 GENERAL LEDGER Input Form Problem No. 9-S FORM GL-2

BATCH TOTALS 9577 23 | 9577 23

Figure 9.33 General Ledger Input Form for Adjusting Entries (Problem 9-S)

5.31) means that Hardware Plus owns $5.31 in current assets for each $1.00 needed to pay current liabilities.

Step 49 Select Option O, *Period-End Closing*, from the General Ledger Main Menu. When prompted to do so, select the **Y** option (for Yes) to instruct the computer to perform period-end closing.

Step 50 Select Option P, *Post-Closing Trial Balance*, and print or display a post-closing trial balance. Your post-closing trial balance should match the one shown in Figure 9.38 (page 291). If your trial balance is different, make the necessary corrections.

Step 51 Return to the System Selection Menu.

Step 52 Once back in the System Selection Menu, save your work as a work in progress file on your own data disk (recommend file name **AA9-S**) and shut down the computer. Then complete the student exercise and transaction problem which follow.

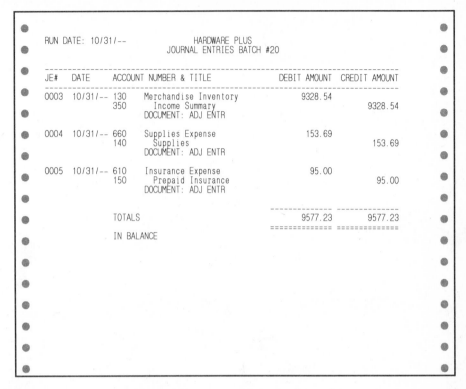

```
RUN DATE: 10/31/--                    HARDWARE PLUS
                                 JOURNAL ENTRIES BATCH #20


----------------------------------------------------------------------
JE#   DATE      ACCOUNT NUMBER & TITLE           DEBIT AMOUNT   CREDIT AMOUNT
----------------------------------------------------------------------
0003  10/31/-- 130    Merchandise Inventory         9328.54
               350      Income Summary                              9328.54
                     DOCUMENT: ADJ ENTR


0004  10/31/-- 660    Supplies Expense               153.69
               140      Supplies                                     153.69
                     DOCUMENT: ADJ ENTR


0005  10/31/-- 610    Insurance Expense               95.00
               150      Prepaid Insurance                             95.00
                     DOCUMENT: ADJ ENTR


                                                  --------------  --------------
                     TOTALS                          9577.23        9577.23
                                                  ==============  ==============
                     IN BALANCE
```

Figure 9.34   Journal Entries Report for Adjusting Entries (Problem 9-S)

```
RUN DATE: 10/31/--                    HARDWARE PLUS
                                      TRIAL BALANCE


----------------------------------------------------------------------
ACCOUNT    ACCOUNT
NUMBER     TITLE                    DEBIT AMOUNT     CREDIT AMOUNT
----------------------------------------------------------------------
110        Cash                       18995.82
120        Accounts Receivable         9633.92
130        Merchandise Inventory     118417.50
140        Supplies                     502.00
150        Prepaid Insurance            475.00
210        Accounts Payable                            25135.00
220        Sales Tax Payable                            2749.67
310        Dennis Siegel, Capital                      58811.98
320        Dennis Siegel, Drawing      1150.00
330        Ruth Hines, Capital                         58746.43
340        Ruth Hines, Drawing         1150.00
350        Income Summary                               9328.54
410        Sales                                       28305.89
420        Sales Discounts              187.00
430        Sales Returns & Allowance    110.00
510        Purchases                  30890.00
520        Purchases Discounts                           169.90
530        Purchases Returns & Allow                     350.00
601        Advertising Expense          370.50
605        Delivery Expense             200.00
610        Insurance Expense             95.00
620        Legal & Prof. Fees Ex.       116.98
640        Rent Expense                1150.00
660        Supplies Expense             153.69
                                     --------------   --------------
           TOTALS                    183597.41        183597.41
                                     ==============   ==============
```

Figure 9.35   Trial Balance after Adjusting Entries (Problem 9-S)

```
                        HARDWARE PLUS
                       INCOME STATEMENT
                   FOR PERIOD ENDED 10/31/--

                                                         % OF NET
    R E V E N U E                                        REVENUE
    --------------
    Sales                          28305.89               101.06
    Sales Discounts                 -187.00                 -.67
    Sales Returns & Allowance       -110.00                 -.39
                                 ---------------
    NET REVENUE                                 28008.89   100.00

    C O S T   O F   M D S E .   S O L D
    -------------------------------------
    BEGINNING INVENTORY            109088.96               389.48
    Purchases                       30890.00               110.29
    Purchases Discounts             -169.90                 -.61
    Purchases Returns & Allow       -350.00                -1.25
                                 ---------------
    MDSE. AVAILABLE FOR SALE        139459.06              497.91
    LESS ENDING INVENTORY           118417.50              422.79
                                 ---------------
    COST OF MDSE. SOLD                          21041.56    75.12
                                            ---------------
    GROSS PROFIT ON OPERATIONS                   6967.33    24.88

    E X P E N S E S
    ---------------
    Advertising Expense               370.50                1.32
    Delivery Expense                  200.00                 .71
    Insurance Expense                  95.00                 .34
    Legal & Prof. Fees Ex.            116.98                 .42
    Rent Expense                     1150.00                4.11
    Supplies Expense                  153.69                 .55
                                 ---------------
    TOTAL EXPENSES                               2086.17     7.45
                                            ---------------
    NET INCOME                                   4881.16    17.43
                                            ===============
```

Figure 9.36   Income Statement (Problem 9-S)

```
                        HARDWARE PLUS
                        BALANCE SHEET
                          10/31/--

    A S S E T S
    -----------
    Cash                            18995.82
    Accounts Receivable              9633.92
    Merchandise Inventory          118417.50
    Supplies                          502.00
    Prepaid Insurance                 475.00
                                 ---------------
    TOTAL ASSETS                                148024.24
                                            ===============
    L I A B I L I T I E S
    ---------------------
    Accounts Payable                25135.00
    Sales Tax Payable                2749.67
                                 ---------------
    TOTAL LIABILITIES                           27884.67

    O W N E R S '   E Q U I T Y
    ---------------------------
    Dennis Siegel, Capital          58811.98
    Dennis Siegel, Drawing          -1150.00
    SHARE OF NET INCOME @ 50%         2440.58
    Ruth Hines, Capital             58746.43
    Ruth Hines, Drawing             -1150.00
    SHARE OF NET INCOME @ 50%         2440.58
                                 ---------------
    TOTAL CAPITAL                              120139.57
                                            ---------------
    TOTAL LIABILITIES & CAPITAL                148024.24
                                            ===============

    NET WORKING CAPITAL:      120139.57
    CURRENT RATIO:            5.31 TO 1
```

Figure 9.37   Balance Sheet (Problem 9-S)

```
RUN DATE: 10/31/--                    HARDWARE PLUS
                               POST-CLOSING TRIAL BALANCE

----------------------------------------------------------------------
ACCOUNT     ACCOUNT
NUMBER      TITLE                      DEBIT AMOUNT      CREDIT AMOUNT
----------------------------------------------------------------------
110         Cash                          18995.82
120         Accounts Receivable            9633.92
130         Merchandise Inventory        118417.50
140         Supplies                        502.00
150         Prepaid Insurance               475.00
210         Accounts Payable                                 25135.00
220         Sales Tax Payable                                 2749.67
310         Dennis Siegel, Capital                           60102.56
330         Ruth Hines, Capital                              60037.01
                                      ---------------   ---------------
            TOTALS                        148024.24         148024.24
                                      ===============   ===============
```

Figure 9.38   Post-Closing Trial Balance (Problem 9-S)

Name _____

Class _____ Date _____

CHAPTER 9
STUDENT EXERCISE

I. Matching   For each of the following definitions, write the letter of the term which best fits that definition in the space provided.

a. Purchases discount   c. Sales discount
b. Debit memorandum   d. Credit memorandum

1. _____ Credit granted to a buyer for returned or damaged merchandise which results in a deduction from the accounts payable account. (Obj. 2)

2. _____ A deduction given to customers on the invoice amount of sales on account in order to encourage early payment. (Obj. 3)

3. _____ A deduction given to buyers on the invoice amount of credit sales in order to encourage early payment. (Obj. 1)

4. _____ Credit granted to customers for returned or damaged merchandise which results in a deduction from the accounts receivable account. (Obj. 4)

II. Short Answer   1. Which input form is used to record debit memorandums? (Obj. 2)

_____

2. Which input form is used to record credit memorandums? (Obj. 4)

_____

3. Assume that a purchase invoice for $700.00, subject to a 2 percent discount, is key-entered into the Accounts Payable System. Show the journal entry or entries that will be generated automatically by the computer. (Obj. 5)

Account	Debit	Credit
_____	_____	_____
_____	_____	_____

4. Show the journal entry or entries that will automatically be generated by the computer when the purchase invoice in Question 3 is released for payment. (Obj. 5)

Account	Debit	Credit
_____	_____	_____
_____	_____	_____
_____	_____	_____

5. Assume that a debit memorandum for $100.00 is key-entered into the Accounts Payable System. Show the journal entry or entries that will be generated automatically by the computer. (Obj. 5)

Account	Debit	Credit

6. Assume that a sales invoice for $200.00, subject to 6 percent sales tax and a 1 percent discount, is key-entered into the Accounts Receivable System. Show the journal entry or entries that will be generated automatically by the computer. (Obj. 5)

Account	Debit	Credit

7. Show the journal entry or entries that will be generated automatically by the computer when cash is received ($209.88) for the sales invoice in Question 6. Assume that the cash is received within the discount period. (Obj. 5)

Account	Debit	Credit

8. Assume that a credit memorandum for $120.00 is entered into the Accounts Receivable System. Show the journal entry or entries that will be generated automatically by the computer. (Obj. 5)

Account	Debit	Credit

DISCOUNTS, DEBIT MEMORANDUMS, AND CREDIT MEMORANDUMS TRANSACTION PROBLEM 9-1

Problem 9-1 is a continuation of Problem 9-S. The sample problem covered the month of October. Problem 9-1 covers the month of November. Therefore, if you did not complete the sample problem, you must load the opening balances for Problem 9-1 from disk. (Objs. 1-5)

Instructions

Step 1 Remove the blank input forms and the Chapter 9 Audit Test from the end of this chapter. Fill in the answers to the audit test as you work through Problem 9-1.

Step 2 The following transactions occurred for Hardware Plus during the month of November. Record the transactions on the proper input forms.

Nov 01   Released Purchase Invoice No. 560 to DataPro Paper Supply for payment, no discount.

02   Released Purchase Invoice No. 566 to Computer Distribution Co. for payment, 1 percent discount to be taken.

02   Purchased merchandise on account from Computer Executive Ltd., $780.20 (Purchase Invoice No. 571).

03   Sold merchandise on account to Dakota County Inquirer, $1,730.50, plus 6 percent sales tax (Sales Invoice No. 786).

03   Released Purchase Invoice No. 565 to Computer Executive Ltd., 2 percent discount to be taken.

05   Received cash on account from Dakota County Inquirer, $1,091.47, covering Sales Invoice No. 785, less 2 percent discount (Customer Check No. 1531).

09   Received cash on account from Dakota County Inquirer, $1,113.53, covering Sales Invoice No. 780, less credit memorandum, no discount (Customer Check No. 1534).

10   Received cash on account from Galactic Insurance, $416.28, covering Sales Invoice No. 760, no discount (Customer Check No. 1173).

11   Sold merchandise on account to Summer Wear, Inc., $3,050.00, plus 6 percent sales tax (Sales Invoice No. 787). Assigned Customer No. 180 to Summer Wear, Inc.

12   Purchased merchandise on account from Software Support Co., $856.45 (Purchase Invoice No. 572). Assigned Vendor No. 180 to Software Support Co.

12   Received cash on account from Dakota County Inquirer, $1,797.64, covering Sales Invoice No. 786, less 2 percent discount (Customer Check No. 1545).

15   Cash sales, $7,710.00, plus sales tax, $462.63. Total, $8,172.63 (Cash Register Tape No. 17).

16   Issued Credit Memorandum No. 93 to Summer Wear, Inc., $45.00, for merchandise returned (Sales Invoice No. 787).

17   Deleted A-1 Electronics Supply from the vendor master file.

17   Deleted Robert Fox from the customer master file.

18   Recorded Purchase Invoice No. 573 to Digital Discount Depot for miscellaneous expense, $7.75. Released this purchase invoice for payment, no discount.

21   Sold merchandise on account to Sounds Around, Inc., $103.02, plus 6 percent sales tax (Sales Invoice No. 788).

22   Software Support Co. granted us credit for damaged merchandise, $102.00 (Purchase Invoice No. 572, Debit Memorandum No. 12).

23   Recorded Purchase Invoice No. 574 to A & K Advertising Co., $350.00, for advertising services. Released this purchase invoice for payment, no discount.

24   Recorded Purchase Invoice No. 575 to Park Ave. Development for rent, $1,150.00. Released this purchase invoice for payment, no discount.

24   Recorded Purchase Invoice No. 576 to Etter and Panozza for legal services, $235.60. Released this purchase invoice for payment, no discount.

26   Sold merchandise on account to Harmon Furniture Co., $7,810.69, plus 6 percent sales tax (Sales Invoice No. 789).

29   Purchased merchandise on account from Digital Electronics Co., $5,797.38 (Purchase Invoice No. 577).

29   Sold merchandise on account to Key City Realty Co., $5,710.00, plus 6 percent sales tax (Sales Invoice No. 790).

30   Recorded Purchase Invoice No. 578 to Rocket Delivery Service for delivery services, $100.32. Released this purchase invoice for payment, no discount.

30   Cash sales, $7,752.20, plus sales tax, $465.13. Total, $8,217.33 (Cash Register Tape No. 18).

30   Dennis Siegel, partner, wishes to withdraw $1,750.00 for personal use (Purchase Invoice No. 579). Released this purchase invoice for payment.

30   Ruth Hines, partner, wishes to withdraw $1,750.00 for personal use (Purchase Invoice No. 580). Released this purchase invoice for payment.

Step   3   Bring up the System Selection Menu.

Step   4   If you did not complete the sample problem, select the *Load Data from Disk* option and choose Problem 9-1 by key-entering the file name **AA9-1** when the directory list appears. If you did complete Problem 9-S, load the data from your work in progress file.

Step   5   Set and record the run date as **November 30** of the current year. Set and record the *Problem Number* field as **Problem 9-1**.

Step   6   Select the *General Ledger* option.

Step   7   Set the batch number to **21**.

Step   8   Key-enter and post the general ledger transactions from the General Ledger input form.

Step   9   Display or print a Journal Entries report and verify that the data key-entered is correct. If errors are detected, make the necessary corrections and print or display a new Journal Entries report.

Step 10   Return to the System Selection Menu.

Step 11   Select the *Accounts Payable* option.

Step 12   Key-enter the data from the Accounts Payable File Maintenance input form.

Step 13   Display or print a new vendor list.

Step 14   Set the batch number to **11**.

Step 15   Key-enter the data from the Accounts Payable input form.

Step 16   Display or print a Purchases on Account report. Verify that the data you key-entered is correct and that the totals of the Invoice Amount columns on the input form and computer printout are equal. If errors are detected, make the necessary corrections and print a new Purchases on Account report.

Step 17   Display or print a Cash Payments report. Verify that the data you key-entered is correct. If errors are detected, make the necessary corrections and print or display a new Cash Payments report.

Step 18   Display or print a general ledger posting summary.

Step 19   Display or print a schedule of accounts payable.

Step 20   Display or print a check register.

Step 21   Display or print the checks.

Step 22   Return to the System Selection Menu.

Step 23   Select the *Accounts Receivable* option.

Step 24   Key-enter the data from the Accounts Receivable File Maintenance input form.

Step 25   Display or print a new customer list.

Step 26   Set the batch number to **11**.

Step 27   Key-enter the data from the Accounts Receivable input form.

Step 28   Display or print a Sales on Account report. Verify that the data you key-entered is correct and that the totals of the Invoice Amount columns on the input form and computer printout are equal. If errors are detected, make the necessary corrections and display or print a new report.

Step 29   Display or print a Cash Receipts report. Verify that the data you key-entered is correct and that the total of the Cash Received column on the input form and the Total Cash Receipts on the computer printout are equal. If errors are detected, make the necessary corrections and display or print a new report.

Step 30   Display or print a general ledger posting summary.

Step 31   Display or print a schedule of accounts receivable.

Step 32   Display or print the customer statements.

Step 33   Return to the System Selection Menu.

Step 34   Select the *General Ledger* option.

Step 35   Display or print a trial balance.

Step 36   Compare the control account balances with the totals from the schedule of accounts receivable prepared in Step 31 and the schedule of accounts payable prepared in Step 19.

Step 37   Prove cash. The checkbook balance is $9,558.88.

Step 38   The information needed to complete the adjusting entries for Hardware Plus is shown below. Record the adjusting entries on the General Ledger input form as Batch No. 22.

Adjustment Information for November 30

Ending Merchandise Inventory $97,470.00
Supplies Inventory........................ $460.00
Value of Insurance Policies $340.00

Step 39   Set the batch number to **22**.

Step 40   Key-enter and post the adjusting entries.

Step 41   Display or print a Journal Entries report and verify that the data key-entered is correct. Make any necessary corrections.

Step 42   Display or print a trial balance to verify that the general ledger is still in balance.

Step 43   Display or print an income statement.

Step 44   Display or print a balance sheet.

Step 45   Be certain that all answers have been filled in on the Chapter 9 Audit Test before closing the ledger in the following step.

Step 46   Select the *Period-End Closing* option and instruct the computer to perform the period-end closing process.

Step 47   Display or print a post-closing trial balance.

Step 48   Return to the System Selection Menu.

Step 49   Save your work as a work in progress file (recommend file name **AA9-1**). Then shut down the computer.

Step 50   Hand in the completed student exercise sheets, input forms, the audit test, and any printouts to your instructor.

You have now completed the computer exercise for Chapter 9.

Name _____

Class _____ Date _____

				GENERAL LEDGER			Problem No. _____

RUN DATE ____/____/____
MM   DD   YY

BATCH NO. [   ]

GENERAL LEDGER
Input Form

Problem No. _____

FORM GL-2

	1	2	3	4	5	
	DAY	DOC. NO.	ACCOUNT NUMBER	DEBIT AMOUNT	CREDIT AMOUNT	
1						1
2						2
3						3
4						4
5						5
6						6
7						7
8						8
9						9
10						10
11						11
12						12
13						13
14						14
15						15
16						16
17						17
18						18
19						19
20						20
21						21
22						22
23						23
24						24
25						25

BATCH TOTALS [   ] [   ]

ACCOUNTS PAYABLE
FILE MAINTENANCE
Input Form

Problem No. _____

FORM AP-1

RUN DATE ___/___/___
MM   DD   YY

	VENDOR NUMBER	VENDOR NAME	
1			1
2			2
3			3
4			4
5			5
6			6
7			7
8			8
9			9
10			10
11			11
12			12
13			13
14			14
15			15
16			16
17			17
18			18
19			19
20			20
21			21
22			22
23			23
24			24
25			25

Name _____

Class _____ Date _____

ACCOUNTS PAYABLE
Input Form

Problem No. _____

FORM AP-3

RUN DATE MM / DD / YY

BATCH NO.

		1	2	3	4	5	6	7	8	9	10	11	12

PURCHASES

PURCH. INVOICE NO.	VEND. NO.	DATE (MO. DAY YR.)	GEN. LEDGER ACCT NO.	INVOICE AMOUNT

DEBIT MEMOS

DATE (MO. DAY YR.)	MEMO. NO.	DEBIT MEMO. AMOUNT

CASH PAYMENTS

DATE (MO. DAY YR.)	DISC. %	DISP. CODE	MANUAL CHECK NO.

Rows 1–20

BATCH TOTALS

DISPOSITION CODE:
A = ON ACCOUNT
M = MANUAL CHECK
P = PAY THIS ITEM
(COMPUTER WRITES CHECK)

ACCOUNTS RECEIVABLE
FILE MAINTENANCE
Input Form

RUN DATE ____ / ____ / ____
        MM   DD   YY

Problem No. _____

FORM AR-1

	1	2
	CUSTOMER NUMBER	CUSTOMER NAME
1		
2		
3		
4		
5		
6		
7		
8		
9		
10		
11		
12		
13		
14		
15		
16		
17		
18		
19		
20		
21		
22		
23		
24		
25		

Name _____

Class _____ Date _____

ACCOUNTS RECEIVABLE
Input Form

Problem No. _____

FORM AR-3

RUN DATE __ MM / DD / YY

BATCH NO.

	SALES						CREDIT MEMOS				CASH RECEIPTS			

BATCH TOTALS

RUN DATE ____/____/____
MM   DD   YY

BATCH NO. [ ]

GENERAL LEDGER
Input Form

Problem No. _____

FORM GL-2

	1	2	3	4	5	
	DAY	DOC. NO.	ACCOUNT NUMBER	DEBIT AMOUNT	CREDIT AMOUNT	
1						1
2						2
3						3
4						4
5						5
6						6
7						7
8						8
9						9
10						10
11						11
12						12
13						13
14						14
15						15
16						16
17						17
18						18
19						19
20						20
21						21
22						22
23						23
24						24
25						25

BATCH TOTALS [ ]

Name _____

Class _____ Date _____

CHAPTER 9
AUDIT TEST

1. What were the total cash receipts from the Journal Entries report for Batch No. 21?

   _____

2. What was the amount of Purchase Invoice No. 572?

   _____

3. What was the total of all purchase invoices for the month of November?

   _____

4. To what account title was Purchase Invoice No. 578 charged?

   _____

5. To what vendor was a check written to pay Purchase Invoice No. 566?

   _____

6. What was the total amount of discounts allowed on invoices paid during November?

   _____

7. From the general ledger posting summary, what was the total amount of merchandise purchased during November?

   _____

8. List the numbers of the purchase invoices which were still unpaid at the end of November.

   _____

9. What was the amount of Check No. 4421?

   _____

10. To whom was Check No. 4427 written?

   _____

11. What was the total amount of all checks written for November?

_____

12. To which customer were goods sold for Sales Invoice No. 787?

_____

13. What was the total amount of sales tax charged to customers for November sales on account?

_____

14. What were the total sales on account for November?

_____

15. What was the total cash received on account during November?

_____

16. What was the total amount received from Galactic Insurance during November?

_____

17. List the sales invoice numbers of all outstanding sales invoices on November 30.

_____

18. What was the net accounts receivable on November 30?

_____

19. From the Journal Entries report for Batch No. 22 (adjusting entries), determine the amount of supplies used during November.

_____

20. What was the amount of insurance which expired during November?

_____

21. Did the value of merchandise inventory increase or did it decrease during November? What was the amount of increase or decrease?

Increase or decrease: _____

Amount: _____

22. What was the cost of merchandise sold for November?

_____

Name _____

Class _____ Date _____

23. What were the total assets as of November 30?

_____

24. What was Ruth Hines' share of net income for November?

_____

25. What was the balance in Dennis Siegel's capital account after period-end closing?

_____

Part 5

PAYROLL

10 PAYROLL SETUP

LEARNING OBJECTIVES

Upon completion of this chapter, you will be able to:

1. Describe the differences between manual and computerized payroll methods.
2. Build employee data.
3. Display or print an employee list.
4. Set the beginning check number.
5. Enter the beginning balances.
6. Display or print a Beginning Balances report.
7. Save data to the disk.
8. Perform system shutdown.
9. Identify the components of and procedures for payroll setup.

INTRODUCTION

Payroll is one of the oldest and most common data processing applications. It is an application which lends itself to the computer because of its repetitive procedures and calculations. Computerized payroll systems basically perform the same functions as those performed manually by payroll clerks. The important differences are the computer's speed, accuracy, reliability, and ability to generate many special reports.

The primary functions of a computerized payroll system are to accurately calculate gross pay, deductions, and net pay; print paychecks; and maintain cumulative payroll records for all employees. To do this, the computer requires the same information required in a manual system. In a manual payroll accounting system, an earnings record is used to record each employee's payroll information. Included on this record are the employee's name, social security number, address, marital status, number of withholding allowances, gross pay, and withholdings for payroll taxes and other deductions. In a computerized payroll system, the computer stores the same information for each employee in individual records. All these employee payroll records together are stored in the **payroll data file**. This file is the basis for a computerized payroll system and is updated by the computer at the end of each pay period.

At the end of each pay period, all payroll transaction data for each employee to be paid during the current pay period, such as regular and overtime hours worked, is key-entered into the computer. Transaction data for each employee to be paid during the current pay period makes up a **transaction record**. (All transaction records are stored along with the employee data in the payroll data file.) As this data is entered into the computer, all withholding taxes and other deductions are calculated, and the quarter-to-date and year-to-date earnings and withholdings are accumulated and updated in the computer's memory. This updated information remains in the computer's memory until it is saved to disk as an updated payroll data file. A payroll proof may be displayed or printed to check batch totals. If printed, this report may be used as an audit trail. The payroll register and checks are then printed. When processing the payroll register, the computer calculates the totals needed to make the necessary journal entries for salary expense, payroll tax expense, and various withholding liabilities. This information is displayed or printed on the payroll register. These amounts are then used to record the payroll entries on the General Ledger input form to be key-entered into the general ledger system. After the payroll register and checks have been printed, the payroll transaction records are cleared and the cycle continues to the next pay period.

At the end of the quarter, the Quarterly report is displayed or printed from the cumulative quarterly earnings and tax withholdings data in the payroll data file. Similarly, at the end of the year, the W-2 statements are displayed or printed from the year-to-date earnings and tax withholdings data in the payroll data file.

The payroll data file is the basis for the computerized payroll system and contains all of the employee payroll records for the company. Each item in an employee record, such as the employee number, name, etc., is referred to as a **field.** All of the fields which define the payroll data for one employee form an **employee record.** All of the employee records for a company are stored in the company's payroll data file. This file has a maximum capacity of 40 employee records (25 employee records for the Apple microcomputer).

In order to build the employee records, all data for each employee must be recorded on a **Payroll File Maintenance input form** (Form PR-1) and then key-entered into the computer. As each employee's data is key-entered into the computer, space is allocated to store additional fields of information, such as tax withholding calculations and quarterly/yearly accumulations, on each employee's record. Next, the beginning check number is established. Once set, all subsequent payroll checks will be numbered consecutively beginning with this check number. After the employee data has been entered and the beginning check number is set, beginning balances for each employee with quarterly and yearly balances are recorded on a **Payroll Beginning Balances input form** (Form PR-2). This task needs to be performed only if a manual, ongoing payroll system is changed to a computerized payroll system during the calendar year. These opening balances are key-entered into the computer, and the employee records are updated, completing the payroll setup procedure. This setup procedure, as illustrated in Figure 10.1, will not be required again until another company is created.

COMPLETING THE INPUT FORMS
As you have just learned, the data required to perform payroll setup is recorded on two different input forms. These forms are the Payroll File Maintenance input form (Form PR-1) and the Payroll Beginning Balances input form (Form PR-2). In this chapter, you will learn how each of these forms is utilized to record the data required to set up the payroll data file.

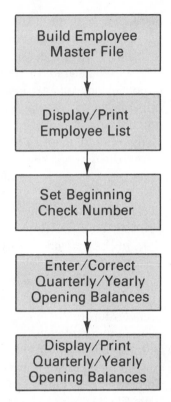

Figure 10.1   Payroll Setup Procedures

Payroll File Maintenance Input Form (Form PR-1)   The Payroll File Maintenance input form serves two separate functions. First, it is used to record the employees to be established in the payroll data file during payroll setup. Second, it is used to record additions, changes, and deletions to the payroll data file after payroll setup has been completed and during the ongoing processing of each pay period. The second use of this form will be discussed further in Chapter 11.

The Payroll File Maintenance input form shown in Figure 10.2 illustrates how the employee information is recorded to set up employee data for Bell Corporation.

The run date recorded in the upper left corner of the form, 12/15/--, is the month, day, and year the form was completed and key-entered into the computer. Each line on the form represents the data required to set up one employee payroll record in the payroll data file. The Employee Number column contains a three-digit number assigned to the employee for the purpose of identification. The Employee Name column contains the name of the employee. The Department Number column contains a one- or two-digit number which identifies the department of the company in which the employee works.. If departments are not used, this column may be left blank. Notice that Bell Corporation has two departments (10 and 11). The next column, Social Security Number, contains the employee's social security number. This number is required for tax purposes. The Marital Status column is used to record the employee's marital status as **M** (for married) or **S** (for single). This information is also needed for tax purposes. The next column, Withholding Allowances, contains the number of allowances

	EMP NO.	EMPLOYEE NAME	DEPT NO.	SOC. SEC. NUMBER	MAR. STAT.	W/H ALLOW.	PAY PER/YR.	TYPE PAY	RATE/ SALARY	ONE	TWO	THREE	
1	110	Bauer, Mary	10	472051799	S	1	26	H	9.25	18.00	12.00		1
2	120	Duncan, Richard	10	564421860	S	1	26	H	9.75	18.00	15.00		2
3	130	Ludwick, Thelma	10	751661251	S	1	26	H	10.50	18.00	20.00	12.50	3
4	140	Nash, Suzanne	11	519637720	M	4	26	S	961.54	20.00	7.50		4
5	150	Parsons, Roger	11	464328217	M	3	26	S	1346.15	25.00	12.00	6.00	5
6	160	Sauer, Beverly	11	476223842	M	2	26	S	1346.15	18.00	12.25	12.00	6
7	170	Weber, Keith	10	721419953	S	1	26	H	9.75	18.00	12.00		7

RUN DATE 12/15/-- MM DD YY

PAYROLL FILE MAINTENANCE Input Form

Problem No. Sample / FORM PR-1

M = MARRIED S = SINGLE   H = HOURLY S = SALARIED

Figure 10.2   Payroll File Maintenance Input Form (Form PR-1)

claimed by the employee and is used for income tax withholding calculation. The Pay Periods per Year column contains the number of times per year the employee is to be paid. All Bell Corporation employees are paid every two weeks (26 times per year). The Type of Pay column contains either an **S** (for salaried employees) or an **H** (for hourly employees). The Rate/Salary column contains the gross amount the employee is to be paid for the pay period (for salaried employees) or the employee's hourly rate (for hourly employees). The last three columns contain voluntary deductions which are withheld from the employee's check each pay period. Examples of voluntary deductions include union dues, charitable contributions, or insurance premium payments.

Payroll Beginning Balances Input Form (Form PR-2)

After the employee data has been key-entered and the beginning check number has been established, the quarter-to-date and year-to-date opening balances may be entered. These opening balances need to be entered only if required at the time the computerized payroll system is established. For example, if the computerized payroll system is set up on January 1 (prior to the first pay period of the new calendar year), the previous year's end-of-quarter and end-of-year balances have been cleared and the payroll reporting is complete. Therefore, neither the quarter-to-date nor year-to-date data is required. If the computerized payroll system is set up during the calendar year immediately after

Quarter-to-Date reports are completed and before the first pay period of the new quarter, the quarter-to-date balances have been cleared and only the year-to-date data is required. If the computerized payroll system is set up after at least one pay period has been processed for a quarter, both the quarter-to-date and year-to-date data is required.

Because Bell Corporation is being set up on a computerized payroll system on December 15 of the current year, both quarter-to-date and year-to-date opening balances must be entered. These opening balances are taken from the employees' payroll earnings records which were used in the manual payroll system. The Payroll Beginning Balances input form shown in Figure 10.3 illustrates how the opening balances for Bell Corporation are recorded.

Problem No. *Sample*

RUN DATE *12/15/--*
MM DD YY

PAYROLL BEGINNING BALANCES
Input Form

FORM PR-2

	1	2	3	4	5	6	7	8	9	
	EMPLOYEE NUMBER	QUARTER-TO-DATE				YEAR-TO-DATE				
		GROSS	FEDERAL	STATE	FICA	GROSS	FEDERAL	STATE	FICA	
1	110	3700 00	465 60	186 25	277 85	18500 00	2328 00	931 25	1389 25	1
2	120	3900 00	495 60	198 25	292 90	19500 00	2478 00	991 25	1464 50	2
3	130	4095 00	524 85	209 95	307 55	20475 00	2624 25	1049 75	1537 75	3
4	140	4807 70	398 10	159 25	361 05	24038 50	1990 50	796 25	1805 25	4
5	150	6730 75	744 25	297 70	505 50	33653 75	3721 25	1488 50	2527 50	5
6	160	6730 75	801 90	320 75	505 50	33653 75	4009 50	1603 75	2527 50	6
7	170	3729 40	470 00	188 00	280 10	18647 00	2350 00	940 00	1400 50	7
8										8
9										9
10										10
11										11
12										12
13										13
14										14
15										15
16										16
17										17
18										18
19										19
20										20
21										21
22										22
23										23
24										24
25										25

Figure 10.3   Payroll Beginning Balances Input Form (Form PR-2)

The run date, located in the upper left corner of the form, is the date the opening balances are recorded and key-entered into the computer. Each line on the body of the form represents the data required to establish the opening balance for one employee. The Employee Number column contains a three-digit number for each employee with an opening balance. These employee numbers can be located by referring to the Payroll File Maintenance input form prepared earlier or by viewing an employee window display. The rest of the form is divided into two major sections: (1) the Quarter-To-Date section contains fields for gross earnings and tax withholdings (federal, state, and FICA), and (2) the Year-To-Date section contains the same fields for the year-to-date totals. The data recorded in these fields is key-entered into the computer and, in turn, updates each employee's record.

PAYROLL SETUP OPERATIONAL PROCEDURES Once the payroll file maintenance and Payroll Beginning Balances input forms are completed, the data contained on them must be key-entered into the computer and various reports may be generated. However, before the computerized payroll system can be set up, the following tasks must be completed:

1. The initial start-up procedures must be performed.
2. The accounting system setup data fields must be set (if they have not already been set).
3. The *Load Data to Disk* option must be selected and the computer informed that a new file is to be created.
4. The Company Information data fields must be set.
5. The *Payroll* option must be selected from the System Selection Menu.

Once the Payroll System is selected, it will be loaded into computer memory and the Payroll Main Menu will appear as shown in Figure 10.4.

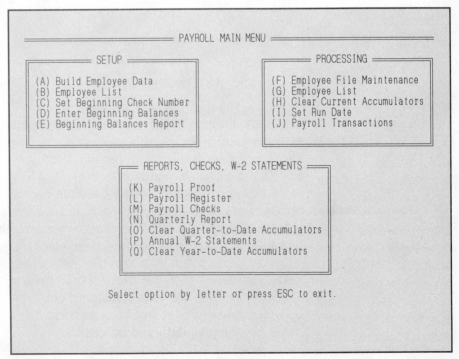

Figure 10.4   Payroll Main Menu

Any option may be selected from the Payroll Main Menu by simply keying the appropriate letter. When a selection is made, a new display will appear on the screen allowing you to enter appropriate data (data entry display) or choose a course of action (decision prompt). The following sections explain how Options A through E of the Payroll Main Menu are used to set up the Payroll System. Each of these options should be performed in sequence in order to complete the setup process.

Build Employee Data Option A

When you select Option A, *Build Employee Data*, from the Payroll Main Menu, the Build Employee Data screen shown in Figure 10.5 will appear. An employee (Mary Bauer) has been entered to illustrate how the data appears.

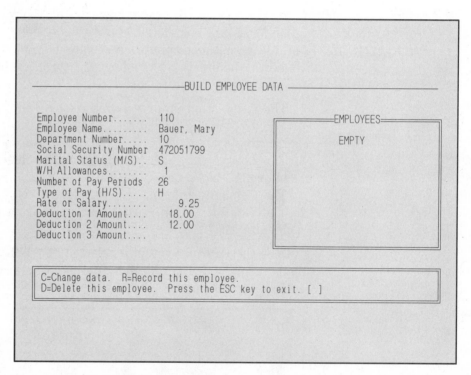

Figure 10.5   Build Employee Data Screen

Notice the Employees window displays **EMPTY** to indicate that there are no employees currently in computer memory. However, if the computer detects employees currently stored in its memory, a decision prompt message will appear and you will be asked to strike the **Y** key (for Yes) or **N** (for No) to erase the employee data currently in memory. Also, because of the serious consequences of selecting this option, a warning decision prompt message is displayed on the screen when the option is selected. The **N** option should be selected if you were unable to key-enter all of your employee data during a previous work session. When you are ready to finish entering the employee data, you may select the *Build Employee Data* option, choose the **N** option, and key-enter the remaining employee data. This option may also be used to add an employee or correct errors. Strike the **Y** key to erase all previous data and proceed.

The data recorded on the Payroll File Maintenance input form is used as the source document from which the employee data fields are keyed. In order to key-enter the data for each employee, complete the following procedures:

1. Key-enter an employee number from one to three digits in length. At this time, the computer will check to see if the employee number key-entered already exists in its memory. If the employee data exists, all the data for the employee will be displayed, and you will be permitted to make corrections. If the employee number entered does not exist, the computer will assume that you wish to build the employee's data record.
2. Key-enter the employee name.
3. Key-enter the department number (if used) as a one- or two-digit number.
4. Key-enter the social security number as a nine-digit number (without hyphens).
5. Key-enter the marital status code (**M** for married, **S** for single).
6. Key-enter the number of withholding allowances as a one- or two-digit number.
7. Key-enter the number of pay periods per year (from 1 to 52).
8. Key-enter the type of pay code (**H** for hourly, **S** for salaried).
9. Key-enter the hourly rate for hourly employees or the amount to be paid each pay period for salaried employees.
10. The remaining fields are used for any voluntary deductions specified by the employee. As many as three voluntary deductions may be entered. Key-enter the amount of each deduction to be withheld per pay period. If no deductions are required, press the ENTER/RETURN key without keying any data in these fields. When the cursor is positioned in the last data field (*Deduction 3 Amount*), press ENTER/RETURN and the computer will check the validity of all the data as it appears on the screen. If no errors are detected, the data will be displayed once again. If errors are detected, an error code and message will be displayed, and you will be given an opportunity to make corrections.
11. A decision prompt will appear asking if you wish to change, record, or delete the employee data. Strike **C** to make changes or corrections, **R** to record the data as displayed, or **D** to delete the data.

    Note: After the employee data has been key-entered and recorded, the employee number and name will appear in the Employees window indicating that a record for that employee has been created.

12. Continue this process until all employees or corrections have been key-entered. When finished, press the Esc key to exit this data entry screen and return to the Payroll Main Menu.

***Employee List
Option B***   When you select Option B, *Employee List*, from the Payroll Main Menu, you will be able to print or display an employee list. When this option is chosen, the usual decision prompt will appear which permits you to display or print the employee list or to exit this option. Select the option of your choice. Figure 10.6 illustrates a displayed employee list for Bell Corporation.

```
RUN DATE: 12/15/--          BELL CORPORATION                    EMPLOYEE LIST
EMP NAME              DEPT  MAR   PAY TYPE    RATE    -------DEDUCTIONS-------
NO. SOC SEC           NO.   ST  W/H PER  PAY   SAL    DED #1   DED #2   DED #3
--------------------------------------------------------------------------------
110 Bauer, Mary       10    S    1  26   H    9.25    18.00    12.00      .00
    472-05-1799

120 Duncan, Richard   10    S    1  26   H    9.75    18.00    15.00      .00
    564-42-1860

130 Ludwick, Thelma   10    S    1  26   H   10.50    18.00    20.00    12.50
    751-66-1251

140 Nash, Suzanne     11    M    4  26   S  961.54    20.00     7.50      .00
    519-63-7720

150 Parsons, Roger    11    M    3  26   S 1346.15    25.00    12.00     6.00
    464-32-8217

160 Sauer, Beverly    11    M    2  26   S 1346.15    18.00    12.25    12.00
    476-22-3842

170 Weber, Keith      10    S    1  26   H    9.75    18.00    12.00      .00
    721-41-9953

    TOTAL EMPLOYEES  7

                Press SPACE BAR to continue.
```

Figure 10.6   Employee List

Set Beginning Check Number Option C

The purpose of this option is to allow you to establish a starting check number. This check number will be assigned to the first payroll check printed. The checks will be numbered consecutively thereafter. The Set Beginning Check Number data entry screen is shown in Figure 10.7.

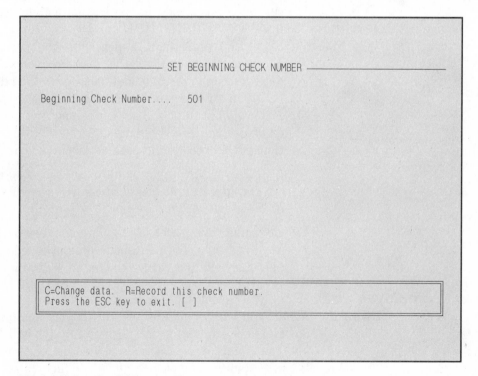

Figure 10.7   Set Beginning Check Number Data Entry Screen

When the Set Beginning Check Number data entry screen appears, key-enter the desired beginning check number. After the beginning check number is key-entered, a decision prompt will appear at the bottom of the screen telling you to strike **C** to change the data, strike **R** to record the check number, or press Esc to ignore the data and return to the Payroll Main Menu.

Enter Beginning Balances Option D

After the employee data has been entered and the beginning check number has been established, the quarter-to-date and year-to-date opening balances must be key-entered for each employee with a balance. A Payroll Beginning Balances input form should be completed and used as the source document from which these opening balances are keyed. When Option D is selected, the Enter Beginning Balances data entry screen will appear. In Figure 10.8 shown below, the beginning balances have been key-entered to illustrate how the data appears.

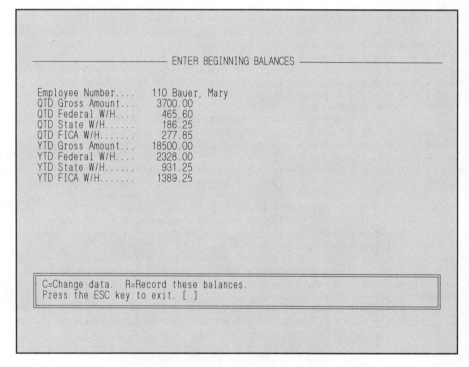

Figure 10.8   Enter Beginning Balances Data Entry Screen

In addition to entering opening balances, the *Enter Beginning Balances* option can be used to make corrections to opening balances which were previously keyed in error. This can be done by key-entering the employee's number whose data is in error, positioning the cursor on the incorrect opening balance, then simply key-entering the correct data. The computer will replace the incorrect data stored in the employee's record with the correct data. A window may be opened to view the employees currently stored in the computer's memory. You will find this window function helpful in verifying valid employee numbers during this data entry activity. To establish opening balances or make corrections to incorrect opening balances, complete the following procedures:

1. Key-enter the employee number. At this time, the computer will check to see if the employee number key-entered already contains beginning balance data. If it does, all the beginning balance data will be displayed and you will be permitted to make corrections (proceed to No. 7). If no beginning balance data exists for the designated employee, the computer will assume you wish to set up opening balance data for that employee.

   *Note: If the employee number does not exist, a decision prompt message will appear asking if you wish to set up this employee. If you respond **Yes**, the Build Employee Data screen will appear and you will be permitted to set up the employee. After the employee has been set up and recorded in the computer's memory, the Enter Beginning Balances data entry screen will again appear and you will be permitted to continue.*

2. Key-enter the quarter-to-date gross earnings amount.
3. Key-enter the quarter-to-date federal withholding amount.
4. Key-enter the quarter-to-date state withholding amount.
5. Key-enter the quarter-to-date FICA withholding amount.
6. Repeat Numbers 2 through 5 for the corresponding year-to-date data fields. After the last field (*Year-to-Date FICA Withholding*) is keyed, the computer will check the validity of the data as it appears on the screen. If errors are detected, an error code and message will be displayed, and you will be given an opportunity to make corrections.
7. A decision prompt will appear asking if you wish to make a change, record the opening balances, or ignore the displayed data. Strike **C** to make changes or corrections, **R** to record the data as displayed, or press Esc to ignore the data and display a blank Enter Beginning Balances data entry screen.
8. Continue this process until all opening balances have been key-entered. When finished, press the Esc key to exit this data entry screen and return to the Payroll Main Menu.

Beginning Balances Report Option E

When you select Option E, *Beginning Balances Report*, from the Payroll Main Menu, you will be able to print or display a Beginning Balances report. This report consists of the employee names, employee numbers, and the quarter-to-date and year-to-date balances of the employees' gross earnings and federal, state, and FICA withholding amounts.

When this option is selected the usual decision prompt message will appear in which you will be permitted to display or print the Beginning Balances report or to exit this option. Select the option desired. Figure 10.9 illustrates a displayed Beginning Balances report for Bell Corporation.

It is recommended that the Beginning Balances report be selected and run after the opening balances are set up and after making any corrections. This will help verify that all data has been recorded properly and provide an audit trail (if printed) for future reference.

Save Data to Disk

As with all the work you completed while using each of the previous accounting systems, be sure to save your payroll data to disk as a work

```
RUN DATE: 12/15/--        BELL CORPORATION              BEGINNING BALANCES
EMP                   --------QUARTERLY & YEARLY--------
NO. NAME                GROSS  FEDERAL     STATE     FICA
-----------------------------------------------------------------------
110 Bauer, Mary         3700.00   465.60   186.25   277.85
                       18500.00  2328.00   931.25  1389.25

120 Duncan, Richard     3900.00   495.60   198.25   292.90
                       19500.00  2478.00   991.25  1464.50

130 Ludwick, Thelma     4095.00   524.85   209.95   307.55
                       20475.00  2624.25  1049.75  1537.75

140 Nash, Suzanne       4807.70   398.10   159.25   361.05
                       24038.50  1990.50   796.25  1805.25

150 Parsons, Roger      6730.25   744.25   297.70   505.50
                       33653.75  3721.25  1488.50  2527.50

160 Sauer, Beverly      6730.75   801.90   320.75   505.50
                       33653.75  4009.50  1603.75  2527.50

170 Weber, Keith        3729.40   470.00   188.00   280.10
                       18647.00  2350.00   940.00  1400.50


         Press SPACE BAR to continue.
```

Figure 10.9   Beginning·Balances Report

in progress file prior to computer shutdown. If you fail to run this option prior to ending the automated accounting session or before loading another file from disk, all data keyed and processed during your computer session will be lost.

PAYROLL SETUP (SAMPLE PROBLEM)

This sample problem illustrates the procedures required to establish a computerized payroll system. The step-by-step procedures for establishing a computerized payroll system for Bell Corporation are provided in the following sections.

The employee data for Bell Corporation has been recorded for you on the Payroll File Maintenance input form (Form PR-1) shown in Figure 10.10. Each employee has been assigned a three-digit number. The beginning balances have been recorded for you on the Payroll Beginning Balances input form (Form PR-2) shown in Figure 10.11.

Instructions

Step 1   Bring up the System Selection Menu according to the instructions for your microcomputer.

Step 2   Select Option B, *Accounting System Setup*, from the System Selection Menu. Set and record each field as follows:

Simplified/Expanded General Ledger .... S
Simplified/Expanded Accounts Payable .... S

	1	2	3	4	5	6	7	8	9	10	11	12	
	EMP NO.	EMPLOYEE NAME	DEPT NO.	SOC. SEC. NUMBER	MAR. STAT.	W/H ALLOW.	PAY PER/YR.	TYPE PAY	RATE/ SALARY	ONE	TWO	THREE	
1	110	Bauer, Mary	10	472051799	S	1	26	H	9:25	18:00	12:00		1
2	120	Duncan, Richard	10	564421860	S	1	26	H	9:75	18:00	15:00		2
3	130	Ludwick, Thelma	10	751661251	S	1	26	H	10:50	18:00	20:00	12:50	3
4	140	Nash, Suzanne	11	519637720	M	4	26	S	961:54	20:00	7:50		4
5	150	Parsons, Roger	11	464328217	M	3	26	S	1346:15	25:00	12:00	6:00	5
6	160	Sauer, Beverly	11	476223842	M	2	26	S	1346:15	18:00	12:25	12:00	6
7	170	Weber, Keith	10	721419953	S	1	26	H	9:75	18:00	12:00		7

PAYROLL FILE MAINTENANCE Input Form — RUN DATE 12/15/-- — Problem No. 10-S — FORM PR-1

M = MARRIED S = SINGLE   H = HOURLY S = SALARIED

Figure 10.10   Payroll File Maintenance Input Form (Problem 10-S)

Simplified/Expanded Accounts Receivable . . . . S
Each Report on New Page . . . . N
Checks on Preprinted Forms . . . . N
Statements on Preprinted Forms . . . . N

Step 3 From the System Selection Menu, select Option C (*Load Data from Disk*). When the Load Data from Disk menu appears, select Option D, *Create Empty File.*

Step 4 Select Option D, *Company Information*, from the System Selection Menu. Key-enter and record each field as follows:

Run Date . . . . 12/15/-- (use the current year)
Company Name . . . . Bell Corporation
Problem Number . . . . Problem 10-S
Type of Business C

Step 5 Select Option I, *Payroll*, from the System Selection Menu.

Step 6 After the Payroll System has loaded into the computer, select Option A, *Build Employee Data*, from the Payroll Main Menu.

Step 7 When the Build Employee Data screen appears, key-enter and record the data for each employee from the Payroll File Maintenance input form shown in Figure 10.10. Key-enter each employee name with the last name first, a comma, and then the first name.

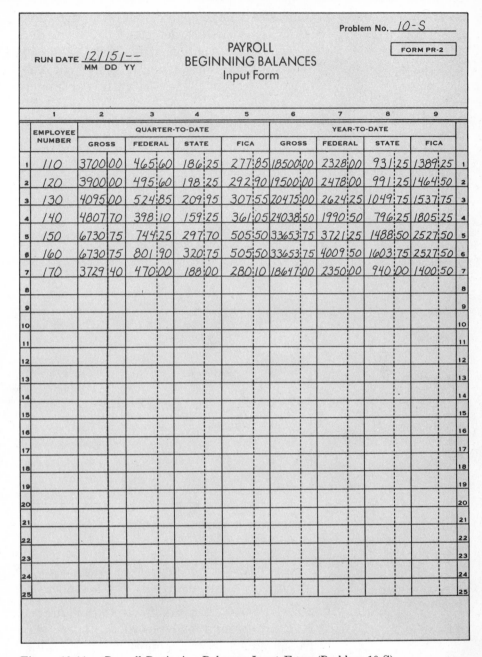

	EMPLOYEE NUMBER	QUARTER-TO-DATE				YEAR-TO-DATE				
		GROSS	FEDERAL	STATE	FICA	GROSS	FEDERAL	STATE	FICA	
1	110	3700 00	465 60	186 25	277 85	18500 00	2328 00	931 25	1389 25	1
2	120	3900 00	495 60	198 25	292 90	19500 00	2478 00	991 25	1464 50	2
3	130	4095 00	524 85	209 95	307 55	20475 00	2624 25	1049 75	1537 75	3
4	140	4807 70	398 10	159 25	361 05	24038 50	1990 50	796 25	1805 25	4
5	150	6730 75	744 25	297 70	505 50	33653 75	3721 25	1488 50	2527 50	5
6	160	6730 75	801 90	320 75	505 50	33653 75	4009 50	1603 75	2527 50	6
7	170	3729 40	470 00	188 00	280 10	18647 00	2350 00	940 00	1400 50	7
8										8
9										9
10										10
11										11
12										12
13										13
14										14
15										15
16										16
17										17
18										18
19										19
20										20
21										21
22										22
23										23
24										24
25										25

Figure 10.11   Payroll Beginning Balances Input Form (Problem 10-S)

Step 8   When the data for all employees has been key-entered, press Esc to exit and return to the Payroll Main Menu. If you exit before all employees have been key-entered, the remaining employees may be key-entered later by completing the following procedures:

1. Select the *Build Employee Data* option.
2. When the decision prompt to erase payroll data appears, select **N** (for No).
3. Key-enter the remaining employee data.

Step 9   Select Option B, *Employee List*, from the Payroll Main Menu.

Step 10   Display or print the employee list.

Step 11   Compare your employee list with the correct one shown in Figure 10.12. If errors are detected on your employee list, select the *Build Employee Data* option, strike **N** so the employee list will not be erased, and key-enter the missing or correct data for the incorrect employee records. Repeat Steps 9-11 until your employee list is correct.

EMP NO.	NAME SOC SEC	DEPT NO.	MAR ST	W/H	PAY PER	TYPE PAY	RATE SAL	DED #1	DED #2	DED #3
	RUN DATE: 12/15/--	BELL CORPORATION EMPLOYEE LIST								
110	Bauer, Mary 472-05-1799	10	S	1	26	H	9.25	18.00	12.00	.00
120	Duncan, Richard 564-42-1860	10	S	1	26	H	9.75	18.00	15.00	.00
130	Ludwick, Thelma 751-66-1251	10	S	1	26	H	10.50	18.00	20.00	12.50
140	Nash, Suzanne 519-63-7720	11	M	4	26	S	961.54	20.00	7.50	.00
150	Parsons, Roger 464-32-8217	11	M	3	26	S	1346.15	25.00	12.00	6.00
160	Sauer, Beverly 476-22-3842	11	M	2	26	S	1346.15	18.00	12.25	12.00
170	Weber, Keith 721-41-9953	10	S	1	26	H	9.75	18.00	12.00	.00
	TOTAL EMPLOYEES 7									

Figure 10.12   Employee List (Problem 10-S)

Step 12   Select Option C, *Set Beginning Check Number*, from the Payroll Main Menu. Key-enter and record the beginning check number as **501**.

Step 13   Select Option D, *Enter Beginning Balances*, from the Payroll Main Menu. Key-enter and record the opening quarterly/yearly balances from the Payroll Beginning Balances input form shown in Figure 10.11.

Step 14   Select Option E, *Beginning Balances Report*, from the Payroll Main Menu. Display or print the Beginning Balances report.

Step 15   Compare your report with the correct one shown in Figure 10.13. If you detect an error on your Beginning Balances report, select Option D, *Enter Beginning Balances*, from the Payroll Main Menu. Make the necessary corrections to the beginning balances by key-entering the correct data for each field that is in error, and display or print a new Beginning Balances report. When all corrections have been made, press Esc to return to the Payroll Main Menu.

Step 16   Press Esc to exit from the Payroll Main Menu and return to the System Selection Menu.

```
 ●
 ●   RUN DATE: 12/15/--        BELL CORPORATION
 ●                            BEGINNING BALANCES
 ●
 ●   -----------------------------------------------------------
 ●   EMP                     ---------QUARTERLY & YEARLY---------
 ●   NO. NAME                 GROSS   FEDERAL    STATE     FICA
 ●   -----------------------------------------------------------
 ●   110 Bauer, Mary          3700.00   465.60   186.25   277.85
 ●                           18500.00  2328.00   931.25  1389.25
 ●
 ●   120 Duncan, Richard      3900.00   495.60   198.25   292.90
 ●                           19500.00  2478.00   991.25  1464.50
 ●
 ●   130 Ludwick, Thelma      4095.00   524.85   209.95   307.55
 ●                           20475.00  2624.25  1049.75  1537.75
 ●
 ●   140 Nash, Suzanne        4807.70   398.10   159.25   361.05
 ●                           24038.50  1990.50   796.25  1805.25
 ●
 ●   150 Parsons, Roger       6730.25   744.25   297.70   505.50
 ●                           33653.75  3721.25  1488.50  2527.50
 ●
 ●   160 Sauer, Beverly       6730.75   801.90   320.75   505.50
 ●                           33653.75  4009.50  1603.75  2527.50
 ●
 ●   170 Weber, Keith         3729.40   470.00   188.00   280.10
 ●                           18647.00  2350.00   940.00  1400.50
 ●
 ●
 ●
 ●
 ●
 ●
```

Figure 10.13   Beginning Balances Report (Problem 10-S)

Step 17   From the System Selection Menu, select Option E, *Save Data to Disk*, and save your data as a work in progress file (recommend file name **AA10-S**).

Step 18   Press Esc to end your automated accounting session. Then, complete the student exercise and transaction problem which follow.

Name _____

Class _____ Date _____

CHAPTER 10
STUDENT EXERCISE

I. Matching   For each of the following definitions, write the letter of the term which best fits that definition in the space provided.

a. Transaction record
b. Payroll File Maintenance input form
c. Payroll Beginning Balances input form

d. Payroll data file
e. Employee record
f. Field

1. _____ All of the transaction data entered for each employee who is to be paid during the current pay period, such as regular and overtime hours worked. (Objs. 1, 2)

2. _____ Each item of data in an employee record, such as the employee number, name, etc. (Obj. 9)

3. _____ All of the fields which define the payroll data for one employee. (Objs. 1, 2, 9)

4. _____ Used to record quarterly and yearly opening balances. (Objs. 5, 9)

5. _____ Used to record all data for each employee record. (Objs. 2, 9)

6. _____ Contains all of the employee payroll records for the company. (Obj 9)

II. Short Answer   1. Identify and describe the steps involved in payroll setup. (Obj. 9)

_____
_____
_____
_____
_____
_____

2. Describe the differences between manual and computerized payroll systems. (Obj. 1)

_____
_____
_____
_____
_____

3. Why must the *Save Data to Disk* option be the last option selected prior to ending the automated accounting system? (Obj. 8)

_____

_____

_____

_____

4. What is the purpose of the *Employee List* option? (Obj. 3)

_____

_____

5. What is the purpose of the Beginning Balances report? (Obj. 6)

_____

_____

PAYROLL SETUP
TRANSACTION PROBLEM 10-1

As of December 1 of the current year, Chase Corporation wishes to convert their manual payroll system to a computerized payroll system. Chase Corporation is a manufacturer of automotive parts, and is organized as a corporation type of business. Your task is to set up an automated payroll system from the employee and beginning balances data provided in the following tables: (Objs. 2-9)

Emp No. Name	Dept. No.	Soc. Sec. Number	Marital Status	W/H Allow.	Pay Per./Yr.	Type Pay	Rate/ Sal.	Deductions		
								One	Two	Three
510 Burns, Lynne	20	497087631	M	4	24	H	12.50	22.00	7.50	
520 Ellis, Scott	30	417375499	S	1	24	H	10.20	17.00	15.00	7.50
530 Levey, Larry	30	539416823	M	2	12	S	2,500.00	28.00		
540 Phelps, Nora	30	748521226	S	1	24	H	12.00	7.00	12.00	
550 Travis, Beth	20	442015639	S	1	12	S	2,666.67	28.00	17.00	12.00
560 York, Douglas	20	729683454	S	1	24	H	11.25	15.00	7.50	

As of December 1 of the current year, the quarter-to-date and year-to-date withholdings for each of the Chase Corporation employees are as follows:

Employee Number	Quarter-to-Date				Year-to-Date			
	Gross	Federal	State	FICA	Gross	Federal	State	FICA
510	4075.00	331.24	132.48	306.04	22412.20	1821.82	728.64	1683.22
520	3223.20	406.00	162.40	242.08	17727.60	2233.00	893.20	1331.44
530	5000.00	570.00	228.00	375.50	27500.00	3135.00	1254.00	2065.25
540	3840.00	528.60	211.44	288.40	21120.00	2907.30	1162.92	1586.20
550	5333.34	946.76	378.70	400.54	29333.37	5207.18	2082.85	2202.97
560	3600.00	462.52	185.00	270.36	19800.00	2543.86	1017.50	1486.98

Instructions

Step 1 Remove the blank input forms and the Chapter 10 Audit Test from the end of this chapter. Fill in the answers to the audit test as you work through Problem 10-1.

Step 2 Record the employee data on the Payroll File Maintenance input form (Form PR-1).

Step 3 Record the employee quarter-to-date and year-to-date data on the Payroll Beginning Balances input form (Form PR-2).

Step 4 Bring up the System Selection Menu.

Step 5 Select the *Accounting System Setup* option and set each field as follows:

Simplified/Expanded General Ledger .... S
Simplified/Expanded Accounts Payable .... S
Simplified/Expanded Accounts Receivable .... S
Each Report on New Page .... N
Checks on Preprinted Forms .... N
Statements on Preprinted Forms .... N

Step **6**   Select the *Load Data from Disk* option and create an empty payroll file.

Step **7**   Select the *Company Information* option, and key-enter and record each field as follows:

Run Date .... 12/01/-- (use the current year)
Company Name .... Chase Corporation
Problem Number .... Problem 10-1
Type of Business C

Step **8**   Select Option I, *Payroll*, from the System Selection Menu.

Step **9**   After the Payroll System has loaded into the computer, select Option A, *Build Employee Data*, from the Payroll Main Menu.

Step **10**   Key-enter and record the employee data from the Payroll File Maintenance input form prepared in Step 2.

Step **11**   Print or display an employee list and correct any errors that are found.

Step **12**   Set the beginning check number to **801**.

Step **13**   Key-enter and record the quarterly and yearly data from the Payroll Beginning Balances input form prepared in Step 3.

Step **14**   Print or display a Beginning Balances report and correct any errors that are found.

Step **15**   Return to the System Selection Menu.

Step **16**   From the System Selection Menu, select Option E, *Save Data to Disk*, and save your data as a work in progress file (recommend file name **AA10-1**).

Step **17**   Press Esc to end your automated accounting session.

Step **18**   Hand in the completed student exercise sheets, input forms, the audit test, and any printouts to your instructor.

You have now completed the computer exercise for Chapter 10.

Name _____

Class _____ Date _____

	PAYROLL	Problem No._____
RUN DATE __/__/__ MM DD YY	**BEGINNING BALANCES** Input Form	**FORM PR-2**

	1	2	3	4	5	6	7	8	9	
	EMPLOYEE NUMBER	QUARTER-TO-DATE				YEAR-TO-DATE				
		GROSS	FEDERAL	STATE	FICA	GROSS	FEDERAL	STATE	FICA	
1										1
2										2
3										3
4										4
5										5
6										6
7										7
8										8
9										9
10										10
11										11
12										12
13										13
14										14
15										15
16										16
17										17
18										18
19										19
20										20
21										21
22										22
23										23
24										24
25										25

Problem No. _____

FORM PR-1

PAYROLL
FILE MAINTENANCE Input Form

RUN DATE ___/___/___
MM DD YY

									DEDUCTIONS		
1	2	3	4	5	6	7	8	9	10	11	12
EMP. NO.	EMPLOYEE NAME	DEPT NO.	SOC. SEC. NUMBER	MAR. STAT.	W/H ALLOW.	PAY PER/YR.	TYPE PAY	RATE/ SALARY	ONE	TWO	THREE
1											
2											
3											
4											
5											
6											
7											
8											
9											
10											
11											
12											
13											
14											
15											
16											

M = MARRIED
S = SINGLE

H = HOURLY
S = SALARIED

Name _____

Class _____ Date _____

CHAPTER 10
AUDIT TEST

1. What is Larry Levey's social security number?

   _____

2. How many of the employees are married?

   _____

3. How many of the employees are paid hourly?

   _____

4. What are the year-to-date gross earnings for Larry Levey?

   _____

5. What is the quarter-to-date state income tax withheld for Beth Travis?

   _____

11 PAYROLL TRANSACTIONS AND REPORTS

LEARNING OBJECTIVES

Upon completion of this chapter, you will be able to:

1. Perform employee file maintenance.
2. Display or print an employee list.
3. Set the run date.
4. Enter and correct payroll transactions.
5. Display or print a payroll proof.
6. Display or print a payroll register.
7. Display or print payroll checks.
8. Display or print a Quarterly report.
9. Display or print annual W-2 statements.
10. Perform the system shutdown procedure.
11. Identify the components and procedures required to generate payroll reports.

INTRODUCTION

In Chapter 10, you learned how to set up employees and beginning balances in the payroll data file. This chapter will cover the payroll pay-period cycle used in an automated accounting system. You will soon learn how payroll transactions are stored in the payroll data file. You will also see how this data is used to update the employee records and generate the payroll reports required to keep track of the company's payroll records. The procedure used in *Automated Accounting for the Microcomputer* to perform payroll processing is illustrated in Figure 11.1.

Once the employee data has initially been built, it must be maintained. New employees must be added and existing employee data may need to be changed. For instance, after all W-2 statements are printed at the end of the calendar year, employees who are no longer with the company must be deleted. The process of making additions, changes, and deletions to the employee data is referred to as **employee file maintenance**. This process is essential for maintaining accurate payroll information.

Data for each employee which may change from one pay period to another, such as regular or overtime hours, is termed **payroll transaction data.** This data is analyzed and recorded on a Payroll input form. The regular and overtime hours for all employees entered on the Payroll input form are totaled and recorded as **batch totals** on the bottom of the form. Later, these batch totals are compared to the **proof totals** printed at the bottom of a computer-generated payroll proof to verify that the payroll transaction data was key-entered correctly.

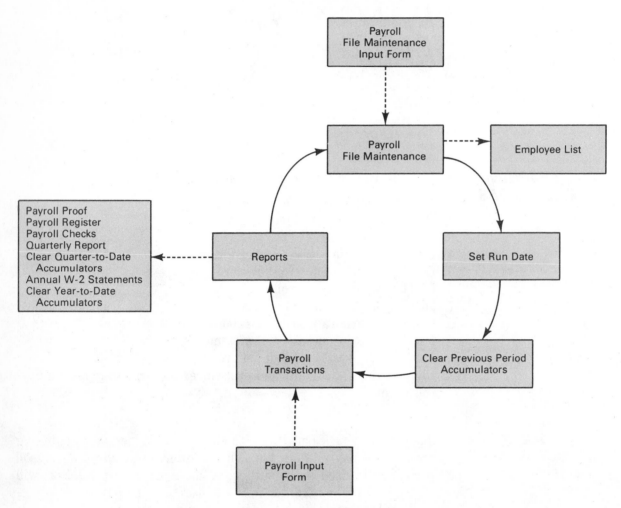

Figure 11.1   Payroll Transaction Processing Procedure

After all data has been analyzed, recorded, and totaled on the Payroll input form, the computer must be instructed to clear the accumulated data (transaction data) from its files. This will erase all the transaction data which is no longer needed. After this data has been erased, the transaction data recorded on the Payroll input form for the current pay period must be key-entered into the computer. Once entered into the computer, the data is checked for errors. First, the employee number is checked to verify that a record exists for that employee. Second, each remaining field of data is verified to determine that it is numeric and within a maximum numeric limit (for example, the number of regular hours entered must be less than or equal to 999.99). After all transaction data for a particular employee has been key-entered and checked, a final check is performed based on the type of pay (hourly or salaried) recorded in the employee's record. If the employee is hourly, the number of regular hours and overtime hours must be entered. If the employee is salaried, a check is made to ensure that the amount of salary was entered when the employee data was initially established.

If no errors are detected in the payroll transaction data, the computer will perform all payroll calculations (gross earnings, tax with-holdings, voluntary deductions, and net pay); create a record of this transaction; and update the employee's record. This cycle continues until the data for all employees to be paid for the current pay period has been keyed into the computer. Thus, only those employees whose employee numbers and transaction data are entered, verified through a payroll proof, and updated will be paid during the current pay period. After the payroll transactions have been key-entered, a payroll proof should be printed or displayed and checked against the Payroll input form. Finally, a payroll register and payroll checks can be generated by the computer to complete the payroll process.

At the end of each quarter, a Quarterly report must be generated. This report is used by the company to report to the Internal Revenue Service the amount of employee wages which are taxable for FICA. After producing this report, the quarter-to-date fields are reset to zero (using the *Clear Quarter-to-Date Accumulators* option) so that the totals for the next quarter can be accumulated. Similarly, at the end of the year, each employee paid by the company during the year must be provided with a W-2 statement for individual tax-reporting purposes. The computer accumulates the earnings and withholdings data for each employee throughout the year. After the W-2 statements are run, the year-to-date fields are also reset to zero (using the *Clear Year-to-Date Accumulators* option) so that the totals for the next year can be accumulated.

GENERAL LEDGER PAYROLL ENTRIES

The payroll register for each pay period contains information which is required to make payroll journal entries in the General Ledger System. The payroll register displays the total gross pay, the totals for all withholdings and deductions, and the total net pay for all employees. In addition, the amount of the employer's federal and state unemployment tax liability is calculated and displayed. These totals are needed to record the payroll and to record the employer's payroll taxes in the General Ledger System. This data is then recorded on a General Ledger input form (Form GL-2) and key-entered as journal entries into the General Ledger System.

COMPLETING THE INPUT FORMS

Information for processing the payroll is recorded on two different input forms. These forms are the Payroll File Maintenance input form (Form PR-1) and the Payroll input form (Form PR-3). You have already worked with the Payroll File Maintenance input form in Chapter 10 to build employee data in the payroll data file. In this chapter, you will learn how this form and the Payroll input form are utilized to process a typical company's payroll.

Payroll File Maintenance Input Form (Form PR-1)

Employee data must be maintained on an ongoing basis. New employees must be added, and changes, such as marital status, number of withholding allowances, and deduction amounts, must be made. After the annual W-2 statements are printed at the end of the calendar year, those employees who are no longer employed with the company must be deleted from the payroll data file. The employee list established for Bell Corporation in Chapter 10 is illustrated in Figure 11.2.

Employee Number	Employee Name
110	Bauer, Mary
120	Duncan, Richard
130	Ludwick, Thelma
140	Nash, Suzanne
150	Parsons, Roger
160	Sauer, Beverly
170	Weber, Keith

Figure 11.2   Bell Corporation Employee List

Let's suppose that during the course of the current pay period the following changes have occurred which require file maintenance in order to update the employee data:

1. Added Rhonda Ritter as a new employee, Employee No. 155 (to place in alphabetic order), Department No. 11, Social Security No. 575-67-8812, married, two withholding allowances, 26 pay periods per year, salaried, $975.00 per pay period, two voluntary deductions of $20.00 and $18.00.
2. Changed Suzanne Nash's number of withholding allowances to 3.
3. Changed Keith Weber's social security number to 721-14-9953.
4. Changed Mary Bauer's Deduction No. 2 to $15.00.
5. Deleted Richard Duncan, Employee No. 120, from the employee data.

In order to record these changes, the Payroll File Maintenance input form (Form PR-1) shown in Figure 11.3 must be completed. Notice that this is the same form you used to build employee data during payroll setup activities.

The run date recorded in the upper left corner of the form represents the date the file maintenance data is key-entered into the computer. Each line on the main body of the form represents the data required to establish and maintain one employee. The first entry is an addition of an employee. The second, third, and fourth entries are changes to existing employee data. An entry to delete an employee is shown on line 5 of the Payroll File Maintenance input form in Figure 11.3. To delete an employee, the letter **D** is entered in the Employee Name column. An employee may be deleted under only two circumstances: (1) If, after the W-2 statements are prepared, the employee no longer works for the company, or (2) If an individual is added to the employee data and then for some reason does not work for the company or does not earn wages.

The first column on the Payroll File Maintenance input form, Employee Number, contains a three-digit number which is used to identify the employee. The Employee Name column contains the name of the employee with the last name first, a comma, and then the first name. The Department Number column contains a one- or two-digit number which identifies the department in which the employee works. The computer will provide earnings totals for each department within the company for the purpose of recording the payroll entries in the General Ledger System. If department numbers are not used, this col-

	1	2	3	4	5	6	7	8	9	10	11	12	

PAYROLL FILE MAINTENANCE Input Form

RUN DATE 12/31/1-- MM DD YY

FORM PR-1

Problem No._____

	EMP NO.	EMPLOYEE NAME	DEPT NO.	SOC. SEC. NUMBER	MAR. STAT.	W/H ALLOW.	PAY PER/YR.	TYPE PAY	RATE/ SALARY	ONE	TWO	THREE	
1	155	Ritter, Rhonda	11	575678812	M	2	26	S	975:00	20:00	18:00		1
2	140					3							2
3	170			721149953									3
4	110										15:00		4
5	120	D											5
6													6
7													7
8													8
9													9
10													10
11													11
12													12
13													13
14													14
15													15
16													16

M = MARRIED S = SINGLE   H = HOURLY S = SALARIED

Figure 11.3   Completed Payroll File Maintenance Input Form

umn may be left blank. The Social Security Number column contains the employee's social security number, which is required for tax purposes. The Marital Status column is used to record the employee's marital status as **M** for married or **S** for single. This information is also used by the computer for tax calculation. The Withholding Allowances field contains the number of allowances to be used during tax calculations.

The Pay Periods per Year column contains the number of times the employee is to be paid per year. For example, if an employee is paid once each month during the calendar year, a 12 would be recorded in this column. If the employee is paid every two weeks during the calendar year, this field would contain a 26. The Type of Pay column contains either an **S** for salaried employees or an **H** for hourly employees. The Rate/Salary column contains either the salary per pay period or the hourly rate for the employee. If the employee is salaried, this column would contain the gross amount of salary to be paid for this pay period. If the employee is hourly, this field would contain his or her hourly rate. The last three columns on the Payroll File Maintenance input form are for recording voluntary deductions which are to be withheld from the employee's check each pay period. Examples of voluntary deductions include union dues, charitable contributions, and insurance.

Payroll Input Form (Form PR-3) In a computerized payroll system, items of information which may change from one pay period to another, such as the number of regular hours and overtime hours worked, are analyzed and recorded on the Payroll input form. The payroll transactions for each employee to be paid during the current pay period are then key-entered into the computer. As you have already learned, these payroll transactions are stored in the payroll data file and used by the computer for processing the payroll. They remain in the payroll data file until the computer is directed to erase them before processing the transactions for the next pay period. Figure 11.4 illustrates a partially completed Payroll input form.

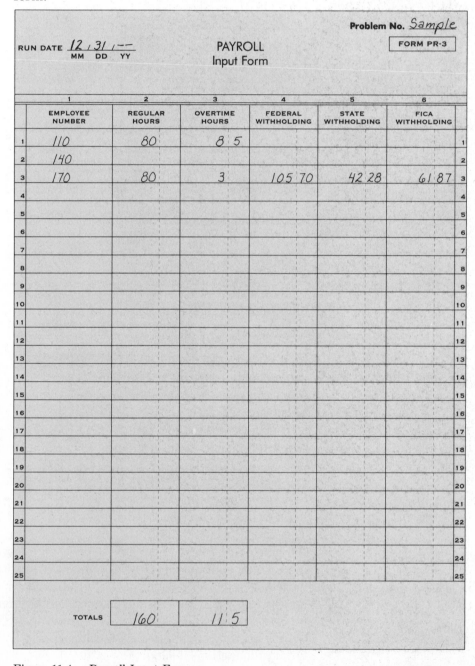

	1 EMPLOYEE NUMBER	2 REGULAR HOURS	3 OVERTIME HOURS	4 FEDERAL WITHHOLDING	5 STATE WITHHOLDING	6 FICA WITHHOLDING	
1	110	80	8 5				1
2	140						2
3	170	80	3	105 70	42 28	61 87	3
4							4
5							5
6							6
7							7
8							8
9							9
10							10
11							11
12							12
13							13
14							14
15							15
16							16
17							17
18							18
19							19
20							20
21							21
22							22
23							23
24							24
25							25
TOTALS		160	11 5				

RUN DATE 12 / 31 / -- (MM DD YY) — PAYROLL Input Form — Problem No. *Sample* — FORM PR-3

Figure 11.4   Payroll Input Form

The run date located in the upper left corner of the form contains the date of the end of the pay period. For example, if the pay period is for one month, the run date should be the last working day of the month, even if the payroll is actually run a few days before this date. The run date is key-entered into the computer and appears on all payroll reports and paychecks generated by the computer.

Each line on the Payroll input form represents one payroll transaction. The first column on the form contains the Employee Number from the employee list which identifies the employee to whom the transaction belongs. Recorded in the Regular Hours column is the number of hours an hourly employee worked during the current pay period for the normal hourly rate. Recorded in the Overtime Hours column is the number of hours an hourly employee worked during the current pay period over and above the regular hours (usually 40 hours per week). In this payroll system, overtime hours are computed at 1 1/2 (1.5) times the hourly rate. Notice that the Regular Hours and Overtime Hours columns are used only for hourly employees.

The three remaining columns on the Payroll input form are used only if you wish to supply the federal, state, or FICA withholdings rather then let the computer calculate them. Finally, at the bottom of the form, the totals for the regular and overtime hours for this pay period are calculated and entered. These batch totals will be used later to verify the accuracy of the data once it is key-entered into the computer.

Three transactions are illustrated in Figure 11.4 on the Payroll input form for Bell Corporation. Line 1 illustrates how an hourly employee is recorded on the form. Employee No. 110 worked 80 regular hours (40 hours per week for a two-week period) and 8 1/2 (8.5) hours overtime. For these overtime hours, the employee will be paid 1 1/2 times the regular hourly rate.

Line 2 illustrates how a salaried employee is recorded on the input form. Notice that only the appropriate employee number (140) is recorded in the Employee Number column.

Line 3 illustrates how an hourly employee with federal, state, and FICA withholding amounts is recorded. Remember, the federal, state, and FICA withholding amounts are only required if you want to supply this data rather than have the computer automatically calculate these values. Employee No. 170 (Keith Weber) worked 80 regular hours and 3 hours overtime. The computer is to deduct the amounts of $105.70 for federal withholding, $42.28 for state withholding, and $61.87 for FICA withholding.

A listing of the transaction data which is entered and stored in the payroll data file may be displayed or printed at any time; however, it is usually printed after all transactions have been keyed into the computer. This payroll proof is useful in detecting and correcting errors. It also serves as an audit trail whereby payroll transactions may be traced to their original source documents. Proof totals for regular and overtime hours are printed at the bottom of the payroll proof. These totals should equal the batch totals recorded at the bottom of the Payroll input form.

**PAYROLL
OPERATIONAL
PROCEDURES**

Once the Payroll File Maintenance input form and the Payroll input form are completed, the data contained on them must be key-entered into the computer. Various reports may then be printed in order to complete the processing of payroll transactions. The following sections explain how Payroll Main Menu Options F through Q (illustrated in Figure 11.5) are used to accomplish this task.

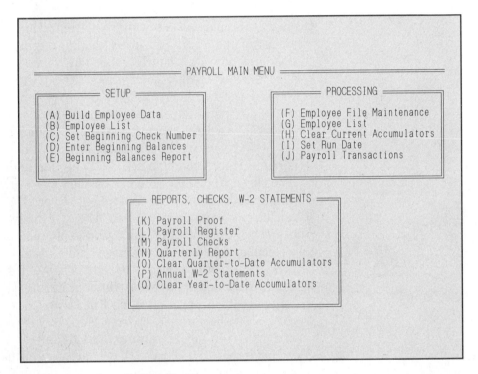

Figure 11.5   Payroll Main Menu

In order to process payroll transactions, the options on the Payroll Main Menu should be selected in the same sequence in which they appear.

**Employee File
Maintenance
Option F**

The *Employee File Maintenance* option permits additions, changes, and deletions to be made to the employee data. When this option is selected, the Employee File Maintenance data entry screen shown in Figure 11.6 will appear.

In order to add, change, or delete employees, complete the following procedures:

1. Key-enter an employee number. The computer will check to see if the employee number key-entered already exists. If not, the computer will assume that you wish to add a new employee. If the employee number already exists, the computer will assume that you wish to delete the employee or make a change to the employee's record. In this case, skip to 11.
2. If you are adding a new employee, key-enter the employee name.
3. Key-enter a two-digit department number. If a department number is not being used, press ENTER/RETURN without key-entering any data to move the cursor to the next field.
4. Key-enter the employee's social security number. Do not use

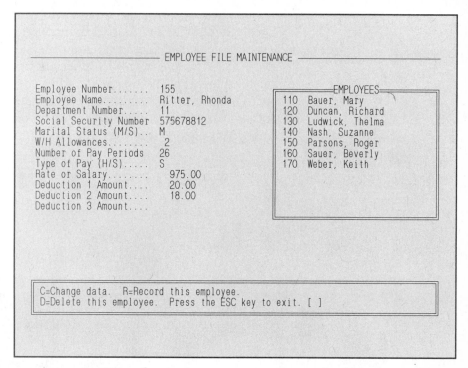

```
┌────────────────────────────────────────────────────────────┐
│                                                              │
│  ──────────────── EMPLOYEE FILE MAINTENANCE ──────────────   │
│                                                              │
│   Employee Number....... 155                  ┌─EMPLOYEES─┐  │
│   Employee Name......... Ritter, Rhonda       │110 Bauer, Mary     │
│   Department Number..... 11                   │120 Duncan, Richard │
│   Social Security Number 575678812            │130 Ludwick, Thelma │
│   Marital Status (M/S).. M                    │140 Nash, Suzanne   │
│   W/H Allowances........    2                 │150 Parsons, Roger  │
│   Number of Pay Periods  26                   │160 Sauer, Beverly  │
│   Type of Pay (H/S).....  S                   │170 Weber, Keith    │
│   Rate or Salary........   975.00             │                    │
│   Deduction 1 Amount....    20.00             └────────────────────┘
│   Deduction 2 Amount....    18.00                            │
│   Deduction 3 Amount....                                     │
│                                                              │
│   ┌───────────────────────────────────────────────────────┐ │
│   │ C=Change data.  R=Record this employee.               │ │
│   │ D=Delete this employee.  Press the ESC key to exit. [ ]│ │
│   └───────────────────────────────────────────────────────┘ │
│                                                              │
└────────────────────────────────────────────────────────────┘
```

Figure 11.6   Employee File Maintenance Data Entry Screen

hyphens or slashes. The computer will insert them later.

5. Key-enter the marital status code (**M** for married, **S** for single).

6. Key-enter the number of withholding allowances as a one- or two-digit number.

7. Key-enter the number of pay periods per year for this employee (from 1 to 52).

8. Key-enter the type of pay code (**H** for hourly, **S** for salaried).

9. Enter the hourly rate for hourly employees or the salary amount to be paid each pay period for salaried employees.

10. Key-enter the amount of the deduction per pay period for each deduction. Each employee may have up to three voluntary deductions, as specified by the employee. If no deductions are required, simply press ENTER/RETURN without key-entering any data to move the cursor past the last deduction amount.

11. A decision prompt will appear asking if you wish to make a change, record this employee, delete this employee, or ignore the displayed data. Strike **C** to make changes or corrections, **R** to record this employee's data, **D** to delete this employee, or press Esc to ignore the data and exit this data entry screen. Remember, an employee cannot be deleted if he or she has been paid by the company during the calendar year or if the annual W-2 statements have not yet been run.

12. Repeat this procedure until all additions, changes, and deletions have been key-entered. Then press Esc without keying any data in the next empty *Employee Number* field to exit this data entry screen and return to the Payroll Main Menu.

Employee List
Option G   An employee list is a report showing employee data stored in the payroll data file. The employee list may be displayed or printed at any

time to verify file maintenance data which has been entered into the Payroll System. Whenever an addition, change, or deletion occurs, an updated employee list should be generated.

Option G is identical to the *Employee List* option you used in Chapter 10 during payroll setup. When this option is chosen, a decision prompt will appear which permits you to display or print the employee list or to exit this option. Select the option of your choice. Figure 11.7 illustrates a displayed employee list for Bell Corporation.

```
RUN DATE: 12/31/--          BELL CORPORATION                     EMPLOYEE LIST
EMP NAME          DEPT MAR     PAY TYPE    RATE    -------DEDUCTIONS-------
NO. SOC SEC       NO.  ST W/H  PER  PAY    SAL     DED #1   DED #2   DED #3
-----------------------------------------------------------------------------
110 Bauer, Mary    10  S  1    26   H      9.25    18.00    15.00     .00
    472-05-1799

120 Duncan, Richard 10 S  1    26   H      9.75    18.00    15.00     .00
    564-42-1860

130 Ludwick, Thelma 10 S  1    26   H     10.50    18.00    20.00    12.50
    751-66-1251

140 Nash, Suzanne  11  M  3    26   S    961.54    20.00     7.50     .00
    519-63-7720

150 Parsons, Roger 11  M  3    26   S   1346.15    25.00    12.00    6.00
    464-32-8217

155 Ritter, Rhonda 11  M  2    26   S    975.00    20.00    18.00     .00
    575-67-8812

160 Sauer, Beverly 11  M  2    26   S   1346.15    18.00    12.25    12.00
    476-22-3842

170 Weber, Keith   10  S  1    26   H      9.75    18.00    12.00     .00
    721-14-9953

    TOTAL EMPLOYEES  8

              Press SPACE BAR to continue.
```

Figure 11.7   Employee List

Clear Current Accumulators Option H

The purpose of the *Clear Current Accumulators* option is to erase the pay period transaction data from the payroll data file before key-entering the current pay period data. When this option is selected, a decision prompt will appear asking if you indeed wish to clear the current period accumulators. Strike **Y** (for Yes) to clear the current period accumulators. Strike **N** (for No) or press the Esc key to exit this option and return to the Payroll Main Menu.

As you have learned, the computer only processes payroll for those employees who have been recorded on the Payroll input form, key-entered into the computer, and stored in the payroll data file. Once the data has been entered and stored in the payroll data file, the computer uses the data to update the employee records, to identify the employees to be paid, and to process the payroll. If the *Clear Current Accumulators* option is not selected prior to processing the payroll transactions for the current pay period, all the payroll transaction data remaining in this file from the previous pay period, plus the data key-entered for the current pay period, will be processed together. This will cause those employees who were paid during the previous pay period and who are not to be paid during the current pay period to be paid again. As a result, these employees will receive a check they have not earned, and their employee records will be updated incorrectly. The computer does not know who to pay or when to pay employees unless you give it instructions. Therefore, it is very important that Option H be selected prior to entering the transactions for the current pay period.

Set Run Date Option I   The purpose of this option is to provide the computer with the run date to be used on payroll reports and paychecks. This date should correspond to the date on the Payroll input form in that it should reflect the end of the pay period. If the pay period covers the last portion of the month, the run date should be the last working day of the month even though the payroll may be run a few days before this date. The run date will appear on all computer-generated payroll reports and paychecks run during the current pay period. The Set Run Date data entry screen is shown in Figure 11.8.

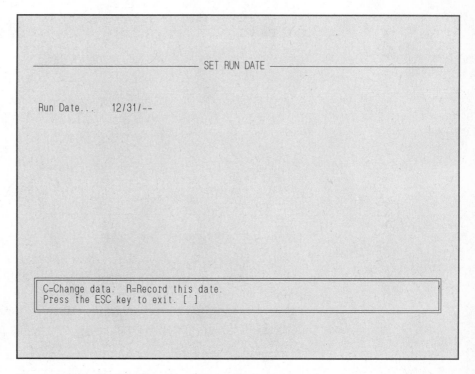

Figure 11.8   Set Run Date Data Entry Screen

In order to key-enter the run date, complete the following procedures:

1. Check the run date displayed. If the date is correct as is, exit this menu and return to the Payroll Main Menu by pressing the Esc key.
2. If the run date must be changed, key-enter the correct date in the MMDDYY format.
3. At this time, a decision prompt will appear at the bottom of the screen telling you to strike **C** to change the data, **R** to record the run date as it appears, or Esc to ignore the data and return to the Payroll Main Menu.

Payroll Transactions Option J

When you select Option J, *Payroll Transactions*, from the Payroll Main Menu, the Payroll Transactions data entry screen will appear. The purpose of this data entry screen is to permit you to (1) identify employees to be paid during the current pay period, (2) enter the regular and overtime hours for hourly employees, (3) key-enter tax withholding data if desired, and (4) cancel payment to employees who have previously been coded and key-entered to be paid. When this option is selected, the first Payroll Transactions data entry screen, shown in Figure 11.9, will be displayed.

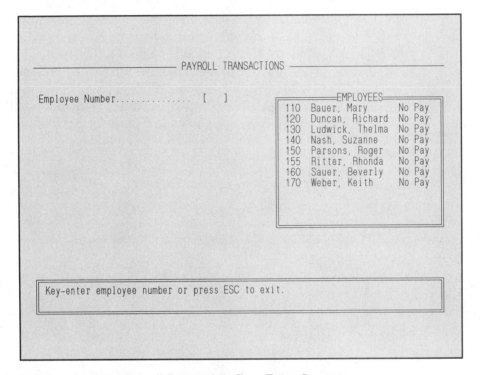

```
 ──────────────────────── PAYROLL TRANSACTIONS ────────────────────────



                                                      ┌────EMPLOYEES────┐
   Employee Number.............. [    ]                │110  Bauer, Mary      No Pay │
                                                       │120  Duncan, Richard  No Pay │
                                                       │130  Ludwick, Thelma  No Pay │
                                                       │140  Nash, Suzanne    No Pay │
                                                       │150  Parsons, Roger   No Pay │
                                                       │155  Ritter, Rhonda   No Pay │
                                                       │160  Sauer, Beverly   No Pay │
                                                       │170  Weber, Keith     No Pay │
                                                       │                             │
                                                       └─────────────────────────────┘




 ┌───────────────────────────────────────────────────────────────────────┐
 │ Key-enter employee number or press ESC to exit.                         │
 └───────────────────────────────────────────────────────────────────────┘
```

Figure 11.9   First Payroll Transactions Data Entry Screen

Notice that an Employees window automatically appears that contains current employee numbers and names and an indication whether or not each employee has been activated to be paid.

When key-entering payroll transactions or making corrections, complete the following procedures:

1. Key-enter the employee number.

At this time, the computer will check to see if the employee number key-entered exists. If it does not exist, a decision prompt message will appear asking if you wish to add this employee. If you respond **Yes**, the Employee File Maintenance data entry screen will appear and you will be permitted to add the employee. After the employee has been added and recorded, the Payroll Transactions data entry screen will again appear and you will be permitted to continue. If the employee number does exist, the employee's name will appear to the right of the *Employee Number* field. Finally, the computer will check to see if transaction data for this employee already exists in the payroll transaction file. If it does exist, all transaction data will be displayed and you will be permitted to make corrections. If no transaction data exists for the designated employee, the computer will assume you wish to enter data for the employee. One of the two data entry screens shown in Figure 11.10 will then be displayed, depending on the employee's type of pay (hourly or salaried).

```
 _____ PAYROLL TRANSACTIONS _____



  Employee Number...............   110  Bauer, Mary
    (Hourly)
  Regular Hours.................    [     ]
  Overtime Hours................    [     ]
  Federal Withholding...........   [CALC    ]
  State Withholding.............   [CALC    ]
  FICA Withholding..............   [CALC    ]







   _____
  | Enter data (withholding: amount, 0=Calculate, or -1=No tax), then press      |
  | ENTER.  Press the ESC key to exit.                                           |
  |_____|

```

Figure 11.10a   Data Entry Screen A for Hourly Wage Earner

```
 _____ PAYROLL TRANSACTIONS _____



  Employee Number...............   140  Nash, Suzanne
    (Salaried)
  Federal Withholding...........   [CALC    ]
  State Withholding.............   [CALC    ]
  FICA Withholding..............   [CALC    ]










   _____
  | Enter data (withholding: amount, 0=Calculate, or -1=No tax), then press      |
  | ENTER.  Press the ESC key to exit.                                           |
  |_____|

```

Figure 11.10b   Data Entry Screen B for Salaried Wage Earner

2. If the employee is an hourly wage earner to be paid this pay period, Data Entry Screen A will appear. Key-enter the regular hours worked by the employee for the pay period. Next, key-enter any overtime hours worked by the employee for the pay period.

3. If the employee is a salaried employee to be paid this pay period, Data Entry Screen B will appear. The last three fields on this data entry screen are used to indicate to the computer how the federal, state, and FICA withholdings will be determined. The term *CALC* will appear in all three withholding fields. This is the default value and means that the withholdings will be calculated based on tax tables stored in the computer. The cursor will appear in the first withholding field. If you want to use the *CALC* default value and have the computer calculate the withholdings, simply press ENTER/RETURN three times to tab through the three withholding fields.

4. Three types of entries may be key-entered in the withholding fields:

   a. A specific dollar amount to be withheld.
   b. A zero to indicate that the computer is to calculate the withholdings.
   c. A negative one (-1) to indicate that no withholding amount is to be deducted.

   Because a zero has the same effect as the default value (*CALC*), you would probably key-enter a zero only when you wanted to override a zero amount or a specific dollar amount for a withholding which had already been key-entered.

5. When the ENTER/RETURN key is pressed with the cursor in the last field (*FICA Withholding*), the computer will calculate and display the withholding amounts, display a zero amount for the withholdings, or display the amounts which were key-entered for the withholdings. A decision prompt will also appear asking if you wish to make a change, record the transaction, or ignore the displayed data (do nothing). Strike **C** to make changes or corrections. When the data is correct, strike **R** (to record), and the computer will create a transaction record with this data in the payroll data file and update the employee's record in the same file.

   *Note: As each employee's payroll transaction data is entered and recorded, a **Pay** status is indicated in the Employees window display.*

6. Continue this procedure for all employees to be paid for the current pay period.

If an employee who has already been designated to be paid must be removed from the pay status, simply key-enter the employee's number. The computer will display the payroll transaction data and a prompt message that permits you to strike **C** to cancel pay, strike **E** to edit (change) the transaction data as it appears, or press the Esc key to exit. When you strike **C**, another prompt message will appear asking you to verify that you indeed wish to cancel the designated employee's pay. Strike **Y** (for Yes), and the computer will remove the employee from active pay status and display an informational message at the bottom of the screen to inform you the action is complete. Press the Space

Bar to continue. Repeat this procedure for each employee to be canceled for the current pay period.

Payroll Proof
Option K

Only employees with data in the payroll transaction file for a particular pay period will be paid. Therefore, transaction data must be created with careful thought to assure that the right people get paid and that they get paid on time. To assist in this process, the computer provides a proof of all employees to be paid. This **payroll proof** lists the payroll transaction data for all employees to be paid during the current pay period. When this option is selected, the usual decision prompt will appear in which you will be permitted to display or print the payroll proof or to exit this option. Select the option desired. Figure 11.11 illustrates a displayed payroll proof for Bell Corporation.

```
RUN DATE: 12/31/--            BELL CORPORATION                      PAYROLL PROOF
EMP                    REG.    OVT.   HOURLY -------------CURRENT------------
NO.    NAME            HRS.    HRS.   SALARY    GROSS FEDERAL   STATE    FICA
-------------------------------------------------------------------------------
110 Bauer, Mary        80.00    .00   HOURLY   740.00   93.12   37.25   55.57
120 Duncan, Richard    80.00   5.50   HOURLY   860.44  114.79   45.92   64.62
130 Ludwick, Thelma    68.00    .00   HOURLY   714.00   89.22   35.69   53.62
140 Nash, Suzanne        .00    .00   SALARY   961.54   91.15   36.46   72.21
150 Parsons, Roger       .00    .00   SALARY  1346.15  148.85   59.54  101.10
155 Ritter, Rhonda       .00    .00   SALARY   975.00  104.71   41.88   73.22
160 Sauer, Beverly       .00    .00   SALARY  1346.15  160.38   64.15  101.10
170 Weber, Keith       80.00   3.00   HOURLY   823.88  105.70   42.28   61.87

    PROOF TOTALS      308.00   8.50




                     Press SPACE BAR to continue.
```

Figure 11.11   Payroll Proof

It is recommended that a payroll proof be run after payroll transactions are entered and after making any corrections. The proof totals printed at the bottom of the report for regular and overtime hours should match the batch totals at the bottom of the Payroll input form. If they do not, chances are that a keying error occurred during data entry. Corrections can be made to the payroll transaction file using Option J, *Payroll Transactions*, if errors are found on the payroll proof.

Payroll Register
Option L

The **payroll register** lists, in detail, the current pay period earnings and withholdings and cumulative quarter-to-date and year-to-date information for each employee paid. A payroll register must be printed each pay period by the computer. When printing this report, the computer reads the payroll transaction data, finds the employees to be paid this pay period, locates the employees' records, and extracts the information required for the report. When this option is selected, a decision prompt will appear in which you may display, print, or exit the payroll register. Select the option of your choice. Figure 11.12 illustrates a displayed payroll register for Bell Corporation.

```
RUN DATE: 12/31/--          BELL CORPORATION                    PAYROLL REGISTER
                    CHK#   NET-AMT  DED #1 ------CURRENT, QTRLY, & YRLY------
EMP NAME        MAR W/A    REG-HRS  DED #2    GROSS   FEDERAL    STATE     FICA
NO. SOC SEC     PAY TYP    OVT-HRS  DED #3   AMOUNT      W/H      W/H      W/H
--------------------------------------------------------------------------------
110 Bauer, Mary   S 501    521.06   18.00    740.00    93.12    37.25    55.57
    472-05-1799  26   1     80.00   15.00   4440.00   558.72   223.50   333.42
                     H        .00     .00  19240.00  2421.12   968.50  1444.82

120 Duncan, Richard S 502  602.11   18.00    860.44   114.79    45.92    64.62
    564-42-1860  26   1     80.00   15.00   4760.44   610.39   244.17   357.52
                     H       5.50     .00  20360.44  2592.79  1037.17  1529.12

130 Ludwick, Thelma S 503  484.97   18.00    714.00    89.22    35.69    53.62
    751-66-1251  26   1     68.00   20.00   4809.00   614.07   245.64   361.17
                     H        .00   12.50  21189.00  2713.47  1085.44  1591.37

140 Nash, Suzanne  M 504    734.22   20.00    961.54    91.15    36.46    72.21
    519-63-7720  26   3       .00    7.50   5769.24   489.25   195.71   433.26
                     S        .00     .00  25000.04  2081.65   832.71  1877.46

          Press SPACE BAR to continue or press ESC to exit.
```

Figure 11.12a   Payroll Register (Screen 1)

```
RUN DATE: 12/31/--          BELL CORPORATION                    PAYROLL REGISTER
                    CHK#   NET-AMT  DED #1 ------CURRENT, QTRLY, & YRLY------
EMP NAME        MAR W/A    REG-HRS  DED #2    GROSS   FEDERAL    STATE     FICA
NO. SOC SEC     PAY TYP,   OVT-HRS  DED #3   AMOUNT      W/H      W/H      W/H
--------------------------------------------------------------------------------
150 Parsons, Roger M 505   993.66   25.00   1346.15   148.85    59.54   101.10
    464-32-8217  26   3       .00   12.00   8076.40   893.10   357.24   606.60
                     S        .00    6.00  34999.90  3870.10  1548.04  2628.60

155 Ritter, Rhonda M 506   717.19   20.00    975.00   104.71    41.88    73.22
    575-67-8812  26   2       .00   18.00    975.00   104.71    41.88    73.22
                     S        .00     .00    975.00   104.71    41.88    73.22

160 Sauer, Beverly M 507   978.27   18.00   1346.15   160.38    64.15   101.10
    476-22-3842  26   2       .00   12.25   8076.90   962.28   384.90   606.60
                     S        .00   12.00   4711.90  4169.88  1667.90  2628.60

170 Weber, Keith   S 508   584.03   18.00    823.88   105.70    42.28    61.87
    721-14-9953  26   1     80.00   12.00   4553.28   575.70   230.28   341.97
                     H       3.00     .00  19470.88  2455.70   982.28  1462.37

          Press SPACE BAR to continue or press ESC to exit.
```

Figure 11.12b   Payroll Register (Screen 2)

```
RUN DATE: 12/31/--      BELL CORPORATION                PAYROLL REGISTER SUMMARY
DEPARTMENT    GROSS
------------------
     10      3138.32
     11      4628.84

      TOTALS
------------------
GROSS AMT   7767.16
Vol Ded #1   155.00
Vol Ded #2   111.75
Vol Ded #3    30.50
FED W/H      907.92
STATE W/H    363.17
FICA W/H     583.31
            ---------
NET AMT     5615.51
            =========
St Unemp     125.34
Fed Unemp     14.40




                        Press SPACE BAR to continue.
```

Figure 11.12c   Payroll Register (Screen 3)

The totals at the bottom of the payroll register provide the necessary information to make journal entries to record the payroll and the employer's payroll taxes in the General Ledger System. In addition, the payroll register becomes a control and audit trail document (when printed) used to balance the Quarterly FICA report and W-2 statements. Therefore, the payroll register for each pay period during the year should be filed for future reference.

Payroll Checks Option M

Employee paychecks displayed or printed by the computer are composed of two parts: (1) The check stub, which contains all current quarter-to-date and year-to-date earnings and withholding information and (2) The check itself, with the employee name, net pay, company name, bank name, and a space for an authorized signature. When Option M, *Payroll Checks*, is selected, the usual decision prompt will appear which permits you to display or print the checks or exit this option. If the option to print is chosen, the computer will check to see if preprinted check forms are required (as specified during accounting system setup). If check forms are required, the computer will prompt you to insert the forms and align them properly before continuing. Align the check forms on the printer so that the first line of print will fall between the two short black lines shown in the upper left corner of the check stub. The two short horizontal lines are printed at the left edge of the paper, outside the tractor feed perforation.

If preprinted check forms are not being used, the computer will draw an outline of a check as it prints the data on standard continuous-form paper. Examples of a preprinted check and check stub and a computer-drawn check and check stub are illustrated in Figure 11.13.

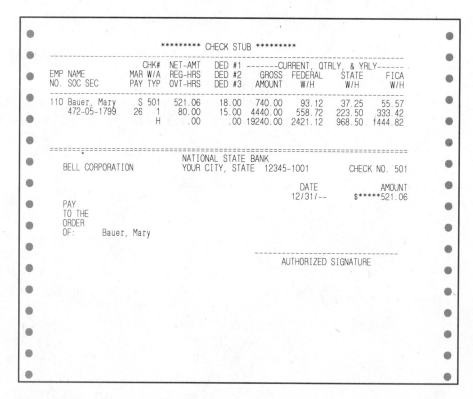

Figure 11.13   Check Stub and Check

The computer will display or print payroll checks for all employees who have been coded on the payroll transaction input form, key-entered into the computer, and stored in the payroll data file. The checks are numbered by the computer beginning with the check number set with the *Set Beginning Check Number* option. This check number field is automatically updated by the computer.

Quarterly Report Option N

Once each quarter, the Quarterly FICA report must be run. This report is used by the company to report FICA-taxable wages to the Internal Revenue Service. When this option is selected, a decision prompt will appear which permits you to display or print the Quarterly report or to exit this option. Select the desired option. Figure 11.14 illustrates a displayed quarterly report for Bell Corporation.

```
RUN DATE: 12/31/--          BELL CORPORATION            QUARTERLY REPORT
SOC SEC #     NAME                   TAXABLE FICA
------------------------------------------------------
472-05-1799   Bauer, Mary              4440.00
564-42-1860   Duncan, Richard          4760.44
751-66-1251   Ludwick, Thelma          4809.00
519-63-7720   Nash, Suzanne            5769.24
464-32-8217   Parsons, Roger           8076.40
575-67-8812   Ritter, Rhonda            975.00
476-22-3842   Sauer, Beverly           8076.90
721-14-9953   Weber, Keith             4553.28

              FINAL TOTAL             41460.26
              TOTAL EMPLOYEES  8




                        Press SPACE BAR to continue.
```

Figure 11.14   Quarterly Report

After the Quarterly report is run, it must be verified for accuracy. It is recommended that this report be printed if possible and filed as a control and audit trail document for future reference.

Clear Quarter-to-Date Accumulators Option O

After the Quarterly report is run and verified for accuracy, and before processing the first payroll of the new quarter, the quarterly accumulators must be reset to zero so that totals for the next quarter can be accumulated. When you select Option O, *Clear Quarter-to-Date Accumulators*, the quarterly accumulator amounts in the employee records stored in the payroll data file (gross earnings, federal withholding, state withholding, and FICA withholding) will be reset to zero. Because of the serious consequences of this option, or in case you accidentally press the wrong key, the computer will ask a second time (with a decision prompt) if you indeed want to perform this task. Strike **Y** (Yes) to instruct the computer to erase all quarterly accumulators. Strike **N** (No) or press the Esc key if you wish to leave the accumulators as they are and return to the Payroll Main Menu.

Annual W-2 Statements Option P

At the end of the year, each employee paid by the company during the year must be provided with a W-2 statement for individual tax-reporting purposes. The computer accumulates this data (earnings and withholdings) for each employee for each pay period. When Option P,

Annual W-2 Statements, is chosen, the usual decision prompt will appear in which you will be permitted to display or print the annual W-2 statements, or to exit this option. Select the desired option. Figure 11.15 illustrates a displayed annual W-2 statement.

```
RUN DATE: 12/31/--        BELL CORPORATION                  ANNUAL W-2 STATEMENTS

**************************************************************
*                                                            *
*    W-2 (WAGE AND TAX STATEMENT)                            *
*                                    WAGES        FICA TAX   *
*  BELL CORPORATION                 19240.00      1444.82    *
*                                                            *
*                                                            *
*                                                            *
*                                                            *
*  SOCIAL SECURITY NO.           FEDERAL TAX     FICA WAGES  *
*    472-05-1799                    2421.12       19240.00   *
*                                                            *
*                                 STATE TAX                  *
*  Bauer, Mary                      968.50                   *
*                                                            *
**************************************************************




              Press SPACE BAR to continue or press ESC to exit.
```

Figure 11.15   Annual W-2 Statement

After the annual W-2 statements are run, they should be verified for accuracy. In an actual business, these statements must be printed so that each employee can receive his or her copy for income tax-reporting purposes.

Clear Year-to-Date Accumulators Option Q

After the annual W-2 statements are run and verified for accuracy, and before processing the first payroll of the new year, the year-to-date accumulators must be reset to zero so the totals for the next year can be accumulated. When you select Option Q, *Clear Year-to-Date Accumulators*, the year-to-date accumulator amounts in the employee records stored in the payroll data file (gross earnings, federal withholding, state withholding, and FICA withholding) will be reset to zero. Because of the serious consequences of this action, or in case you accidentally press the wrong key, the computer will ask a second time (with a decision prompt) if you indeed want to perform this task. Strike **Y** (Yes) to instruct the computer to erase all year-to-date accumulators. Strike **N** (No) or press Esc if you wish to leave the accumulators as they are and return to the Payroll Main Menu.

Save Data to Disk

After all payroll processing has been completed, or if you are interrupted during your work session, return to the System Selection Menu and save your data to disk as a work in progress file. Remember that this option must be the last option selected prior to ending the payroll session or before loading another file from disk. If you fail to follow this procedure, all data keyed and processed during your computer session will be lost.

PAYROLL TRANSACTIONS AND REPORTS (SAMPLE PROBLEM)

This sample problem illustrates the principles and procedures required to process payroll transactions using an automated accounting system. The employees, beginning balances, and beginning check number for Bell Corporation as discussed and prepared in Chapter 10 will be the basis of this sample problem. The data for Bell Corporation has been stored as Problem 11-S under the file name **AA11-S** on disk. To complete this problem, you will be shown the step-by-step procedure for processing the final payroll for the month of December (which includes end-of-quarter and year-end reports).

The following payroll file maintenance data for the week ending December 31 has already been recorded for you on the Payroll File Maintenance input form shown in Figure 11.16.

Problem No. *11-S*

RUN DATE *12/31/--*
MM DD YY

PAYROLL
FILE MAINTENANCE
Input Form

FORM PR-1

	EMP NO.	EMPLOYEE NAME	DEPT NO.	SOC. SEC. NUMBER	MAR. STAT.	W/H ALLOW.	PAY PER/YR.	TYPE PAY	RATE/ SALARY	DEDUCTIONS ONE	DEDUCTIONS TWO	DEDUCTIONS THREE	
	1	2	3	4	5	6	7	8	9	10	11	12	
1	155	Ritter, Rhonda	11	575678812	M	2	26	S	975:00	20:00	18:00		1
2	140					3							2
3	170			721149953									3
4	110										15:00		4
5													5
6													6
7													7
8													8
9													9
10													10
11													11
12													12
13													13
14													14
15													15
16													16

M = MARRIED   H = HOURLY
S = SINGLE   S = SALARIED

Figure 11.16   Payroll File Maintenance Input Form for December 31 (Problem 11-S)

1. Added Rhonda Ritter as a new employee, Employee No. 155 (to maintain alphabetic order), Department No. 11, social security number 575-67-8812, married, two withholding allowances, 26 pay periods per year, salaried, $975.00 per pay period, two voluntary deductions of $20.00 and $18.00.
2. Changed the number of Suzanne Nash's withholding allowances to 3.
3. Changed Keith Weber's social security number to 721-14-9953.
4. Changed Mary Bauer's Deduction No. 2 to $15.00.

The following payroll transaction data for the week ending December 31 has been recorded for you on the Payroll input form shown in Figure 11.17.

Problem No. _11-S_						
RUN DATE _12/31/--_ MM DD YY		**PAYROLL** Input Form			**FORM PR-3**	
	1	2	3	4	5	6
	EMPLOYEE NUMBER	REGULAR HOURS	OVERTIME HOURS	FEDERAL WITHHOLDING	STATE WITHHOLDING	FICA WITHHOLDING
1	110	80				
2	120	80	5 5			
3	130	68				
4	140					
5	150					
6	155					
7	160					
8	170	80	3			
9						
10						
11						
12						
13						
14						
15						
16						
17						
18						
19						
20						
21						
22						
23						
24						
25						
TOTALS	308	8 5				

Figure 11.17   Payroll Input Form for December 31 (Problem 11-S)

1. Mary Bauer worked 80 regular hours, no overtime hours.
2. Richard Duncan worked 80 regular hours, 5.5 overtime hours.
3. Thelma Ludwick worked 68 regular hours, no overtime hours.
4. Enter Suzanne Nash to be paid (salaried).
5. Enter Roger Parsons to be paid (salaried).
6. Enter Rhonda Ritter to be paid (salaried).
7. Enter Beverly Sauer to be paid (salaried).
8. Keith Weber worked 80 regular hours, 3 overtime hours.

Instructions

Step 1   Compare the payroll file maintenance data and the payroll transaction data with the completed input forms shown in Figures 11.16 and 11.17.

Step 2   Bring up the System Selection Menu according to the instructions for your microcomputer.

Step 3   Select Option C, *Load Data from Disk*. When the Load Data from Disk menu appears, select Option A, *Load Opening Balances from the Program Disk*.

Step 4   When the directory of Opening Balances contained on the disk appears, select Problem 11-S by key-entering the file name **AA11-S**.

Step 5   Select Option D, *Company Information*, from the System Selection Menu, and change the run date to **December 31** of the current year. Verify that the *Company Name* field contains **Bell Corporation**, that the *Problem Number* field contains **Problem 11-S**, and that the type of business is set to **C** (for Corporation). If these data fields are not correct, you may have loaded the incorrect file from disk. If so, repeat Steps 3 through 5.

Step 6   Select Option I, *Payroll*, from the System Selection Menu.

Step 7   Select Option F, *Employee File Maintenance*, from the Payroll Main Menu.

Step 8   Key-enter and record the employee file maintenance data from the Payroll File Maintenance input form in Figure 11.16.

Step 9   Select Option G, *Employee List*, from the Payroll Main Menu and display or print a revised employee list. Verify that the data you entered is correct. The revised employee list for Bell Corporation is shown in Figure 11.18.

Step 10   If your employee list contains errors, make the necessary corrections and display or print a new employee list.

Step 11   Select Option H, *Clear Current Accumulators*, and respond **Y** to clear the accumulators.

Step 12   Select Option I, *Set Run Date*, and verify that the run date has been set to **December 31** of the current year. If not, make the necessary change.

Step 13   Select Option J, *Payroll Transactions*, and key-enter and record the payroll transaction data from the Payroll input form in Figure 11.17. Notice that the computer is being instructed to calculate all taxable withholdings.

Step 14 Select Option K, *Payroll Proof,* and display or print a payroll proof. Compare your payroll proof with the correct one shown in Figure 11.19.

```
RUN DATE: 12/31/--          BELL CORPORATION
                              EMPLOYEE LIST

------------------------------------------------------------------------
EMP  NAME            DEPT  MAR  PAY  TYPE   RATE   -------DEDUCTIONS-------
NO.  SOC SEC         NO.   ST  W/H PER  PAY   SAL    DED #1   DED #2   DED #3
------------------------------------------------------------------------
110  Bauer, Mary      10   S   1   26   H     9.25   18.00    15.00      .00
     472-05-1799

120  Duncan, Richard  10   S   1   26   H     9.75   18.00    15.00      .00
     564-42-1860

130  Ludwick, Thelma  10   S   1   26   H    10.50   18.00    20.00    12.50
     751-66-1251

140  Nash, Suzanne    11   M   3   26   S   961.54   20.00     7.50      .00
     519-63-7720

150  Parsons, Roger   11   M   3   26   S  1346.15   25.00    12.00     6.00
     464-32-8217

155  Ritter, Rhonda   11   M   2   26   S   975.00   20.00    18.00      .00
     575-67-8812

160  Sauer, Beverly   11   M   2   26   S  1346.15   18.00    12.25    12.00
     476-22-3842

170  Weber, Keith     10   S   1   26   H     9.75   18.00    12.00      .00
     721-14-9953

     TOTAL EMPLOYEES  8
```

Figure 11.18   Revised Employee List (Problem 11-S)

```
RUN DATE: 12/31/--          BELL CORPORATION
                              PAYROLL PROOF

------------------------------------------------------------------------
EMP               REG.   OVT.  HOURLY --------------CURRENT-------------
NO.   NAME        HRS.   HRS.  SALARY  GROSS FEDERAL   STATE    FICA
110 Bauer, Mary     80.00    .00  HOURLY   740.00   93.12   37.25   55.57
120 Duncan, Richard 80.00   5.50  HOURLY   860.44  114.79   45.92   64.62
130 Ludwick, Thelma 68.00    .00  HOURLY   714.00   89.22   35.69   53.62
140 Nash, Suzanne     .00    .00  SALARY   961.54   91.15   36.46   72.21
150 Parsons, Roger    .00    .00  SALARY  1346.15  148.85   59.54  101.10
155 Ritter, Rhonda    .00    .00  SALARY   975.00  104.71   41.88   73.22
160 Sauer, Beverly    .00    .00  SALARY  1346.15  160.38   64.15  101.10
170 Weber, Keith    80.00   3.00  HOURLY   823.88  105.70   42.28   61.87

    PROOF TOTALS   308.00   8.50
```

Figure 11.19   Payroll Proof (Problem 11-S)

Step 15 If your payroll proof is incorrect, select Option J, *Payroll Transactions*, rekey the incorrect data, and print a new payroll proof.

Step 16 Select Option L, *Payroll Register,* and display or print a payroll register. A payroll register summary will also be displayed or printed. This summary shows the totals needed to record the payroll data and the employer's payroll tax expense in the General Ledger System. The payroll register for Bell Corporation for the week ending December 31 is shown in Figure 11.20.

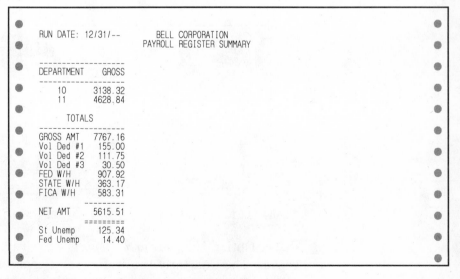

Figure 11.20   Payroll Register (Problem 11-S)

Step 17   Select Option M, *Payroll Checks*, and display or print the payroll checks. Two of the payroll checks for the pay period ending December 31 for Bell Corporation are shown in Figure 11.21.

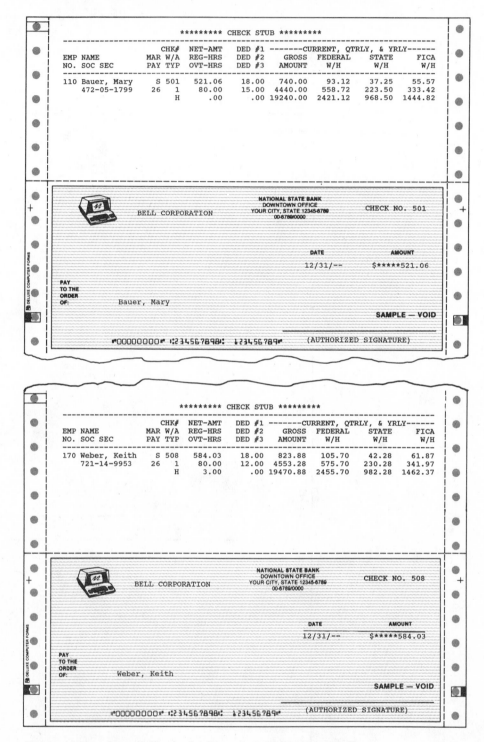

Figure 11.21   Payroll Checks for December 31 (Problem 11-S)

Step 18   Select Option N, *Quarterly Report*, and display or print a Quarterly report. The Quarterly report for Bell Corporation is shown in Figure 11.22. Check to be sure your Quarterly report is correct. If not, make the necessary corrections using the *Enter Beginning Balances* option. Be sure your report is in balance before proceeding. *Once the next step is performed, the quarter-to-date data will be erased from the payroll data file.*

```
  RUN DATE: 12/31/--        BELL CORPORATION
                            QUARTERLY REPORT

  ---------------------------------------------------
  SOC SEC #    NAME                 TAXABLE FICA
  ---------------------------------------------------
  472-05-1799  Bauer, Mary              4440.00
  564-42-1860  Duncan, Richard          4760.44
  751-66-1251  Ludwick, Thelma          4809.00
  519-63-7720  Nash, Suzanne            5769.24
  464-32-8217  Parsons, Roger           8076.40
  575-67-8812  Ritter, Rhonda            975.00
  476-22-3842  Sauer, Beverly           8076.90
  721-14-9953  Weber, Keith             4553.28

               FINAL TOTAL            41460.26
               TOTAL EMPLOYEES   8
```

Figure 11.22   Quarterly Report for December 31 (Problem 11-S)

Step 19   Select Option O, *Clear Quarter-to-Date Accumulators*, and respond **Y** to clear the quarter-to-date accumulators.

Step 20   Select Option P, *Annual W-2 Statements*, and display or print the annual W-2 statements. Two of the W-2 statements for Bell Corporation are shown in Figure 11.23. Check to be sure your statements are correct. If not, make the necessary corrections using the *Enter Beginning Balances* option. Be sure your statements are correct before proceeding. *Once the next step is performed, the year-to-date data will be erased from the payroll data file.*

Step 21   Select Option Q, *Clear Year-to-Date Accumulators*, and respond **Y** to clear the year-to-date accumulators.

Step 22   Return to the System Selection Menu.

Step 23   Once back in the System Selection Menu, select Option E, *Save Data to Disk*, and save your data as a work in progress file (recommend file name **AA11-S**).

Step 24   Press Esc to end your computer session. Then, complete the student exercise and transaction problem which follow.

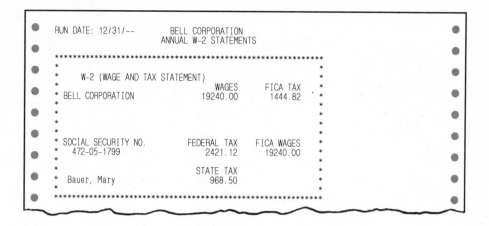

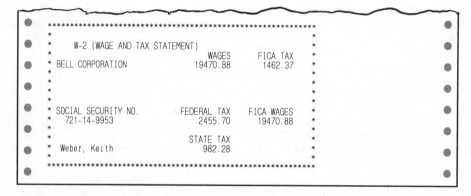

Figure 11.23   Annual W-2 Statements (Problem 11-S)

Name _____

Class _____ Date _____

CHAPTER 11
STUDENT EXERCISE

I. Matching   For each of the following definitions, write the letter of the term which best fits that definition in the space provided.

a. Employee file maintenance   c. Proof totals
b. Batch totals   d. Payroll transaction data

1. _____ Totals located on the bottom of the Payroll input form for the purpose of verifying that the payroll transaction data was key-entered correctly. (Obj. 5)

2. _____ The process of making additions, changes, and deletions to employee data. (Obj. 1)

3. _____ Totals printed on the bottom of the computer-generated payroll proof for the purpose of verifying that the data was key-entered correctly. (Obj. 5)

4. _____ Items of information for each employee which may change from one pay period to another, such as the number of regular hours and overtime hours worked. (Obj. 4)

II. Short Answer 1. What is payroll transaction data? (Objs. 4, 11)

_____

_____

2. Why should the batch totals on the Payroll input form be checked against the proof totals on the payroll proof? (Objs. 4, 5)

_____

_____

3. Briefly explain the purpose of each of the following reports: (Objs. 5-9).

a. Payroll proof: _____

_____

_____

b. Payroll register: _____

_____

c. Payroll checks: _____

_____

_____

d. Quarterly report: _____

_____

e. Annual W-2 statements: _____

_____

4. Explain the purpose of each of the following options: (Objs. 4, 8, 9)
   a. *Clear Current Accumulators:*

   _____

   _____

   b. *Clear Quarter-to-Date Accumulators:*

   _____

   _____

   _____

   c. *Clear Year-to-Date Accumulators:*

   _____

   _____

PAYROLL TRANSACTIONS AND REPORTS
TRANSACTION PROBLEM 11-1

In this transaction problem, you will be completing the payroll for Chase Corporation for December 15 and December 31. (Objs. 1-11)

Instructions

Step 1 Remove the blank input forms and the Chapter 11 Audit Test from the end of this chapter. Fill in the answers to the audit test as you work through the transaction problem.

Step 2 On December 15 of the current year, Chase Corporation's hourly employees are to be paid according to the payroll transaction data which follows. All taxes are to be calculated by the computer. Record the payroll transaction data for each employee to be paid on the first Payroll input form.

Employee Number	Employee Name	Regular Hours	Overtime Hours
510	Burns, Lynne	80	
520	Ellis, Scott	80	4.5
540	Phelps, Nora	80	4.5
560	York, Douglas	72	

Step 3 Bring up the System Selection Menu.

Step 4 Select Option C, *Load Data from Disk*. When the Load Data from Disk Menu appears, select Option A, *Load Opening Balances from the Program Disk*.

Step 5 When the directory of Opening Balances contained on the disk appears, select Problem 11-1 by key-entering the file name **AA11-1**.

Step 6 Select Option D, *Company Information*, and set the run date to **December 15** of the current year. Verify that the *Company Name* field contains **Chase Corporation**, that the *Problem Number* field contains **Problem 11-1**, and that the type of business is set to **C** (for Corporation). If these data fields are not correct, you may have loaded the incorrect file from disk. If so, repeat Steps 4 through 6.

Step 7 Select Option I, *Payroll*.

Step 8 When the Payroll Main Menu appears, clear the current accumulators.

Step 9 Select the *Set Run Date* option. Verify that the run date has been set to **December 15** of the current year. If not, make the appropriate change.

Step 10 Key-enter and record the payroll transaction data from the Payroll input form prepared in Step 2.

Step 11 Display or print a payroll proof. If errors are detected, make the necessary corrections and display or print a new payroll proof.

Step 12 Display or print the payroll register.

Step 13   Display or print the payroll checks.

Step 14   Return to the System Selection Menu.

Step 15   Once back in the System Selection Menu, save your data to disk as a work in progress file (recommend file name **AA11-1A**), then either press Esc to end your computer session or continue on to the next step if you're instructed to do so.

Step 16   On December 31 of the current year, Chase Corporation's employees are to be paid according to the payroll file maintenance and transaction data which follows. All taxes are to be calculated by the computer. Record the payroll file maintenance information on the Payroll File Maintenance input form and the payroll transaction data on the second Payroll input form.

   1. Add Gale Miller as a new employee, Employee No. 535 (to maintain alphabetic order), Department No. 20, social security number 547-82-9759, married, four withholding allowances, 24 pay periods per year, hourly, $12.25 per hour, two voluntary deductions of $12.00 and $7.50.
   2. Change Scott Ellis's marital status to **M** and his withholding allowances to 2.
   3. Change Nora Phelps's hourly rate of pay to $12.25.
   4. Lynne Burns worked 80 regular hours, 5.5 overtime hours.
   5. Scott Ellis worked 80 regular hours, no overtime hours.
   6. Enter Larry Levey to be paid (salaried).
   7. Gale Miller worked 80 regular hours, no overtime hours.
   8. Nora Phelps worked 78 regular hours, no overtime.
   9. Enter Beth Travis to be paid (salaried).
   10. Douglas York worked 80 regular hours, 5 overtime hours.

Step 17   Bring up the System Selection Menu.

Step 18   Load your work in progress file from Step 15 into your computer's memory.

Step 19   Set the run date to **December 31** of the current year. Verify that the *Problem Number* field contains **Problem 11-1** and that the company name is still **Chase Corporation**.

Step 20   Select Option I, *Payroll*.

Step 21   Key-enter and record the employee file maintenance data from the Payroll File Maintenance input form prepared in Step 16.

Step 22   Display or print an employee list and make any necessary corrections.

Step 23   Clear the current pay period accumulators.

Step 24   Verify that the run date has been set to **December 31** of the current year. If not, make the appropriate change.

Step 25   Key-enter and record the payroll transactions from the Payroll input form prepared in Step 16. Notice that the computer is being instructed to calculate all withholding taxes.

Step 26   Display or print a payroll proof and make corrections, if necessary.

Step 27   Display or print a payroll register.

Step 28   Display or print the payroll checks.

Step 29   Display or print a Quarterly report.

Step 30   Clear the quarter-to-date accumulators.

Step 31   Display or print the annual W-2 statements.

Step 32   Clear the year-to-date accumulators.

Step 33   Return to the System Selection Menu and save your work to disk as a work in progress file (recommend file name **AA11-1B**).

Step 34   Press Esc and end your computer session.

Step 35   Hand in the completed student exercise sheets, input forms, the audit test, and any printouts to your instructor.

You have now completed the computer exercise for Chapter 11.

Name _____

Class _____ Date _____

Problem No. _____

RUN DATE ___/___/___
        MM   DD   YY

PAYROLL
Input Form

FORM PR-3

	1 EMPLOYEE NUMBER	2 REGULAR HOURS	3 OVERTIME HOURS	4 FEDERAL WITHHOLDING	5 STATE WITHHOLDING	6 FICA WITHHOLDING	
1							1
2							2
3							3
4							4
5							5
6							6
7							7
8							8
9							9
10							10
11							11
12							12
13							13
14							14
15							15
16							16
17							17
18							18
19							19
20							20
21							21
22							22
23							23
24							24
25							25
TOTALS							

Problem No. ___

FORM PR-1

PAYROLL
FILE MAINTENANCE
Input Form

RUN DATE ___/___/___
         MM DD YY

| | 1 | 2 | 3 | 4 | 5 | 6 | 7 | 8 | 9 | DEDUCTIONS | | |
| | | | | | | | | | | 10 | 11 | 12 |
	EMP NO.	EMPLOYEE NAME	DEPT NO.	SOC. SEC. NUMBER	MAR. STAT.	W/H ALLOW.	PAY PER/YR.	TYPE PAY	RATE/ SALARY	ONE	TWO	THREE
1												
2												
3												
4												
5												
6												
7												
8												
9												
10												
11												
12												
13												
14												
15												
16												

M = MARRIED
S = SINGLE

H = HOURLY
S = SALARIED

Name _____

Class _____ Date _____

RUN DATE ___/___/___ MM DD YY	**PAYROLL** Input Form	**Problem No.** _____ FORM PR-3	

	1 EMPLOYEE NUMBER	2 REGULAR HOURS	3 OVERTIME HOURS	4 FEDERAL WITHHOLDING	5 STATE WITHHOLDING	6 FICA WITHHOLDING	
1							1
2							2
3							3
4							4
5							5
6							6
7							7
8							8
9							9
10							10
11							11
12							12
13							13
14							14
15							15
16							16
17							17
18							18
19							19
20							20
21							21
22							22
23							23
24							24
25							25
TOTALS							

CHAPTER 11
AUDIT TEST

1. From the December 15 payroll information, what were the total regular hours for all employees?

   _____

2. From the December 15 payroll information, what were the total overtime hours for all employees?

   _____

3. From the December 15 payroll information, what was Lynne Burns's gross pay?

   _____

4. From the December 15 payroll information, what was the federal withholding amount for Employee No. 520?

   _____

5. From the December 15 payroll information, what was the state withholding amount for Employee No. 540?

   _____

6. From the December 15 payroll information, what was Lynne Burns's yearly gross income?

   _____

7. From the December 15 payroll information, what was the amount of total gross earnings of all employees?

   _____

8. From the December 15 payroll information, what was the total net pay for all employees?

   _____

9. From the December 31 payroll information, how many withholding allowances did Douglas York claim?

   _____

10. From the December 31 payroll information, what were the quarterly gross wages for Employee No. 520?

   _____

Name _____

Class _____ Date _____

11. From the December 31 payroll information, how many regular hours did Gale Miller work?

   _____

12. From the December 31 payroll information, what was the gross amount of pay for Department No. 20?

   _____

13. From the December 31 payroll information, what was the total net pay for all employees?

   _____

14. From the December 31 payroll information, what was the total amount of Beth Travis's FICA-taxable wages for the quarter?

   _____

15. From the December 31 payroll information, what was Douglas York's total federal income tax withheld?

   _____

APPENDIX A
ERROR CODES, MESSAGES, AND OPERATOR ACTION

This appendix lists all error codes and messages which might be displayed while using *Automated Accounting for the Microcomputer*. An explanation of the operator action that should be taken is also given for each error code.

101   *Insert program disk into disk drive X.*

Insert your *Automated Accounting for the Microcomputer* disk into the first disk drive and press the Space Bar to continue. Refer to the start-up procedures for your microcomputer found in Chapter 1 if necessary.

102   *The date field is incorrect. Key in the format MM/DD/YY.*

Press the Space Bar, then rekey the date in the MMDDYY format (where MM is a two-digit month, DD is a two-digit day, and YY is a two-digit year).

103   *Out of range error.*

The value of the data is too small or too large. Press the Space Bar and key-enter the correct data.

104   *Entries limited to 2 decimal places.*

Press the Space Bar and key-enter the correct data.

105   *Disk in drive X is write-protected.*

Remove the disk from the disk drive and remove the write-protect tab. Insert the disk back into the disk drive and retry.

106   *Disk drive X is not ready.*

Check the disk drive to make sure it is on-line and ready to use (for example, make sure the disk drive door is closed). Make the appropriate adjustments and retry.

107   *Disk media error.*

The computer is unable to read or write to the disk. Check to make sure the disk has not been damaged. Try the disk on another machine if possible to determine if the problem is with the disk or the disk drive.

108 Disk is full.

The system has detected that the disk you are using is full. Delete unwanted files from the disk and retry.

109 The printer is not ready.

The system has detected that the attached printer is not in a ready-to-print status. Ready the printer and check to make sure it is properly connected to your computer, then retry. If the problem persists even though the printer is ready, notify your instructor.

110 Invalid drive designation.

The data disk drive designation field contains an invalid disk drive identification. Press the Space Bar and key-enter a valid disk drive identification (i.e. A, B, or C).

111 Disk drive X is not available.

The data disk drive designation field contains a drive identification of a disk drive that is not available for use. Press the Space Bar and key-enter a valid disk drive identification of a drive that is available for use.

112 Invalid path name. Directory name too long.

The path name field contains a path name that does not exist on any of the disks in the disk drives or is too long. Press the Space Bar and key-enter a valid path name or insert the correct data disk and retry.

113 Student name missing or begins with invalid character.

The student name field is blank. Press the Space Bar and key-enter your name.

114 Unable to read student name. No alpha characters.

The computer is unable to accept the data contained in the student name field as a valid field. Press the Space Bar and key-enter a valid name.

115 Invalid student ID code.

The student ID code field contains invalid data. Press the Space Bar and key-enter a valid student ID code (consisting of letters and/or numbers).

116 Problem file not found.

The file name that has been entered does not exist in the directory. Press the Space Bar and key-enter a valid file name from the directory display.

117 Insert template/data disk into disk drive X.

The student data disk (see the data disk designation field) cannot be found in the specified disk drive. Insert the data disk in the designated disk drive, then press the Space Bar and retry.

118   File name must be in directory.

The file name key-entered must be in the directory in order for the computer to load the file's data into memory. Press the Space Bar, then key-enter a valid file name from the directory display.

119   Bad file format.

An attempt has been made to load a data file that is not in the proper *Automated Accounting for the Microcomputer* format. Consult the teacher's manual for information on how to build your own problems and access their data files. Press the Space Bar and key-enter a valid file name or press the Esc key to exit.

120   File name must consist of letters and/or numbers.

An attempt has been made to save a file under an invalid file name. Press the Space Bar, then key-enter a valid file name (avoid the use of special symbols such as *, #, @, etc.). On Apple systems, a file name must begin with a letter.

121   Directory is full.

The maximum capacity of entries has been exceeded in the directory (IBM and Tandy capacity is 105, Apple capacity is 40). To prevent loss of the data currently in memory, remove your data disk, insert another data disk (which has free space), press the Space Bar, then save your file to this disk. (Unwanted files may be deleted from the full disk to free up space for new files.)

122   Invalid path name.

The path name must begin with a letter. Press the Space Bar and key-enter a valid path name.

123   File name must begin with a letter.

The file name entered begins with an invalid character. Press the Space Bar and key-enter a file name beginning with a letter.

124   Insert template disk into disk drive.

The template disk cannot be found in the disk drive. Insert the template disk in the disk drive, then press the Space Bar and retry.

125   Unable to find template/data on disk drive X.

The appropriate files cannot be found on the specified disk drive or the path name cannot be found. Press the Space Bar and key-enter a valid disk drive and path name.

201   Statements option must be either Y or N.

Press the Space Bar and key-enter either a **Y** (for Yes) or an **N** (for No) to continue.

202   New page option must be either Y or N.

Press the Space Bar and key-enter either a **Y** (for Yes) or an **N** (for No) to continue.

203   *Preprinted checks option must be either Y or N.*

Press the Space Bar and key-enter either a **Y** (for Yes) or an **N** (for No) to continue.

204   *Type of business must be S, P, or C.*

Press the Space Bar and set the type of business to **S** for a sole proprietorship, **P** for a partnership, or **C** for a corporation.

208   *Simplified/Expanded option must be S or E.*

Press the Space Bar, then key-enter the correct simplified/expanded code (**S** for simplified, **E** for expanded).

209   *Type of business not set (Option D).*

An attempt has been made to enter an Automated Accounting System before the data for Option D of the System Selection Menu has been set. Each system requires that the type of business (S = Sole proprietorship, P = Partnership, C = Corporation) be key-entered in order to operate properly. Press the Space Bar, then choose the option to set Company Information.

210   *No problem selected (Option C).*

An attempt has been made to enter an Automated Accounting System before data has been loaded from disk. Each system requires that data be loaded from disk or that the system be informed that a new file is to be created in order to operate properly. Press the Space Bar and choose the option to load data from disk.

211   *No work in progress files found with Student ID of XXX.*

An attempt to access work in progress files has been made and no files can be found for the current Student ID code. Check to make sure the correct Student ID code has been entered. Press the Space Bar and take appropriate action.

212   *Run Date not set (Option D).*

An attempt has been made to enter an Automated Accounting System before the data for Option D of the System Selection Menu has been set. Each system requires that the run date be key-entered in order to operate properly. Press the Space Bar, then choose the option to set Company Information.

301   *Control account numbers have not been set.*

Press the Space Bar and select the *Set Control Accounts* option. Refer to the chart of accounts and set the specified control accounts.

302   *Chart of accounts is empty.*

Press the Space Bar, then create the chart of accounts data using the *Build Chart of Accounts* option.

303   *No revenue found.*

During the printing of the income statement, no revenue was found. Verify that all journal entries have been key-entered.

304   *Error in G. L. set control accounts.*

A control account is missing or does not match an account number in the chart of accounts. The account number specified in the *Set Control Accounts* option must be in the chart of accounts. Press the Space Bar and key-enter the correct control account number. If the control account number is correct, press Esc to exit and add the account as a new entry using the *Chart of Accounts File Maintenance* option.

305   *End of file.*

The end of the file has been reached. Press Esc to exit or choose an option which changes the direction of the search.

306   *Beginning of file.*

The beginning of the file has been reached. Press Esc to exit or choose an option which changes the direction of the search.

307   *Account number XXXX is not in the chart of accounts.*

The account number specified does not exist in the chart of accounts. Check to see if the number key-entered is in the chart of accounts. If the number key-entered is incorrect, key-enter the correct account number. If the account has not been opened, strike **Y** and add the account as a new entry. The system will return to where you were interrupted and you will be permitted to continue.

308   *Classification must be 1-9.*

The first digit of each account number must be a digit from 1 to 9. Press the Space Bar and key-enter a valid account number.

309   *Distribution of Income not = to 100%.*

Percent of income distribution to partners in the partnership business is not equal to 100%. Press the Space Bar, then adjust the percentages and continue.

310   *Title must begin with a valid character.*

Press the Space Bar, then key-enter a valid account name.

311   *Account has a balance.*

An attempt has been made to delete an account with an account balance or previous activity. If an incorrect account number has been key-entered, press the Space Bar and key-enter the correct number. The account will not be deleted if an account balance is present or previous data has been entered.

312   *Journal capacity is full. Erase journal file (Y or N)?*

The number of journal entries has reached capacity. Respond **Y** (Yes) to the message about purging data from the previous month. This will free up room for additional journal entries. You may wish to respond **N** (No) to return to the General Ledger Main Menu and print the previous month's journal entries report for an audit trail before purging the files.

313   *The journal entry must contain either a debit or credit amount.*

Press the Space Bar and key-enter a debit or credit amount.

314   *No journal entries found.*

Press the Space Bar to continue.

315   *Journal entry number has been deleted.*

The journal entry number of the journal entry you are attempting to access has been deleted. Press the Space Bar. Refer to your journal entries report and key-enter a valid journal entry number, or press Esc to exit.

316   *Journal capacity is full with current batch. Must delete some entries or do a closing.*

The journal entries capacity has been reached in the current batch. Press the Space Bar. You may wish to return to the General Ledger Main Menu and print the current journal entries report, then delete some entries to free up room, or perform a period-end closing.

317   *Chart of accounts has reached capacity.*

Press the Space Bar, delete any accounts that are not being used, or combine similar accounts to free up additional space.

318   *Account number is missing.*

The general ledger account number field is blank. Press the Space Bar, then key-enter a valid account number.

319   *No journal entries made.*

The system has detected that no journal entries have been made. Press the Esc key to exit.

320   *Journal entry number X not found.*

An attempt to access a journal entry that does not exist has been made. Check for a valid journal entry number, press the Space Bar, then key-enter a valid number.

321   *Current asset account classification must be 1.*

The system has detected that the account classification of the current asset account is not a 1. Press the Space Bar, then key-enter a valid account number with a 1 in the first digit to identify it as an asset account.

322   *Current liability account classification must be 2.*

The system has detected that the account classification of the current liability account is not a 2. Press the Space Bar, then key-enter a valid account number with a 2 in the first digit to identify it as a liability account.

323   *Batch Number must be 1 for opening balances.*

Press the Space Bar. Change the batch number to 1 using the *Set Run Date and Batch Number* option.

324   *Batch Number must be greater than 1 for journal entries.*

Press the Space Bar. Change the batch number using the *Set Run Date and Batch Number* option.

401   *Control account numbers have not been set.*

Press the Space Bar. Set the required control accounts using the *Set Control Accounts* option.

402   *No accounts payable data.*

Press the Space Bar. Verify that accounts payable transaction data has been key-entered into the computer system.

403   *No vendor data.*

Press the Space Bar. Create vendor data using the *Build Vendor Data* option.

404   *Account number XXX is not in the chart of accounts.*

The specified account number is not in the chart of accounts. Press the Space Bar. Check to see if the number key-entered is in the chart of accounts. If the number is incorrect, key-enter the correct number. If the account has not been opened, exit the Accounts Payable System and open the account using the *Chart of Accounts File Maintenance* option in the General Ledger System.

405   *Vendor name must begin with valid character.*

Press the Space Bar and key-enter a valid vendor name.

406   *Error in G.L. Set Control Accounts.*

An error has been detected in the general ledger control accounts. Return to the General Ledger System and verify that the control accounts set in the *Set Control Accounts* option exist in the chart of accounts. Correct any incorrect control accounts. If the control accounts are correct, add the accounts as new entries using the *Chart of Accounts File Maintenance* option before returning to the Accounts Payable System.

407   *Error in A.P. Set Control Accounts.*

An error has been detected in the *Set Control Accounts* option. The account numbers specified in the Set Control Accounts fields must be in the chart of accounts. Press the Space Bar and correct any incorrect control accounts. If the control accounts are correct, press Esc to exit and add the accounts as new entries using the *Chart of Accounts File Maintenance* option in the General Ledger System.

408 *A purchase invoice number is required.*

A purchase invoice number is required before processing can continue. Press the Space Bar and key-enter a valid purchase invoice number.

409 *Vendor number XXX is not in vendor data file.*

Check the number key-entered against the vendor list. If the number is incorrect, press the Space Bar and key-enter the correct vendor number. If the vendor has not been previously entered, strike **Y** and add it to the vendor data as a new entry. The system will return to where you were interrupted and you will be permitted to continue.

410 *A vendor number is required.*

A vendor number is required before processing can continue. Press the Space Bar and key-enter a valid vendor number.

411 *Disposition code must be A, P, or M.*

Press the Space Bar and key-enter a valid disposition code.

412 *Disposition code for opening balances must be an A.*

Press the Space Bar and key-enter the correct disposition code.

413 *A.P. transactions have reached capacity. E = Erase paid items.*

Respond **E** to the prompt to erase all transactions in the accounts payable data file which have been paid. This will free up room for additional transaction data. Before erasing the paid items from the file, press Esc to return to the Accounts Payable Main Menu to obtain any printouts for audit trail purposes.

414 *Cannot delete active vendor.*

An attempt has been made to delete a vendor which has a balance or previous activity. Press the Space Bar and key-enter the correct data. If the vendor is to be deleted, each transaction which is in the computer for that vendor must first be individually deleted so the computer can properly handle the integration of these transactions.

415 *Vendor data has reached capacity.*

To free up space, delete any inactive vendors. Press the Space Bar to exit and take appropriate action.

416 *You must choose to pay some of the invoices.*

The accounts payable data file is full. After attempting to purge the file of previously paid invoices, the computer has been unable to free up additional space. Press the Space Bar to exit and take appropriate action.

417   Manual check number is missing.

An amount has been entered for a manual check and a check number must be entered. Press the Space Bar, then key-enter a valid manual check number.

418   Account number is missing.

The general ledger account number field is blank. Press the Space Bar, then key-enter a valid account number.

419   No invoices marked to be paid for batch number X.

The system has detected that no checks have been recorded to be paid for the current batch number. Press Esc to exit. Release invoices that are to be paid by recording them with a **P** (indicating Pay) and/or check the current batch number.

420   Journal entries have reached capacity.

The system has detected that the journal entries generated by the accounts payable system have caused the journal entries capacity to be exceeded. Return to the General Ledger System and perform period-end closing after generating the desired reports for audit trail purposes.

421   Debit memo amount exceeds invoice amount.

The amount of the debit memo is greater than the amount of the original invoice. Press the Space Bar, then key-enter a valid debit memo amount.

422   Batch Number must be 1 for opening balances.

Press the Space Bar. Change the batch number to 1 using the Set Run Date and Batch Number option.

423   Batch Number must be greater than 1 for transactions.

Press the Space Bar. Change the batch number using the Set Run Date and Batch Number option.

501   Control account numbers have not been set.

Press the Space Bar. Set the required control accounts using the *Set Control Accounts* option before continuing.

502   No accounts receivable data.

Press the Space Bar. Verify that accounts receivable transaction data has been key-entered into the computer system.

503   No customer data.

Press the Space Bar. Create customer data using the *Build Customer Data* option before continuing.

504   Account number XXX is not in the chart of accounts.

Press the Space Bar. Check to see if the number key-entered is in the chart of accounts. If the number key-entered is incorrect, key-enter the correct number. If the account has not been opened, exit the Accounts Receivable System and open the account using the *Chart of Accounts File Maintenance* option in the General Ledger System.

505   Customer name must begin with a valid character.

Press the Space Bar and key-enter a valid customer name.

506   Error in G.L. Set Control Accounts.

An error has been detected in the general ledger control accounts. Return to the General Ledger System and verify that the control accounts set in the *Set Control Accounts* option exist in the chart of accounts. Correct the control accounts. If the control accounts are correct, add the accounts as new entries using the *Chart of Accounts File Maintenance* option before returning to the Accounts Receivable System.

507   Error in A.R. Set Control Accounts.

An error has been detected in the accounts receivable *Set Control Accounts* option. The account numbers specified in the set control accounts fields must be in the chart of accounts. Press the Space Bar and correct the control accounts. If the control accounts are correct, press Esc to exit and add the accounts as new entries using the *Chart of Accounts File Maintenance* option in the General Ledger System.

508   An invoice number is required.

An invoice number is required before processing can continue. Press the Space Bar and key-enter a valid invoice number.

509   Customer number XXX is not in customer data file.

The customer number keyed is not in the accounts receivable data file. Check the number key-entered against the customer list. If the number is incorrect, press the Space Bar and key-enter a valid customer number. If the customer has not been previously entered, strike **Y** and add it to the customer data as a new entry. The system will return to where you were interrupted and you will be permitted to continue.

510   A customer number is required.

A customer number is required before processing can continue. Press the Space Bar and key-enter a valid customer number.

511   Accounts receivable transactions have reached capacity. E=Erase paid items.

Respond **E** to erase all transactions which have previously been paid. This will free up room for additional transaction data. Press Esc to return to the Accounts Receivable Main Menu to obtain any printouts for audit trail purposes before erasing the paid items from the file.

512 *Cannot delete active customer.*

An attempt has been made to delete a customer which has an active balance or previous activity. Press the Space Bar to key-enter the correct data. If the customer is to be deleted, each transaction which is in the computer for that customer must first be individually deleted so the computer can properly handle the integration of these transactions.

513 *Customer data has reached capacity.*

To free up space, delete any inactive customers. Press the Space Bar to exit and take appropriate action.

514 *You must enter cash receipts for some of the invoices.*

The accounts receivable data file is full. After attempting to purge the file of previously paid invoices, the computer is unable to free up additional space. Press the Space Bar to exit and take appropriate action.

515 *Account number is missing.*

The general ledger account number field is blank. Press the Space Bar, then key-enter a valid account number.

516 *No customer statements available.*

The system has detected that there are no customer statements to print and/or there are no accounts receivable transactions on account. Press Esc to exit.

517 *Journal entries have reached capacity. Erase journal entries (Y or N)?*

The system has detected that the journal entries generated by the accounts receivable system have caused the journal entries capacity to be exceeded. Return to the General Ledger System and perform period-end closing after generating the desired reports for audit trail purposes.

518 *Credit memo amount exceeds invoice amount.*

The amount of the credit memo is greater than the amount of the original invoice. Press the Space Bar, then key-enter a valid credit memo amount.

601 *No checks available.*

Checks have been requested; however, no employees have been identified to be paid for the current pay period. Verify that the payroll transaction data has been key-entered into the computer system.

602 *No employee data.*

Press the Space Bar. Create employee data using the *Build Employee Data* option before continuing.

603 *Employee number XXX is not in the payroll data file.*

Check the number key-entered against the employee list. If the number is incorrect, press the Space Bar and key-enter the correct number. If the employee has not been previously entered, strike **Y** and add it to the employee data as a new entry. The system will return to where you were interrupted and you will be permitted to continue.

604   *Employee name missing or begins with invalid character.*

Press the Space Bar and key-enter a valid employee name.

605   *Marital status code must be S=Single or M=Married.*

Press the Space Bar, then key-enter the correct marital status code (**M** for married, **S** for single).

606   *Type of pay code must be S=Salaried or H=Hourly.*

Press the Space Bar, then key-enter the correct type of pay code (**H** for hourly, **S** for salaried).

607   *Employee with year-to-date information cannot be deleted.*

Press the Space Bar. Employees with year-to-date information cannot be deleted until after the annual W-2 statements are processed.

608   *No W-2 statements available.*

The system has detected that there are no employees with a year-to-date gross pay greater then zero. Verify that payroll transaction data has been key-entered into the computer system.

609   *No employees paid.*

Press the Space Bar to continue.

610   *Hourly employee missing hours worked.*

An hourly employee has been released to be paid, but the number of hours worked is missing. Press the Space Bar, then key-enter the employee's hours.

611   *Employee data has reached capacity.*

Delete all employees who have not been paid at least once during the current calendar year. This will free up additional space in the payroll data file. Press the Space Bar to exit and take appropriate action.

DATE DUE

GAYLORD			PRINTED IN U.S.A.